CLASSICS OF
PRACTICING ANTHROPOLOGY
1978 – 1998

Editorial Group

Editors

Patricia J. Higgins, *Practicing Anthropology* Editor 1990-1996, Plattsburgh State University

J. Anthony Paredes, Society for Applied Anthropology President 1993-1995, National Park Service

Advisory Editors

Erve J. Chambers, *Practicing Anthropology* Editor 1978-1986, Society for Applied Anthropology President 1987-1989, University of Maryland

Alexander M. Ervin, *Practicing Anthropology* Editor 1997-2002, University of Saskatchewan

Shirley J. Fiske, National Sea Grant Program

Benita Howell, *Practicing Anthropology* Editor 1986-1990, University of Tennessee

Stanley Hyland, University of Memphis

Edward B. Liebow, Environmental Health and Social Policy Center, Seattle

Anthony Oliver-Smith, University of Florida

John Poggie, Jr., *Human Organization* Editor 1983-1988, University of Rhode Island

Ruth O. Selig, Smithsonian Institution

Donald Stull, *Human Organization* Editor 1999-2001, University of Kansas

Robert T. Trotter II, Northern Arizona University

Maria Luisa Urdaneta, University of Texas - San Antonio

Thomas Weaver, Society for Applied Anthropology President 1976-1977, University of Arizona

Curtis W. Wienker, University of South Florida

Robert M. Wulff, The Peterson Companies, Washington

John A. Young, Society for Applied Anthropology President 1997-1999, Oregon State University

Production Designer

Neil E. Hann, Society for Applied Anthropology, Oklahoma City

Production Manager

J. Thomas May, Society for Applied Anthropology, Oklahoma City

CLASSICS OF
PRACTICING ANTHROPOLOGY
1978 – 1998

Edited by

Patricia J. Higgins
Plattsburgh State University

J. Anthony Paredes
National Park Service

Society for Applied Anthropology
Oklahoma City, Oklahoma

2000

Whatever propensities and values may unite and distinguish anthropologists, first among them is a view of life that is relativistic and pluralistic ... Our central concept of culture, our other-people and long-term perspective, and our fieldwork ethos must influence us in this direction.

... if only one out of five Americans share our values, and if *of these* only one out of a hundred have had enough contact with us to associate their values with anthropology, these would add up to 200,000 adults. But suppose the number in this country is only 50,000 with a commitment to and some relevant knowledge of anthropology. What happens if—through this new journal—these are brought into active intercommunication?

I foresee this possible future: (1) that some thousands of anthropologists and persons interested in anthropology who are in the nonacademic, everyday work force will tell one another publicly that ... they would like to have other anthropologists join them at work; (2) that personnel offices, Civil Service Commissions, and others would begin to recognize the positions for which training in anthropology is beneficial; and (3) that more and more identified anthropologists would enter the occupational structure, and the process would snowball. The inclusion of anthropological understanding and values in bureaucratic organizations of all kinds would itself improve our society. But also it just might trigger a movement which would make a large difference in shaping the next century ...

Sol Tax
A Community of Anthropologists
Practicing Anthropology 1,1(1978)

Contents

Foreword

JOHN A. YOUNG
SfAA PRESIDENT, 1997-1999

I recently finished serving two years as SfAA President, 1997-99. My term coincides with the end point of the twenty years covered by this historically significant volume. It is an appropriate time to assess both the accomplishments of *Practicing Anthropology* and our prospects for the future. How well have we responded to Sol Tax's 1978 admonition to "trigger a movement"? Are we prepared to "make a large difference in shaping the next century"?

The advent of *Practicing Anthropology* marked the first major step in transforming applied anthropology into a profession, an effort that is still progressing. I commend the founding editor, Erve Chambers, for his foresight, and his successors—Benita Howell, Pat Higgins, and Sandy Ervin—for their perseverance in staying the course and developing the full potential of this publication.

Practicing Anthropology is uniquely situated to foster dialogue among academics, practitioners, and others interested in the practical application of anthropological knowledge. The operative word here is "dialogue," as opposed to the mere delivery of information. For example, agents employed by the Cooperative Extension Service engage in one-way communication; their task is to package and deliver research results to the public. In contrast, practicing anthropologists are producers as well as messengers of new knowledge. By either formal or informal means, they have learned valuable lessons and communicated them through many contributions to the pages of *Practicing Anthropology*. Although it is important for practitioners to share information among themselves, perhaps the dialogue in *Practicing Anthropology* has provided the most benefit for applied training programs. The practitioner perspective has changed the way we think, teach, and learn about our subject matter.

What is the primary influence of practitioners on applied anthropology? Their contribution is not fundamentally about writing resumes and securing jobs for an otherwise ill-equipped army of surplus anthropological labor. Rather it is about changing the world.

Critics say that applied anthropology will never amount to anything because it focuses on the "small stuff" and does not tackle the "big issues." My answer is that much of what we do is local, but when our clients and communities endorse it, and we add it up, it takes on global significance. *Classics of Practicing Anthropology* illustrates the additive process by which we share and use our knowledge in increasingly effective ways. This collection of articles shows that real-world applied anthropology, more than solving isolated problems, is beginning to change the behavior and culture of a wide range of public and private institutions.

Several articles in this volume are about self-reflection and soul-searching, which are necessary side-steps that help us to accept greater professional responsibility, solve difficult ethical dilemmas, and fight our own demons. The inclusion of such articles effectively counters the mistaken perception that applied anthropology is merely instrumental and dogmatically uncritical. Applied anthropology is not a petty exercise in career building. There is a moral as well as a scientific basis for our work. We could not consider ourselves to be a "movement" without developing this moral dimension.

What limits do we face as we look to the future? *Classics of Practicing Anthropology* shows that any problem and any social context is fair game. Our influence can continue to spread with no topical or geographical boundaries. *Practicing Anthropology* has laid the groundwork for our knowledge to inform policy, and for policy to be put into action. Consistent with the vision of Sol Tax, we are now poised and have the momentum to play a variety of important roles and make a difference in shaping the future of human society. As we proceed into the next century, we can find strength in our roots and draw continuing inspiration from the articles in this volume.

Key to Authors of Introductory Paragraphs

A. M. E.	Alexander M. Ervin
C. W. W.	Curtis W. Wienker
E. B. L.	Edward B. Liebow
J. A. P.	J. Anthony Paredes
J. A. Y.	John A. Young
P. J. H.	Patricia J. Higgins
R. M. W.	Robert M. Wulff
R. O. S.	Ruth O. Selig
S. J. F.	Shirley J. Fiske

Topical Coverage

	Introduction	Chambers	Wolfe	Schensul
Practicing Anthropology				
Development of Field	x		x	
Relationship with Academic Anthropology		x		
Methods and Perspectives				x
Ethical Issues				
Career Development and Employment Opportunities		x		
Fields of Endeavor		x		
Health and Medical Care				
Social Services				
Education				
Economic Development/Development Anthropology				
International/Intercultural Exchange				
Natural Resources and Environment				x
Historic Preservation and Cultural Resources Management				
Business and Commerce				
Legal Practice				
Intersection with Public Policy				
Government Employment				
Consultation				
Media Relations				
Citizen Action and Advocacy				x
Subfields of Anthropology				
Cultural Anthropology	x			
Physical Anthropology				
Linguistics				
Archaeology				
Geographic Regions				
United States	x		x	x
Native Americans				
Other Minority Populations				x
Latin America				
Europe				
Middle East				
Asia				
Pacific Islands				

Trend	Nash	Davis/Mathews	Wolcott	Langley	Orbach	Singer	Sibley	Joans	Burkhalter	Hanna/Baker	Mukhopadhyay	Lett	Whiteford	Hamada	Stoffle et al.
x					x				x						
x					x	x									
		x	x							x			x		x
x	x			x		x		x	x			x			
									x				x		
													x		
		x	x								x				
		x		x					x						x
		x		x			x							x	
x							x		x					x	
								x						x	
x	x			x											
x									x				x		x
		x										x			
x		x	x	x	x	x	x		x		x	x	x	x	x
								x		x		x			
x	x	x			x		x	x	x	x			x	x	x
	x	x			x			x							
	x	x							x						
		x						x		x					
								x						x	
								x							

Topical Coverage
(continued)

	Fitchen	Boone/Liebow	Anyon/Zunie	Rhoades
Practicing Anthropology				
Development of Field				x
Relationship with Academic Anthropology				
Methods and Perspectives				
Ethical Issues				
Career Development and Employment Opportunities		x	x	
Fields of Endeavor				
Health and Medical Care				
Social Services		x		
Education				
Economic Development/Development Anthropology				x
International/Intercultural Exchange	x			
Natural Resources and Environment			x	
Historic Preservation and Cultural Resources Management				
Business and Commerce				
Legal Practice				
Intersection with Public Policy				
Government Employment			x	x
Consultation	x		x	x
Media Relations		x		
Citizen Action and Advocacy				
Subfields of Anthropology				
Cultural Anthropology	x	x		x
Physical Anthropology				
Linguistics			x	
Archaeology				
Geographic Regions				
United States	x	x	x	
Native Americans			x	
Other Minority Populations				
Latin America				x
Europe				
Middle East				
Asia				
Pacific Islands				

Fiske	Zhai	Dove	Grobsmith	Halper	Garrow	Tongue et al.	McEwan et al.	Johnston	Ruppert	Eisenberg	Gonzalez	MacDonald	Kolar	Jenakovich/Murdoch	Petto/Russell
x			x										x	x	
				x								x		x	
		x				x					x		x		
			x		x										
x			x		x									x	x
						x				x				x	
			x							x			x		
			x	x		x					x		x		
x	x	x	x	x					x				x		
x	x	x						x	x						
x	x				x		x		x						
			x												
x									x						
		x	x		x				x		x	x	x		
			x				x		x		x	x			
x	x	x	x	x		x			x	x	x	x	x	x	x
													x		x
			x				x								
x		x			x	x			x	x	x	x	x		x
		x				x			x		x	x			
						x					x	x			
							x						x		
		x			x										
	x														

Introduction: Context and Vision for *Practicing Anthropology*

J. ANTHONY PAREDES AND PATRICIA J. HIGGINS

In the 1960s academic anthropology was booming. Anthropology—ambitiously devoted to the study of humankind, its products, and its activities, worldwide and at all times—was riding high on a tide of rapidly increasing college enrollments. At mid-decade the first of the "baby boomers" carried forward the swell of college enrollments begun with the GI Bill veterans of World War II and Korea. With an expanding war in Vietnam, college deferments from the draft made higher education an attractive alternative for many young men (who could afford it). Ironically, even as the United States was becoming ever more deeply involved in an unpopular war in Southeast Asia, the government facilitated the post-secondary education alternative to military service through increased funding for higher education and university-based research, particularly in the hard sciences. Area studies and social science research on non-Western societies were also supported at unprecedented levels. These were the years of the United States's "space race" with the Soviet Union, triggered by the USSR's successful launch of the first artificial planetary satellite in 1957. At the same time the U.S. reached out to the Third World trying to demonstrate the superiority of U.S. economic and political systems and to win the Cold War.

In the succeeding decades, changes in the domestic and international scenes have made anthropology all the more relevant, although its usefulness has not always been well recognized. Anthropology as a discipline and a profession has also experienced some dramatic changes, including increased internal diversification and multiplication of subdisciplines, an apparently expanding gap between physical and cultural anthropology and between scientific and humanistic approaches to the study of culture, and the extension of applied anthropology to a full-time, long-term, nonacademic career path for a growing number of anthropologists. This collection of articles selected from the first twenty years of *Practicing Anthropology*, the career-oriented publication of the Society for Applied Anthropology (SfAA), grows out of these changes and in turn reflects upon them.

A New High for Anthropology

In the 1960s anthropology was one of the fastest growing subjects in undergraduate curricula (a fact noted by even such popular magazines as *Mademoiselle*, according to an article one of the editors [Paredes] saw posted on a

2

college bulletin board in the halcyon days of the late sixties). The reasons for anthropology's appeal were many. Through her popular writings, Margaret Mead was spreading the message of the importance of cultural differences far and wide. The writings of other anthropologists such as Clyde Kluckhohn, Ruth Benedict, and Ashley Montague were also reaching an ever-wider audience. In the early 1960s, CBS even broadcast a prime time television program—narrated by Walter Cronkite—on the famous Cornell-Peru Vicos project of applied anthropology.

Americans were becoming much more widely traveled and, superficially at least, more sophisticated and interested in other cultures. John Kennedy's Peace Corps, Lyndon Johnson's "War on Poverty," and the Civil Rights Movement exposed many young people to ways of life abroad and at home different from their own. Many thought anthropology held the key to understanding other cultures and through them understanding ourselves. The popular literati of America had, it seemed, taken up Kluckhohn's "mirror for man"—anthropology (Clyde Kluckhohn, *Mirror for Man: The Relation of Anthropology to Modern Life* [New York: Whittlesey House, 1949]).

Fascination with distant foreign peoples and indigenous cultures closer to home also flourished in the countercurrents of American popular culture of the 1960s. Hippies, communards, anti-establishmentarians, ecology activists, rock musicians, and many others sought inspiration in exotic cultures. In their search for alternative life styles, the disenchanted and disgruntled turned to everything from Boy Scout Indian lore manuals (usually unacknowledged) to experimentation with mind-altering substances— the more exotic the better. The emblematic capstone of the era was publication of anthropologist Carlos Castaneda's highly controversial *Teachings of Don Juan* (New York: Ballantine Books, Inc.) in 1968. In that same year, however, a police assault on political demonstrators in Chicago during the Democratic National Convention, watched by millions on television, signaled the beginning of the end of that peculiar brand of popular social consciousness flavored with exoticism from which anthropology had so much benefited.

Through the 1960s, graduate schools could not keep up with the growing demand for anthropology professors. New graduate programs built to meet the new demand, in turn, fueled even more demand as newly minted anthropologists spread the popularity of the discipline in a seemingly endless feedback loop. Many anthropology graduate students took jobs before finishing their Ph.D.s and wrote dissertations in absentia while teaching a full load of college courses. Even small colleges were beginning to add anthropology to their curriculum and searching for anthropologists. (One of us was receiving invitations to apply for such teaching positions even before completion of the master's degree in 1964.) The trend could not last.

New Roles for Not-So-Old Anthropologists

The bubble burst. By the early 1970s, the number of academic positions open for anthropologists had leveled off, and the prospect of an oversupply of new Ph.D.s loomed on the horizon. (See R. G. D'Andrade, E. A. Hammel, D. L. Adkins, and C. K. McDaniel, "Academic Opportunity in Anthropology, 1974-90," *American Anthropologist* 77,4[1975]:753-773.) More and more anthropologists found their way into nonacademic jobs, sometimes jobs specifically calling for anthropological skills, oftentimes not. Some created their own consulting firms (especially archaeologists) to try to get a piece of the action spun off from such diverse new developments in the 1970s as more stringent historic preservation laws, increasing concern for social impacts in urban planning, ever more vocal calls for improving public schools, corporate expansion into overseas markets, and the relentless march of the new information technology. Others went to work for large, multidisciplinary research or consulting firms, or directly for public or private organizations.

The anthropology profession responded slowly but surely. A few academic departments began preparing students for the task of practicing anthropology in the workaday world of business, commerce, and government. The trend continues. (See *Guide to Training Programs in the Application of Anthropology*, 3rd edition, edited by Stanley Hyland and Sean Kirkpatrick [Memphis, Tenn: SfAA, 1989].) Amidst much controversy, archaeologists formed the Society of Professional Archaeologists in 1976 (supplanted by the Registry of Professional Archaeologists in 1998) to protect the interests of formally trained anthropologist-archaeologists from others trying to cash in on new opportunities in historic preservation. Soon thereafter, as part of the reorganization of the American Anthropological Association (AAA), some of the growing number of nonacademic anthropologists, joined by sympathizers in academia, formed the National Association for the Practice of Anthropology (NAPA).

The venerable Society for Applied Anthropology (SfAA), an international, interdisciplinary organization founded in 1941, also began to reach out to a new clientele. From the outset the society was dedicated to the "scientific investigation of the principles controlling the relations of human beings to one another…and the wide application of these principles to practical problems" (Bylaws of the Society for Applied Anthropology). The SfAA was born of an era when anthropologists and other like-minded social scientists, by choice or by necessity, had strayed from academia (at least temporarily) to help tackle the knotty problems of the Great Depression, the burgeoning needs of a newly urban America, major changes in federal American Indian policy, and winning the war against Fascism and Japanese imperialism. (See Edward Spicer, "Beyond Analysis and Explanation? The Life and Times of the Society for Applied Anthropology," *Human Organization* 35,4[1976]:335-343.)

4

It is one of the ironies of anthropology that the whole discipline had developed, in the nineteenth century and earlier, partly as a very "applied" instrument of government policies for the "civilizing" of native peoples at home and the administration of colonial empires abroad. Museums, too, provided a home and much of the institutional support for anthropology through the early twentieth century. (See Nancy Oestrich Lurie, "Musuemland Revisited," *Human Organization* 40,4[1981]:180-187.) Only later were respectable academic programs of anthropology established, first at a handful of elite universities in the United States and in some European countries. Applied anthropology then slipped into obscurity if not ill repute for several decades, even though anthropologists never withdrew totally from major social issues of their day, such as the eugenics movement.

After World War II, most of the founders of the SfAA, many of whom had been employed by government agencies, established secure bases in expanding academic institutions, though some continued to make periodic forays into nonacademic employment. Unlike these pioneers of applied anthropology, however, the practicing anthropologists of the 1970s worked largely outside the security of academia and often even outside government employ.

A New Publication for a New Kind of Anthropologist

From its inception, the SfAA began publishing a journal, *Applied Anthropology*, retitled *Human Organization* in 1949. The journal quickly achieved visibility and respectability within the anthropological profession at large. Many of the journal's contributors have been well-recognized social scientists. While case studies based on direct observation dominated early issues, the journal became more theoretical and academically oriented in the 1950s and 1960s as the activities and interests of the membership changed. Today the main articles and even some of the lesser contributions to the journal are often replete with methodological explication, meticulous presentation and analyses of data, and mid- to high-level theoretical interpretation and conform to rather formal writing styles, even while (usually) remaining true to the goal of applying anthropological knowledge to the solution of practical problems. Articles published in *Human Organization* are widely cited in other academic publications, and the quarterly has high credibility as a "refereed journal" in the machinations of university tenure and promotion rituals. Certainly within the academic world *Human Organization* continues to be the most visible manifestation of the SfAA.

For the growing number of anthropologists in the 1970s whose workaday world was in government agencies, local community organizations, domestic or international businesses, or independent consulting firms, the scholarly *Human Organization* and, indeed, the academically focused SfAA were of marginal usefulness and relevance. These anthropologists were more immediately involved in the second part of SfAA's mission—"the wide application" of "principles controlling the relations of human beings to one another"—rather than in the "scientific investigation" of these principles. The desire to better serve and hold the interest of the new, growing cadre of nonacademic anthropologists eventually led the SfAA to support the growth of local practitioner organizations, such as the Washington Association of Professional Anthropologists; to establish mechanisms to ensure that practitioners are represented in leadership groups; to sponsor annual meeting sessions devoted to practitioner needs; and to include more practitioner-oriented articles in *Human Organization*.

The SfAA leadership, therefore, listened with special interest in 1977 to a proposal put forward by students and faculty from the University of South Florida (USF). They sought support to explore interest in establishing a new publication that would "provide a forum for all anthropologists (B.A., M.A., and Ph.D.) interested in using their knowledge outside academia…" (See Wolfe, "How It All Began," in this volume.) An SfAA committee had also been considering the need for a new publication addressed to nonacademic anthropologists. While the USF proposal, inspired by Sol Tax's vision of bringing into contact tens of thousands of persons sharing anthropological values whatever their occupation, was somewhat broader than the publication that resulted, *Practicing Anthropology* has proven to be an unqualified success.

As initially produced, *Practicing Anthropology* appeared to be almost a "throw-away" publication. Printed on newsprint stock without a standard cover, *Practicing Anthropology* had the look of something to be read quickly for the latest news and tips on doing anthropology in settings novel and familiar, then tossed in the trash or the recycling bin (just then appearing on the American scene) along with the daily newspaper. This format was selected not only because it signaled currency and liveliness, but also so that *Practicing Anthropology* could be published as quickly and inexpensively as a college newspaper and might be given away as a recruitment tool. Designed to catch ephemeral activities of practitioners and to meet their immediate needs, early editors took pride in the publication being "ideal for lining an average size birdcage" (Erve Chambers, personal communication). Libraries typically discarded back issues after a year or so along with other newsprint serials, and even the packrats among early readers soon found their copies growing yellow and fragile, if not disintegrating completely.

Articles published in *Practicing Anthropology* were intended to be short, direct, comfortably readable, to-the-point, charged with immediacy, and—above all—practical. Extensive literature reviews were discouraged, and bibliographic citations used only sparingly. Seeking to capture and document the activities of people whose employers did not always value or reward publication, *Practicing Anthropology* editors came to rely on guest editors to identify potential authors and assemble articles on particular themes for special issues or sections. In addition, editors sometimes became silent co-authors with practitioners too busy with practical matters to write about them. As another way of publicizing the activities of practitioners, "Sources," a column of brief project profiles edited by John van Willigen and based on materials submitted to the University of Kentucky's Applied Anthropology Documentation Project, became a regular feature beginning in 1981. The shift from conventional to desktop publishing in 1986, just as this new technology became available, made it possible for *Practicing Anthropology* to publish even more current information. Timely policy columns, such as "Washington Week" (soon changed to "Washington Watch") could be inserted literally the day before the issue went to print. Other columns added later were "Practical Computing" and, most recently, "The Real World," devoted to the discussion of anthropological applications to public policy.

In the end, though, it was *Practicing Anthropology*'s journalistic style that proved its greatest asset and a source of enduring value to anthropology. Timely as they were, many articles published in *Practicing Anthropology* were widely read and proved useful to an ever-wider audience of practitioners in anthropology and other fields. Eventually many editors, authors, readers, and instructors of anthropology came to regret that so many articles of enduring interest and high quality were distributed in such a fragile medium.

Recognizing the continuing value of much of the material published in *Practicing Anthropology*, in 1990 the SfAA authorized a major change in the publication's format. With Volume 13 in 1991, *Practicing Anthropology* began publication on letter size paper with a heavier paperstock cover, thus ensuring its place on library shelves and in the "to keep" pile of individual subscribers. A semi-glossy cover featuring striking human-interest photos or artwork was designed to catch the attention of new readers.

Even earlier, the SfAA had indexed Volumes 1-10 and reproduced these volumes and the index on microfilm. These microfilm copies were made available at nominal cost to libraries and to individuals. In 1994 a new cumulative index for Volumes 1-16 was published in paper copy and included in a new updated microfilm. (This microfilm collection is available from the Society for Applied Anthropology, as are a number of back issues of *Practicing Anthropology*. Contact the SfAA Business Office, P.O. Box 24083, Oklahoma City, OK 73124; (405)843-5113, for current selections and prices.)

Nonetheless, it seemed to some members of the SfAA that there were a number of articles from the early years of *Practicing Anthropology* that should be available in a form more accessible than microfilm. When as editor of *Practicing Anthropology* (1991-1996) Patricia Higgins solicited from the SfAA Executive Committee ideas for special issues, Anthony Paredes (then president-elect) proposed a reprint issue of some of the classics from "the newsprint years." His inspiration for this came, quite frankly, from the frequency with which he found himself copying Harry Wolcott's piece, "How to

Look Like an Anthropologist Without Really Being One" (this volume), for the seemingly endless stream of graduate students from the College of Education who wanted to use "ethnographic techniques" in their thesis or dissertation research.

The idea for a volume of *Practicing Anthropology* classics was born. But, it grew to something quite a bit more than just another issue of *Practicing Anthropology*.

About this New Book of Old Articles

Higgins and the SfAA Executive Committee enthusiastically received Paredes's idea. Through contacts with former editors of *Practicing Anthropology* and notices published in the SfAA's quarterly newsletter, Higgins solicited "nominations" of articles for a classics issue. Before there was time to supplement these nominations with a more thorough review of the newsprint issues, Higgins's term as editor ended. She passed along the idea for a reprint number to her successor Alexander Ervin. He was receptive to the idea, but as he, Higgins, and Paredes discussed the proposed issue, they began to believe that perhaps something on a somewhat grander scale might be needed.

Our own review of Volumes 1-12, articles nominated by SfAA members, and articles reprinted elseware convinced us that there were many more selections from the newsprint years worth rescuing than could possibly be included in a single issue of *Practicing Anthropology*. Higgins, Paredes, and Ervin felt that the appeal and usefulness of a collection of such articles could be extended by expanding the scope of the volume to include the entire twenty-year history of *Practicing Anthropology* in an independent book. By selecting articles that displayed intrinsic quality, illustrated diverse areas of anthropological practice, and highlighted developments over the past twenty years, the value of the volume for introductory and applied anthropology courses could be enhanced. The goal became to produce a volume that would simultaneously celebrate the success of *Practicing Anthropology* and the many authors who have contributed to its pages, while introducing new readers to key features of anthropological practice.

Higgins agreed to edit the classics volume, whatever shape it might take, and asked Paredes to assist her in the effort.

When the idea for a book of reprints from *Practicing Anthropology* was formally presented to the SfAA Executive Committee at their fall 1997 meeting, response was favorable, but the committee wanted to broaden the number of people involved in the composition, design, and promotion of the book. Higgins and Paredes organized an advisory editorial board (listed on page ii) and asked members to review the selections tentatively made from the newsprint years, propose articles from Volumes 13-20 for inclusion, and suggest ways to improve the proposed book and ensure its success. Another call was

8

also made to the general membership of the SfAA to suggest articles for the book. At their spring 1998 meeting, the SfAA Executive Committee decided to authorize and fund publication of this volume.

With the help of the editorial board, editors Higgins and Paredes made the final selection of the works included here. This was not easy. The 39 articles republished here constitute less than a third of the 125 articles nominated. In making these selections the editors followed guidelines developed in conjunction with advisory editors:

- each article should be of continuing and/or of historical interest and comprehensible without lengthy prefatory contextualization in now-passé debates;
- articles should be written in an engaging and accessible style and suitable for use as teaching tools;
- more articles from the earlier newsprint issues should be included for preservation's sake;
- various specialties and all four subfields of anthropology should be represented; and
- a variety of issues, geographic regions, and styles of anthropological practice should be represented.

The chart on pages xiv-xvii illustrates how this collection meets our breadth and distribution objectives. While all subfields of anthropology are represented, the vast majority of the articles discuss or describe uses of cultural anthropology—as do most articles published in *Practicing Anthropology.* Similarly, while there is some representation of most of the world's major cultural areas, the majority of the cases are set in the United States—in keeping with the pattern of submission and publication in *Practicing Anthropology.*

Some of the articles are published here in abridged form. Whenever possible, approval for any editing was obtained from the author. Each selection is preceded with a brief introductory statement prepared by one of the editors or advisory editors (acknowledged by initials, see page xiii). These introductory "blurbs," as we came to affectionately call them, are intended to focus attention on the historical and professional context of the piece. Each selection is also accompanied by a brief biographical statement indicating the author's current position and contact information when available. Many of the projects described had a lifespan beyond the original publication dates, and interested readers are invited to contact authors for more up-to-date information. In some cases, a new reference is also included to help readers gain access to recent literature on the subject.

The editors and the advisory board gave much attention to the organization of this volume. There were some strong differences of opinion. Some wanted the collection to be organized by subject matter. Others preferred a structure that would facilitate using the volume in conjunction with a standard textbook in applied anthropology. Yet others preferred a simple chronological organization. Each approach was seen to have some important advantages.

In the end, we opted for a chronological organization. We reasoned that any single subject-matter or conceptual-issue format would be found wanting by many, given the varied approaches of teachers of applied anthropology. We also felt that historical organization would promote an understanding of the unfolding of professional practicing anthropology as it came to be at the end of the twentieth century, distantly echoing the emergence of academic anthropology at the beginning of the century from the primordial applied anthropology of the nineteenth century. Nonetheless, for the convenience of teachers, we do offer a grouping by topical areas, as suggested by members of our advisory board, on pages xiv-xvii.

While we hope this volume will be used in classes, the editors, advisory editorial board, and the SfAA all want the book to be more than just another classroom reader. We hope it will also be a lasting collection of classics in its own right, both from the publication *Practicing Anthropology* and from the profession of practicing anthropology. Hence, we purposefully introduced the ambiguity of the title *Classics of Practicing Anthropology: 1978-1998*.

10

Practicing Anthropology: Hauling in the Future

ERVE J. CHAMBERS

In the inaugural editorial of Practicing Anthropology, *Erve Chambers predicted a future in which anthropology would no longer be an almost exclusively academic discipline. Rather, it would be a profession comprised of practitioners using anthropological methods in a wide variety of fields as well as university-based scholars and teachers. The goals Chambers elucidated for the publication in 1978—that it serve as a vehicle of communication for anthropologists working outside academia, a source of information on nontraditional career opportunities, and a medium for discussing the use of anthropology in policy research and implementation—have continued to guide the editors. In addition, the publication has sought "to encourage a bridge between practice inside and outside the university" and "to serve as a forum for inquiry into the present state and future of anthropology," to quote from the statement of purpose included in every issue since Fall 1980 (Volume 3, Number 1). Examples of articles contributing to the achievement of all these goals are to be found in later pages of this book.* P.J.H.

This first issue of *Practicing Anthropology* appears in the midst of an unsettled period in the development of our profession. Over the past decade there has been considerable speculation and occasional controversy concerning the future of anthropology. Much of the discussion has centered on alternative careers for anthropologists, with a level of argument that ranges from the idealistic (How can anthropology contribute more directly to the public interest?) to the strictly pragmatic (Will training in anthropology help me get a job?). Between these two questions lies a variety of current experiences that we have barely begun to explore. When it is summed up, years of concern have left us with precious little in the way of useful information.

Much of the problem is simply a matter of communication. The few career publications in our profession are almost entirely directed to the interests

Erve J. Chambers is Professor of Anthropology at the University of Maryland (College Park, MD 20742; (301) 405-1439; <echambers@anth.umd.edu>). He was editor of *Practicing Anthropology* from 1978 through 1985 and is a past president of the Society for Applied Anthropology.

Originally published in *Practicing Anthropology* 1,1(1978):9-10, this article has been abridged for republication here.

12

of university-based anthropologists. Individuals who work outside the universities are not well represented. It is true that the *Anthropology Newsletter*, published by the American Anthropological Association, has recently been including more information about anthropologists working outside academia. And a few local organizations, like the Society of Professional Anthropologists in Tucson and the Washington Association of Professional Anthropologists in Washington, D.C., have done an admirable job in organizing practicing anthropologists in their locales. But, without a widely distributed publication devoted expressly to their interests, the contributions and experiences of uncounted numbers of anthropologists have gone largely unnoticed and remain a matter of surmise rather than fact. It is in this way that we see the mission of *Practicing Anthropology* as "hauling in the future."

The time for speculation is over. We need to begin exploring the range of actual practice in modern anthropology. Only as we do so can the isolated experiences of practicing anthropologists become shared professional knowledge. And it is only on the basis of a solid knowledge of the present that we should presume to speak of the next futures of our profession.

We feel *Practicing Anthropology* will interest the entire anthropological community. At the same time, we hope the publication will help us all actively challenge and begin to redefine the parameters of that community. To this end, we start with as few preconceptions as possible concerning the nature of current anthropological practice. We do not believe the work of modern anthropology can be defined simply by the achievement of a certain degree level, by one or a few traditional fields of interest, by a particular kind of training, or by a single product. Neither do we feel that there is any longer, if there ever was, a particular ideological or philosophical bent which clearly identifies the anthropological view. While most of us would agree that anthropologists at least strive to be relativistic and pluralistic in their view of the human condition, we must also recognize that the interpretation of the relativistic perspective by modern anthropologists is itself subject to considerable variation.

Although we deliberately avoid trying to define what a practicing anthropologist is or might be in today's world, we have no difficulty in describing what we will be looking for in the pages of *Practicing Anthropology*. These are our major goals:

- Practicing Anthropology *will serve as a vehicle of communication and source of career information for anthropologists who are currently working outside academic settings.* In this respect, we respond to an urgent need to represent the interests of persons who are actively engaged in forging alternatives to the limited range of career choices anthropologists have traditionally accepted. There have been such people since the beginning of our profession, but they have never been in greater evidence. The need for a national publication directed to their interests is clear.

- *We will explore the variety of career opportunities available to individuals with training in anthropology.* Practicing Anthropology is not only for those who have begun their work, but also for students and others who are preparing for careers in anthropology. We will be describing the kinds of employment which individuals with B.A.s, M.A.s, and Ph.D.s in anthropology are currently obtaining, and we will be offering practical advice for persons newly entering a job market that we believe to be as exciting and promising as it is diverse and, at times, confusing.
- Practicing Anthropology *will represent fields of academic practice which have received little attention in the past.* We will, for example, be exploring teaching opportunities in high schools, community colleges, and university departments other than anthropology. Activities in these areas have received little attention in the profession, even though they have helped significantly in adding to the visibility of anthropology in the world at large.
- *Finally, in relation to each of these goals, we will be describing and critiquing the uses of anthropology in policy research and implementation.* Most practicing anthropologists are working in some area of public policy concern. Through the varied experiences of our readers, we intend to openly explore public issues—always and unabashedly asking, "What's in it for anthropology?" and at the same time asking what the rest of the world stands to gain when anthropologists do become involved in particular concerns.

How It All Began

Alvin W. Wolfe

Each year thousands of students take courses in anthropology, and many others develop an interest in the field through independent reading or television viewing. While very few people pursue graduate training in anthropology, and fewer still ever occupy positions specifically requiring anthropological training, many people have absorbed some anthropological values. Wouldn't these tens of thousands of persons be better able to use anthropology, and in the process help improve the world, if they had a vehicle for communicating with one another? That, Alvin Wolfe tells us, was the vision that motivated University of South Florida (USF) students and faculty in the 1970s to plan an independent, participatory magazine. That vision was lost, or at least seriously diluted, Wolfe suggests, when the USF group joined with the Society for Applied Anthropology to produce Practicing Anthropology—*a publication directed more toward nonacademic professional anthropologists than the much larger number of anthropologists at heart. In his comment on this article (*Practicing Anthropology *1,4[1979]:25-26), editor Erve Chambers expressed his desire to see a wider range of experiences represented in the pages of* Practicing Anthropology *and his belief that institutional affiliation and occupational labels need not constrain broad participation in the publication.*   P. J. H.

As interest in applied anthropology is expanding in the late 1970s, we hear and read various accounts of how it began in the 1940s. Who attended those first meetings in Cambridge, and in New York, which gave birth to the Society for Applied Anthropology and the journal entitled *Applied Anthropology* that later became *Human Organization*? It seems strange that events so important in their consequences, involving persons so literate and so accustomed in other circumstances to documenting their observations, require reconstruction almost forty years later.

If it should happen that *Practicing Anthropology* is still around in 2016, will some of us who shared in its origins be asked to recall who was at the first meeting, what we intended to accomplish, why we did it as we did? In 2016,

Alvin W. Wolfe is Distinguished Service Professor of Anthropology at the University of South Florida (Tampa, FL 33620-9900; (813) 974-0823; <wolfe@chuma1.cas.usf.edu>) and a past president of the Society for Applied Anthropology.

Originally published in *Practicing Anthropology* 1,4(1979):3,19.

16

I will be 88 years old and may not remember what was happening on Tuesday evening, January 25, 1977, when Sol Tax, at the University Restaurant in Tampa, relaxing after a formal lecture on "Action Anthropology," stimulated into action a group of anthropology students and a few faculty members. Tax excited those students, and the faculty members as well, with the idea that tens of thousands of persons in the world hold anthropological values and are without a medium for communicating with one another along lines of mutual interest. Think of all the college graduates who were turned on by anthropology courses but continued in other fields, and are now lost to professional anthropology! They may, at heart, be anthropologists, who interpret events of their daily lives and of the world at large from an anthropological perspective. Yet, the *American Anthropologist* has little in it for them. Neither has *Human Organization*, nor other recognized journals of the discipline. Their anthropological view could influence the world for the better, Tax was suggesting. But these tens of thousands, perhaps hundreds, the world over, needed a way of communicating with one another.

The seed Sol Tax deposited that evening did not fall on barren soil. Within two weeks of his visit to Tampa, plans were underway to implement the idea. A notice went out, locally, to "all persons interested in Anthropology at Work," inviting them to come to an informal meeting on February 12, 1977, "to discuss the development and organization of a newsletter concerning the use of the anthropological perspective in non-academic fields." The suggested title was intended to convey two meanings: "anthropology in one's daily work," but also "the idea of anthropology being effective in the world at large."

According to the announcement of that meeting, "The emphasis of this newsletter will be to publish short articles and communications by individuals who find the concepts of anthropology useful to their careers (jobs, home life, applied research, community action, etc.)." The idea prevalent at that time was a participatory organization, without a formal distinction between editors, authors and readers. The publication, "Anthropology at Work," or "Practicing Anthropology," or whatever it would be called, would be like conversation. The nine of us who met at my house on February 12, 1977 each brought in a little message of the kind we thought might kick off the conversations we hoped would follow.

Following Tax's original suggestion, we discussed how we might get addresses of potential participants from alumni lists of universities where anthropology was taught. By March, we had two such lists and were seeking more.

In the course of those weeks in the spring of 1977, it became obvious that we would need some start-up funding. The University of South Florida (USF) was in no position to help significantly and, in any event, we thought of the enterprise as a people's thing, a national or international thing, but not an institutional thing. I was at the time secretary of the Society for Applied Anthropology, and was up for election to the presidency, and it was decided to present the idea to the Society for their possible support for start-up only. I am quite sure that none of us at the time considered that what we had in mind would become a publication of a professionally oriented association like the Society. Although he had missed that first organizing meeting, Robert Wulff, who was on the USF faculty at the time, had taken considerable initiative during this planning stage. He chaired a committee representing the group who had accepted Tax's challenge, to prepare a request for funding to present to the Society for Applied Anthropology at its April 1977 meeting. The request was for $449.00 "to assess the interest in the proposed new magazine." Quoting from that document dated March 27, 1977: "The goal of the magazine is to provide a public forum for all anthropologists (B.A., M.A., and Ph.D.) interested in using their knowledge outside academia in tasks other than university-based teaching/research. The guiding philosophy of the magazine is that the anthropological perspective can be fruitfully applied in every human endeavor." The magazine, as it was referred to by then, was to be called either *Practicing Anthropology* or *Anthropology at Work*.

Coincidentally, the SfAA Committee on Goals and Organizational Structure, chaired by Art Gallaher, the Society's president-elect, was considering the need for a newsletter that would help "ensure greater participation by non-academic anthropologists in the affairs of the Society." On April 6, 1977, that committee recommended, and the SfAA Executive Committee adopted, a resolution that:

> SfAA develop a practitioner-oriented publication with an identity separate from *Human Organization* ... The intent should be to produce a publication that (1) focuses on jobs, personnel moves, events, 'success stories,' training developments, etc.; (2) is appealing across a broad range of applied interest groups; (3) is so good that any one interested in applied anthropology will not want to be without it; and (4) is aimed toward a monthly or bimonthly distribution.

In the course of discussion, the Executive Committee identified four possible audiences for such a newsletter: basic researchers, applied researchers, practitioners, and users. Thinking of the large population that Sol Tax was concerned about, I suggested that SfAA should also consider all anthropology alumni as a potential audience. The resolution contained no motion for implementation, and none was moved separately. The request from the Tampa group was in hand, but action on it was deferred to the next meeting, which would involve the newly elected officers and members of the Executive Committee.

Another significant event occurred at those SfAA meetings. Sol Tax was the recipient of the 1977 Malinowski Award, and in his Award Lecture he referred to the beginnings that had been made in Tampa as follows:

18

There are thousands of anthropologists in the work force who have had training in anthropology. On the initiative of anthropologists at the University of South Florida, the program will identify as many of these as possible and help them to inaugurate a journal through which they can recognize one another and intercommunicate. It is hoped that this communication network will soon reach both internationally and to (1) academic anthropologists, (2) undergraduate and advanced secondary school students, and (3) interested others, and thus will quickly broaden the base and influence of anthropology.

I talked with Tax during the course of those meetings in San Diego, and he reinforced for me the idea that, instead of starting a journal that persons merely *subscribe* to, it would be more worthwhile to *involve* as many anthropologists as possible in what they would think of as their own enterprise.

On April 9, 1977, the new SfAA Executive Committee met, with the new president, Art Gallaher, in the chair. Upon a motion by past-president Thomas Weaver, seconded by member John Singleton, the Executive Committee authorized President Gallaher to negotiate with the Tampa group "the implementing of their proposal for a practitioner-oriented publication under the auspices of SfAA." The President was authorized to commit up to $2000 for costs within the first year of operation of the publication.

Back in Tampa, on April 12, I put out another local announcement to "Anthropologists interested in *Anthropology at Work/Practicing Anthropology*," informing them of the SfAA actions, telling them of Tax's reference to our efforts, and calling for another planning meeting on April 30, 1977. Ten persons showed up at the Saturday morning session.

A great many decisions were made at that meeting, which was the first for which minutes were recorded. It was decided, tentatively, to call the publication *Practicing Anthropology at Work*, a compromise between two contending titles. It was decided to publish bimonthly, with an ultimate aim of monthly publication. It was decided to seek "ballyhoo from biggies" such as Saul Bellow, Kurt Vonnegut, Shana Alexander, and Jomo Kenyatta, all of whom had anthropological background. It was also decided that all persons participating would be called "contributing correspondents," not "subscribers"— only institutions could simply "subscribe." Robert Wulff was elected Coordinating Editor, and was authorized to negotiate with the president of the Society for Applied Anthropology, "about the funding and other aspects of our relationship." It was clear that the Tampa group had in mind some kind of participatory experience for a very broad range of "anthropologists," not merely a newsletter for professional applied anthropologists.

SfAA president Gallaher visited Tampa during May 1977, and was concerned about many details which had not been previously settled. These involved specification of the support that could be expected from USF students or faculty. Those concerns also included specification of the involvement, if any, of the AAA executive office, which handled all the printing and mailing of SfAA's official publication *Human Organization*. Negotiations on these matters continued on through the summer, with what seems in retrospect a gradual erosion of the original concept of an independent, openly participatory, conversational magazine toward a publication serving applied anthropologists. I am startled to see in the records how even I, who favored the earlier open concept of an independent publication, wrote the USF dean in the course of negotiating for support: "The Society for Applied Anthropology has recently decided to launch a new national journal designed to appeal to anthropologists working in non-academic occupations."

The negotiations went into fall, with President Gallaher turning the issue over to the Society's Publications Policy Committee. The minutes of the SfAA Executive Committee of November 1977 note that Robert Wulff was invited to report on progress with a "practitioner-oriented journal." That report takes up matters of administration, editorial organization, format, costs, and so forth. It speaks of contributing editors, but no longer of contributing correspondents. They had become subscribers, at a fee of $5.00.

In the next six months, development of the journal slowed somewhat, with Robert Wulff planning to leave Tampa to accept a position with Housing and Urban Development (HUD) in Washington, and the SfAA Publications Policy Committee seemingly taking a more proprietary interest in the new enterprise. After lengthy discussion during the 1978 meetings, the Executive Committee adopted a position recommended by its Publication Policy Committee: *Practicing Anthropology* would be edited by Erve Chambers at USF in Tampa, but it should be explicitly recognized as a publication of the Society for Applied Anthropology, which would allocate $10,000 for publication of the first six issues.

Let me make it clear that I believe *Practicing Anthropology*, as it has turned out, is a fine and worthwhile publication, and Erve Chambers has done a wonderful job as editor. Still, I also believe Sol Tax was right. There are tens of thousands of amateur anthropologists out there who are not necessarily interested in the professional practice of anthropology, in skills, competencies, and careers. They found anthropology to be an exhilarating experience as it opened their minds to permit exploration of new ways of life. The values implicit in anthropology—relativism, pluralism, and appreciation of complementarity of both tradition and change—need nurturing if they are to have some positive effect in the world. Professional anthropologists can do some good but, if we could engage all those others who are anthropologists at heart, much more could be done.

Commando Research:
A Rapid Applied Anthropology
Technique

Stephen L. Schensul

"Commando Research" never made it into the standard lexicon of applied anthropology. The subtitle of this article, however, reads like the first draft of a phrase that has become institutionalized in some agencies, e.g., the U.S. National Park Service, as "rapid ethnographic assessment projects." In many ways, Stephen Schensul's report stands as a major turning point in the 1970s debate over "quick-and-dirty" research in ethnography. Here he shows dramatically just how valuable even very short-term field observations can be when carried out by a well-organized team of well-focused workers. His report also documents an early example in applied anthropology of "community-based action research"; community members took the lead in the design, execution, and analysis of the research. Finally, this report neatly illustrates the importance of combining interviews with direct field observation, a hallmark technique by which scientific anthropology avoids the sole reliance on the "hearsay evidence" of surveys and interviews so often encountered in other social sciences. J. A. P.

It was only through a great deal of effort by Latino ethnic and community organizations, including marches and demonstrations, that a Teaching English as a Second Language (TESL) program was instituted in 1967 in the Chicago public school system. While most Latino educational activists considered it far from a true bilingual educational program, it at least represented some recognition of the needs of the fast-growing number of Puerto Rican and Chicano children in the system.

By 1970 serious questions were being raised about the conduct of the TESL program in Latino communities. Reports and memos circulated concerning violations of program guidelines, frequent cancellation of classes, and inept and uncaring TESL teachers. One Chicano organization on the West Side

Stephen L. Schensul is Associate Professor and Director of the Center for International Community Health Studies at the University of Connecticut School of Medicine (263 Farmington Avenue, Farmington, CT 06030; (860) 679-1570; <schensul@nso2.uchc.edu>).

Originally published in *Practicing Anthropology* 1,1(1978):13-14.

decided that something had to be done about the situation—but they first needed the facts upon which to substantiate their allegations. To get those facts they organized a unique research project which has clear implications for applied research methodology. On June 9, 1970 thirty-four people gathered at the organization headquarters. Among these people were four members, including myself, of the Community Research Unit (CRU) of the Community Mental Health Program. The CRU had been in the Chicano community for a year and a half at this point, attempting to generate research results that would be useful in community action and development. When we heard that this community organization was mobilizing this effort we offered our services. Up until we appeared with the rest of the group on that day we had no idea how the gathering of the information would proceed. We were to find that we would be "taken to school," not only literally, but also in the sense of learning an innovative information-gathering technique applied to a community problem.

The action proceeded in the following way:

10:00 am. We were briefed by organization leaders on the operation. They had prepared a set of questions to be answered by observations, by interviews with the principal and TESL teachers, and where possible by the students. We were given instructions on how and when to enter the school, who to talk to, and when to complete our visit. After the school visit, we were to return to organization headquarters and be debriefed.

10:45. We synchronized our watches and left for the nine district schools in teams of three to four.

11:00. All teams entered the school. Our team went right to the principal's office. We announced that we were community residents who wanted (as was our right) to observe unobtrusively the TESL class. We were taken to the class and left on our own. We observed the class for fifteen minutes, and then took the teacher aside for a five-minute conversation while other members of the team talked with students. We then went back to the principal for a fifteen-minute meeting.

11:46. We left the school and returned to the organization headquarters. Our team gathered together our individual observations and results of our interviews and handed them to the organization staff.

We had found the TESL classes lasted only twenty-five minutes rather than the required forty minutes because the teacher had to collect the children from all over the school. In the week before our visit the TESL teacher had substituted for other teachers a total of two and a half days. As a result, only half the TESL classes were held. The children in the class also verified that classes were frequently not held. In contrast to the report of the teacher and the children, the principal had told us that TESL teachers had not substituted for other teachers once during the entire school year!

The TESL teacher reported that the principal did not think the TESL programs were important. When she had first come to the school the classes were held in the lunchroom, then in the boiler room, and then transferred to one of the corridors. The TESL teacher was a temporary teacher and in the entire history of the three-year program at this school the TESL program had only had temporary or substitute teachers.

The members of our team felt that the classroom was not suited for the teaching of English to Spanish-speaking students. The room was small and poorly ventilated. There was no display of symbols or artwork that established a Mexican or Chicano identity. The failure of the teacher to speak Spanish created difficulties in communication between teacher and students which we felt interfered with the learning situation. Finally, the teacher stated that there was hardly any time to give the children individual instruction since they displayed such varying levels of English-speaking capability. The reports from the other schools were the same or worse.

The community group now had a solid factual base demonstrating the violations of federal guidelines for TESL programs on the part of the district schools. A report of the data from the raid was prepared and used as the basis of a suit brought by the organization to the U.S. Civil Rights Commission.

This "Commando Raid" procedure had several advantages:

(1) It caught the schools in the district unaware. Had we done one school each day principals would have alerted the other schools after the first was visited.

(2) The information was provided rapidly. The school term was ending and efforts to improve the program for September depended on accurate information collected before this school year ended.

(3) It allowed us to gain access to the TESL classrooms themselves to talk to the key people involved and to observe classroom procedure. Very often we depend too heavily on "reported behavior" or "key informant interviews" when the impact can be much greater and the results more believable when on-the-scene observations and interviews are carried out.

From the point of view of the CRU staff this was the most productive forty-five minutes in our applied research careers. We learned a great deal about timing, rapid feedback, and the link between research design and action. We began to realize the need for more innovative methods if we wanted to create an ongoing research component in community development activities. This experience was one of many times in which we found our postgraduate training in applied research coming from the Chicano community activists with whom we worked.

24

Anthropology and Contract Research: Managing and Being Managed

M. G. TREND

Federal support for experimental social programs and systematic research to evaluate their impact provided new opportunities in the 1970s for many social scientists, anthropologists among them. Here M. G. Trend compares the conditions of work on large-scale applied research projects to those typically encountered in basic ethnographic research. The focus on specific questions that arise from policy concerns and the importance of producing concrete results within tight time frames and set budgets are also characteristic of small-scale applied research projects. Other features, such as the hierarchical nature of research organizations, their interdisciplinary staffs, and the inclusion of more than one anthropologist and more than one research site, are in part a function of the size of the operations Trend describes. While these conditions of work are somewhat restricting, they also have the potential, in Trend's view, to advance basic as well as applied social science. If anthropologists do not move beyond their usual entry-level position as field researchers, however, to become analysts, research designers, and decision makers in the applied research organizations, anthropological influence on such research will continue to be restricted and anthropologists limited to support positions. Anthropologists are at risk, Trend argues, of becoming the "go-fers" of applied research. P. J. H.

Since the early 1970s, when several federal agencies undertook large social experiments at about the same time, anthropologists have been hired to work in groups on applied social research projects. They work as members of interdisciplinary teams for firms and organizations that specialize in doing research under contract with the federal government. The projects usually involve two parts: the experimental or ongoing program to be evaluated, and the actual research or evaluation itself. The research is usually commissioned with the idea of using the results to modify public policy.

M. G. Trend was Senior Analyst with Abt Associates Inc. at the time this article was published. He is now an independent practitioner who specializes in econometric research, photography, and grant writing. He can be contacted at 2009 El Greco Street, Las Vegas, NV 89102; (702) 248-1382; fax: (702) 248-1838; <trend@intermind.net>.

Originally published in *Practicing Anthropology* 1,2(1978):13-17, this article has been abridged for republication here.

26

By academic standards, the projects are well funded. Those large enough to require teams of anthropological fieldworkers (in addition to economists and survey analysts) may cost several million dollars, and run from two to five years. Smaller research projects sometimes use fieldworkers; however, since the cost of keeping a person in the field is high, fieldwork on that type of project is usually short term and bears little resemblance to the kind of research that most anthropologists have been trained to do.

This article concerns only the large projects, because they afford the best opportunity for anthropologists to become familiar with policy-relevant, applied social research. The work that anthropologists are likely to be offered, at least for entry-level positions, resembles research in a nonapplied setting. That is, extended fieldwork is often involved—a minor difference being that the fieldworker is likely to be located in the offices of a local public agency under study, rather than in the community alone. The site researcher is usually charged with the responsibility of observing the operation of an organization as it administers a new program. Further, the fieldworker may be encouraged to have systematic contact with individuals affected by the program: the local populace, bureaucrats, and program clients.

Working on applied social research projects thus may "feel" like doing basic ethnographic research. There are differences, however, and those considering a tour in this kind of research should be aware of this.

In contrast to basic social science research done under grants, applied social research for the federal government is done under contracts that are awarded on a competitive bidding basis. Most of the awards go to research organizations—some of them profit-making, some of them on a nonprofit basis—rather than to colleges or universities. The successful competitors are all part of the applied social research "industry." Depending on one's definition of "applied social research," the federal market may be as small as $500 million per year, or as large as $1 billion.

Organizations vying for research contracts have adapted to a fearsome marketplace. Their most distinctive features are their hierarchical nature, their interdisciplinary staffs, and their ability to quickly mobilize intellectual and other resources. Policy-relevant research, often quite elaborate, is done under close time schedules and with an eye toward keeping within the budget.

Contract research "houses" excel at planning and executing research designed to answer a set of focused questions that have to do with policy choices. Anthropologists may not be accustomed to such specificity, speed, and normativeness. Farewell to endless long interviews sitting under trees with elderly key informants. Farewell to that easy relativism.

Unlike research done under grants, which may specify only one vague product and which may be allowed to slip indefinitely, contracts have timetables with reports or "contract deliverables" being required at certain intervals.

Often, continued funding for the research is tied to them. Farewell to putting things off until next summer.

The conduct of applied social research is necessarily more disciplined than basic research. As noted above, the contracts are large. A $50,000 research project is a small one. The larger the contract, the more social scientists are involved and the more supervision and coordination are required. Those things all go together. Farewell to Lone Ranger field work.

Because large social experiments are of many parts, and because contracts set deadlines, research must proceed in an orderly fashion. The need for the work to be both focused and empirically sound (since the results and decisions based upon it are open to scrutiny) means that the freedom—some of us would say license—of individual team members is reduced further.

Doing applied social research is not the dreary business that some outsiders contend. One of the major challenges faced by anyone writing a contract research proposal is to show how policy questions can be answered by the research. Even after the contract is awarded, the research may change in an attempt to answer the policy questions more definitively. Once the work is underway, shifting policy interests on the part of the government client, or the early results of the inquiry, may shape the research design further. So, be creative, flexible, rigorous, and wise.

Compared with other social scientists, anthropologists are underrepresented in the federal government and in contract research houses. Blame the fabled, post-World War II "growth spurt" of academic anthropology for this. But in any case, members of our profession are proportionately unlikely to be involved as a government client responsible for specifying the questions to be answered by the proposed research project, or as a staff member of one of the contract research organizations involved in bidding for the award. In the latter case, such "in-house" research staff are responsible for responding to the Request for Proposal (RFP) prepared by the potential client. Once the contract is awarded, the research staff are responsible for producing a polished research design, hiring the necessary additional staff, and doing the work.

The relatively small proportions of anthropologists employed outside the universities means that the kind of work anthropologists can do is determined largely by people outside the profession. Both policy and research questions are formulated and addressed by people with the mind-set of an economist or a political scientist, rather than that of an anthropologist.

Anthropologists are often viewed by other social scientists as people who do fieldwork in exotic societies and write ethnographies about their experiences. A lot of analysts in contract houses also believe that anthropologists are a bit muddleheaded and incompetent in quantitative techniques. Unfortunately, for those anthropologists who want to do applied social research of the type I have described, it really does not matter whether the stereotypes are valid. What does matter is that they are believed.

As things stand now, anthropologists tend to get hired onto research projects that are just getting underway, after the contract has been awarded and the research design has been fairly well fixed. The anthropologist is hired in an entry-level position, commonly as one of several site researchers or observers on a large demonstration where different agencies, located in different parts of the country, try to induce some sort of limited social change. Depending on the sponsoring federal department or bureau, the local organizations may be welfare offices, schools, housing authorities, or correctional institutions.

A typical demonstration project may have a dozen or so agencies, each implementing a different version of a new program. For example, one large effort sponsored by the U.S. Department of Housing and Urban Development required eight agencies to design and effect their own versions of a housing allowance program. Instead of being placed into housing projects, program participants were given cash grants to live in housing available on the private market. Each local agency tried its own ideas about the amount of housing counseling that was required, the stringency of their minimum housing standard, and so forth.

In the more elegant demonstrations or social experiments, the research team may try to reconcile the qualitative information that comes from field workers with quantitative information that comes from surveys, agency records, and management information systems. Most contract researchers like to think of themselves as hard-nosed empiricists. They like to measure things precisely, and the idea of using "triangulation" with varied data to provide more reliable answers is appealing to them. Even "bomber pilot" analysts, the ones who like to work only from computer printouts (preferably in the home office, several hundred miles from the nearest demonstration site), need occasional reassurance from someone who was really there watching it happen. The fieldworker's perspective can do much to inject a bit of realism and sanity into the musings of such individuals.

Turning things around a bit, the cross-site comparative outlook of in-house analysts can enrich the understanding of individual fieldworkers who are each likely to feel that "their" site is special, and that only someone who has lived there for a year or more can really understand. This kind of proprietariness is familiar enough to those who have heard traditional anthropologists talking about "their" people or "their" village.

Just because a project collects both qualitative and quantitative data, there is no guarantee that they will be used together. Particularly in education, where federal influence on local practice has been historically slight, such applied research projects may tend to resemble basic research. That is, the interdisciplinary nature of the work may be de-emphasized if the pressure to produce answers to focused policy questions is off. If you should find yourself doing this sort of work in an applied setting, enjoy it for what it is: the chance to do trail-breaking, basic research outside the university.

On some projects, the qualitative and quantitative information have been kept almost completely apart. These are likely to be far fewer in the future; the trend is toward using both perspectives. One may expect to see a decline in the number of "holistic" case studies or ethnographies commissioned in future years. Similarly, reports that appear to be computer-written may also be on the decline.

The analysis and report writing for large research projects almost invariably extends beyond the time when field data is being collected. In part, this is due to sheer volume of data involved. Also, getting large quantitative data bases into shape is time consuming and really is not complete until the last survey data have been collected. A lot of anthropologists seem to be intimidated by—or are at least suspicious of—quantitative or econometric techniques. My only observation is that no one method or person can do it all. Quantitative techniques are a mainstay of applied social research; however, nonspecialists only have to be able to understand some basic techniques and know when they are in over their heads. They have to know when to call for help.

Having been the supervisor of a number of anthropologists working on large projects, I am impressed by our wide interests and the range of skills we possess collectively. At the same time, this makes us strange to people from other disciplines. Economists, for example, seem to be genuinely confused about what our subject matter really *is*, unless it is everything that has to do with human beings.

As a result, anthropologists are usually hired for the observational skills they are thought to possess rather than for any uniquely anthropological perspectives they might bring to policy-relevant research. They run some risk, therefore, of becoming handmaidens of other disciplines, the go-fers of the applied research world.

Being forever in the field unfortunately means that you get isolated from the home office or the contract research organization, where the applied research is really designed and where most of the analysis takes place. Those who decide to remain solely fieldworkers miss the opportunity of working with professionals from other disciplines in any but the most subordinate fashion. One of the myths of our profession is that anthropology and fieldwork are coterminous. Actually, the fieldwork of academic anthropologists only serves as punctuation to a teaching career. Equally for the applied anthropologist doing contract research, perhaps the bulk of one's time should be spent in the home office working with other professionals.

I am beginning to believe that advances in the social sciences may come at least as readily from applied social research contexts as from basic, disciplinary research from the universities. One of the strengths of the contract houses is that their staffs comprise people from many disciplines. Because of the hierarchical nature of these organizations, staff work together on projects under the direction of a research manager or principal investigator. This kind of cooperation is difficult to negotiate in a university setting where the divisions are departmental. The interchange of ideas may be actually easier to achieve in the contract house than in the university.

Some of us have thrived in the new research setting. It is apparent from reading a few symposium papers and journal articles that others have not. With few exceptions, the journal articles about contract research and anthropology have been written by anthropologists in entry-level, fieldworker positions. Anthropologists will no longer be "new" in contract research when the articles are written by anthropologists who work with in-house analysts on a regular basis, and when the articles themselves focus on research rather than the role of the researchers.

One curious point confronts me. For all our emphasis on depth, holism, extended fieldwork, and insight, and for all our expertise with other cultures, we seem to be no better than other social scientists and journalists in understanding our own society.

Thank God we are no worse.

Anthropologist in the White House

PHILLEO NASH

Philleo Nash is one of a handful of distinguished public service an-thropologists whose careers spanned elective and appointive offices. Nash was Administrative Assistant to the President under President Truman, Lieutenant Governor of Wisconsin, and U.S. Commissioner of Indian Affairs under President Kennedy. Nash argues that anthropology in-formed all his work, such as his opposition to termination of tribal status for the Menominee of Wisconsin and his support for the estab-lishment of a President's Commission on Civil Rights to address race relations (back in 1947!). The number of anthropologists who have en-tered government as civil servants has grown, and many now have senior staff or management positions. Nash's observation about anthro-pologists' role and identity, however, is still accurate: being an anthro-pologist is usually secondary to the other more publicly recognized roles and skills. Nash comments that he was confirmed as U.S. Commissioner of Indian Affairs despite being an anthropologist, rather than because of it. This would probably still be true today—although no other anthro-pologists have tested the waters as potential political appointees with Senate confirmation. There are still challenges for anthropologists! S. J. F.

Like many other anthropologists of my generation, I came to my first ap-plied job in Washington, D.C., during World War II. I liked the place and the work, never missed the academy, and stayed on after the war—filled with a sense of tasks unfinished. The Truman era turned me on and the McCarthy era did not permanently sour me, although it switched my opportunities to zero at the end of the Truman administration. I turned then to the academy, but the departments I approached were fearful, or discounted my thirteen years of government service as a void, or both.

I left Washington feeling somewhat unwanted both in and out of the acad-emy and was gratified to gain acceptance in the rough and tumble of practical politics. In seven years I made my way from County Chairman to Lieutenant

Philleo Nash (1909-1987) was President of Biron Cranberry Company of Wisconsin Rapids and Professor Emeritus at American University when this article was written. He was also a past president of the Society for Applied Anthropology, and in 1986 he received the Society for Ap-plied Anthropology's Bronislaw Malinowski Award.

Originally published as part of a special section on "Public Interest Anthropology," edited by Robert M. Wulff, Kirk L. Gray, and Erve Chambers, in *Practicing Anthropology* 1,3(1979):3,23.

32

Governor of Wisconsin. I visited and revisited every corner of my native state, made innumerable friends, and some enemies, and gained enormous respect for the political process. In my last try for re-election, I was defeated, so I returned to Washington for a second round, this time as U.S. Commissioner of Indian Affairs. This was satisfactory but not eternal, and after a brief period as a consultant to some multinational clients, I returned to the academy in an established department of anthropology, from which I am an emeritus professor today.

It has been an active, turbulent, personally satisfying career—all of it outside the academy except at the beginning and the end. But was it anthropology or politics? I thought it was anthropology at the time and said so when I made my autobiographical entry in the Wisconsin Blue Book. "Applied Anthropologist," I called myself. Was I right?

In the early part of World War II, I headed a small section in a division of the Domestic Branch of the Office of War Information. Our task was to develop criteria for the evaluation of racial tensions. After correctly forecasting riots in a number of cities, we were naively astonished to find that there was no civilian agency of government willing to receive our information. My associates and I, brash and young, took the problem directly to the White House. There we found a willing, albeit skeptical, listener in a new administrative assistant to President Roosevelt. Jonathan Daniels, journalist and editor, and son of FDR's first boss in the U.S. Navy, was and is an authentic southern liberal. Daniels listened, and that began an association with him that continued up to FDR's death.

President Truman quite literally inherited me, for he knew nothing of me or my work. I came along, so to speak, with the man who was to be my immediate boss during most of the Truman Administration—David K. Niles.

Niles was as authentic a northern liberal as Daniels was southern. His credentials went back to Sacco and Vanzetti and, even before, to the LaFollete-Wheeler presidential campaign of 1924.

Niles and President Truman quickly developed a relationship of trust and confidence in the most delicate areas of human rights. Policy and politics were both served, for Niles soon became Truman's ombudsman to the liberal establishment.

Tragically, Niles' health failed during the last years of the Truman Administration. With the support and guidance of others on the Truman staff, I carried on some of his duties, but there could be no real substitute for him.

Truman's Christmas present to me in the last year of his office was the title "Administrative Assistant to the President." But his last day in office was also mine, for I knew there would be no place for me in the new administration.

When I left, I looked back on ten years during which I had worked on one or more aspects of the following national problems: racial tension; civil rights; conscientious objection; self-determination for the Virgin Islands, Puerto Rico,

American Samoa and Guam; civil government in the Trust Territory of the Pacific; American Indian affairs; displaced persons; statehood for Hawaii and Alaska; and technical assistance (Point IV).

To say that I worked on these problems means that I prepared research and program memoranda leading to both executive and legislative action; drafted speeches and correspondence; discussed proposals and complaints with delegations; maintained contact with the executive departments; reviewed budget proposals in assigned areas; prepared draft executive orders; made advance preparation for Presidential trips; and carried out many other duties, some humdrum, but others filled with tension and excitement. Thus, I wrote dozens of letters thanking creative stitchers for their handiwork gifts to the President, but I was also the first to read the letter of instruction found on the body of the Puerto Rican Nationalist who attempted to storm the Blair House and died in an exchange of gunfire with the Secret Service.

The life of the White House staffer is like that of any member of a large organization. Mostly, one tries to be useful from day to day, in whatever areas of opportunity arise. But in the broader sense no one assigned me to duties in detail, and many of the areas into which I ventured were, at the beginning, self-assigned. Those subject areas were consistent with the accepted content of cultural anthropology.

That I was permitted a lot of initiative does not mean that I was unsupervised. The possibility of embarrassing the President by clumsiness or outright failure was ever-present. Of course, I chafed under restraints, but also came to recognize their usefulness. Sharing responsibility with others was a protection. Group effort enhanced the chance of success as much as it reduced the likelihood of failure.

Viewed anthropologically, the Presidency is a belief system based on the premise that the President does everything by himself. As he moves through the day, the President engages in various behaviors appropriate to the multiple roles of his Office. President Truman used to refer to them as Commander-in-Chief, Chief Politician, Chief Economist, Chief Legislator, Chief of State, and Chief Executive. Reason tells us that no one human being could act out all these roles unaided. Yet, the Presidential mystique requires everyone to act as though he did. Media representatives, who are on hand twenty-four hours a day, continuously evaluate the President's capacity to know, to think, and to decide. But, unsupported by staff initiative, the President can do little. Hence, the White House staffer must learn to do everything as though it were being done by the President, and with the certain knowledge that it is the President who will be held accountable. Living in, working with, and studying this unique culture was my field work for ten years.

With the end of World War II came the lapse of the War Powers Act, which meant a limitation on Presidential power and the disappearance of the rationale for our wartime program. Yet, our research suggested that the return of

34

servicemen from overseas would provide the time and place for a repetition of the postwar riots of World War I.

In late 1945 and 1946, our worst predictions came true. It was time to extend theory and practice one more step. My contribution to the program had been deprivation theory: the precursor of violence is protest and the cause is deprivation. Violence can be controlled, but in a democratic society, even one at war, the focus should be on the deprivation and not on the protest. Still, the postwar violence mounted and seemed to be mainly directed at returning black veterans. The fallout, in the form of national indignation, reached President Truman. He really believed in the slogan he kept on his desk—"The Buck Stops Here."—and he demanded a program.

Congress was obviously not ready to act, and neither were the Courts. Civil Rights legislation and the watershed court decisions were still years away. Presidential action was required, yet there were limits on Presidential power. What to do?

In the files, ready for use if the time should ever seem right, was a proposal going back to the early years of the war—a proposal to create a national commission on race relations. It had been rejected then, because it seemed inadequate to the emergency. Now it was all that was possible. Staff work was begun at once under Niles' direction, and the outcome was the President's Committee on Civil Rights.

The Committee's report, "To Secure These Rights," issued in late 1947, was only a report and took no action in and of itself. But it was the first Presidentially based document that dealt directly and across the board with such divisive issues as segregation. Some of its most basic recommendations were not acted upon for seventeen years, and others have never been adopted. But it began a dialogue about human rights that was necessary to start the process of change. It was a key element in the campaign of 1948 and in Truman's victory. The issue was dramatized as never before in modern times, and successor Presidents were bound to follow the lead.

In President Truman's four years, though, there remained the requirement of direct action where opportunities for the Chief Executive were present and results were possible. Developing staff support for such actions was to keep me hard at work for four more years. It was also to bring me into close personal association and eventual friendship with Truman.

Truman kept in close touch and helped me personally in my work after he left the Presidency. He had been out of office six years when I ran, with his approval, for Lieutenant Governor of Wisconsin on a platform that included opposition to federal termination of the Menominee Indian tribe. I served only one term, but before I left office my name as President of Wisconsin Senate was on a Joint Resolution urging Congress to abandon Menominee termination before it was too late. The Congress regrettably did not heed that advice until many years later.

The position I had taken was consistent with the views of anthropology. Yet, I did not run for office as an anthropologist, and when I was defeated for re-election it was not as an anthropologist that I went down.

In 1961, I was nominated by President Kennedy to be U.S. Commissioner of Indian Affairs, and I was confirmed by the U.S. Senate after a prolonged struggle. The struggle had nothing to do with me being an anthropologist, but involved a revival from Wisconsin of the old McCarthy accusations. I was pleased to beat down that smear, and I did not complain about the time it took. But I have to say to other applied anthropologists that I was confirmed in spite of being an anthropologist, not because of it. The Senate of the United States in those days did not think it wise to have a believer in the worth of indigenous cultures serving as Commissioner of Indian Affairs. The Senators confirmed me because President Kennedy, Secretary of the Interior Stewart Udall, and Senator Hubert H. Humphrey refused to back down in the face of diversionary tactics by the opposition.

I was also aided by strong support from the National Congress of American Indians, assembled in convention at just the right time in Lewiston, Idaho. But did these tribal representatives support me because I was known to them as an anthropologist? Not at all. They supported me because I had a clean record on termination, which was then the hottest single issue in American Indian affairs.

There has been a quantum change since World War II. Segregation is on the defensive, and integration, still far from universal, is the norm to be defended. Minority rights are now more often asserted by minority representatives than by elite advocates. Programs for minority benefits are increasingly self-directed. Termination has been replaced by the idea of restoration. Programs that were once developed by Presidential power are directed today by commissions organized under their own statutes.

The anthropological view of social policy—that cultural diversity and respect for cultural differences are a requirement of the good life—has had a big advance since 1942. I am inordinately proud of my part in it, and I am grateful to the political leaders who let me do what I would and could. But it was not done in the name of anthropology. It was done in the name of public policy and forged under conditions of extreme social tension.

It appears that anthropologists are now moving into some of the slots once occupied by lawyers, political scientists, economists, psychologists and sociologists. We are challenged to succeed where others have not succeeded. I wish the current generation of anthropologists well, and I hope their increased visibility will improve their effectiveness in designing and implementing public policy based on anthropological precepts of social justice. But, I wonder…

Public Interest Anthropology: Beyond the Bureaucratic Ethos

SHELTON H. DAVIS AND ROBERT O. MATHEWS

Shelton Davis and Robert Mathews address an issue that has long troubled many anthropologists: For whose benefit is anthropology be-ing applied? Like M. G. Trend (this volume), Davis and Mathews are concerned that the contribution of applied anthropology is too often lim-ited to providing data for decisions made by persons in more powerful positions. Their proposed solution, however, is not for anthropologists to rise to positions of power within research organizations working on government (or corporate) contracts—or even to rise to positions of power within governments and corporations. Rather, they propose that anthropologists focus their research on the structures of power and pow-erlessness, address significant social problems, represent the interests of those most affected by the problems, and put the results of their work in the hands of citizens and citizen groups. They offer brief descriptions of three projects undertaken by the Anthropology Resource Center as examples of the type of applied anthropology they advocate. P. J. H.

To develop the ability to perceive adversity or injustice or constraint or other things that people do not like is a call to any profession to break out of its rigid mode of behavior. Anthropology's mission is to ferment intellectually, physically, economically, and generationally. One of the surest observations we can make is that wherever there is an important problem in our society, we will not find an anthropologist near it.— Ralph Nader, "Anthropology in Law and Civic Action," in Bela C. Maday, ed., *Anthropology and Society* (1975), p. 40.

Consumer advocate Ralph Nader's observations are particularly relevant to the present dilemma of applied anthropology. Although one might argue that applied anthropologists are "near" the problems of contemporary society,

Shelton H. Davis is Sector Manager for Social Development, Latin America and Caribbean Region, at The World Bank (1818 H Street, NW, Washington, D.C. 20433; (202) 473-3413; <sdavis2@worldbank.org>).

Robert O. Mathews is Staff Technical Writer at Rational Software Corporation (20 Maguire Road, Lexington, MA 02421; (781) 676-2712; fax: (781) 676-2640; <rom@rational.com>).

Originally published as part of a special section on "Public Interest Anthropology," guest edited by Robert M. Wulff, Kirk L. Gray, and Erve Chambers, in *Practicing Anthropology* 1,3(1979):5,25-26.

38

they have neither approached them with the "intellectual ferment" of a truly critical discipline nor proposed solutions that have generated public debate and civic action. This failure is due largely to the compromises that applied social researchers have made in serving only the needs of government bureaucrats and corporate managers. There is a certain "liberal practicality" among American social scientists, as C. Wright Mills pointed out, that limits the vision of the applied researcher to the demands of the modern corporation and state.

A recent survey by the Society for Applied Anthropology of jobs held by anthropologists outside academia confirms the persistence of this narrow vision. According to Alvin W. Wolfe, who reported the survey results in the first issue of *Practicing Anthropology* ("The Jobs of Applied Anthropologists," *Practicing Anthropology* 1,1[1978]:14-16), 48 percent of the respondents described their jobs as "evaluation research," while only 6 percent said they were involved in "advocacy anthropology." Their most important tasks were social-impact, demographic, and intervention research and development; the least important were representation, instruction, and policy formation. They spent most of their time in such activities as "interviewing people," "negotiating with people," "monitoring people," "persuading people," and "arranging people."

Although the survey's correlational, cross-tabulation, and cluster analyses are incomplete, three generalizations emerge from an outsider's view of the data. First, most of these anthropologists appear to take for granted the structure of American society; few are analyzing the sources of power and powerlessness. Second, representing the interests of those most affected by social problems seems to be the least common activity of applied anthropologists. Third, posing solutions to these problems and formulating alternative policies are not the aims of research or development. Applied anthropologists have found their way out of the academy and into an Orwellian world of sample surveys, simulation, and cost-benefit analysis.

Public-interest anthropology differs from traditional applied anthropology in what is considered the object of study, whose interests the researcher represents, and what the researcher does with the results of his or her work. Public-interest anthropology grows out of the democratic traditions of citizen activism rather than the bureaucratic needs of management and control. It is based on the premise that social problems—war, poverty, racism, sexism, environmental degradation, misuse of technology—are deeply rooted in social structure, and that the role of the intellectual is to work with citizens in promoting fundamental social change.

The Anthropology Resource Center (ARC) was established in 1975 as the first public-interest anthropology organization in the United States. As part of an evolving program of social research and public education, ARC publishes periodic reports, maintains a data center for use by students and citizen groups, and distributes a quarterly newsletter. In the remainder of this article, we describe three ARC projects and contrast them with traditional applied anthropological research in the same areas. [The ARC was dissolved in 1984 for lack of reliable funding.]

Development Policy in the Amazon

The social and ecological destruction taking place in the Amazon basin has received much attention in the world press. Some anthropologists have responded by making their services available to national Indian bureaus and international development agencies such as USAID and the World Bank. In fact, some anthropologists have argued that the survival of indigenous communities will depend upon these agencies' benevolence toward tribal peoples and continued reliance on anthropological expertise.

Unfortunately, these anthropologists have paid little attention to the activities of the development agencies themselves and their relationships with authoritarian governments and multinational corporations. International aid and lending institutions and multinational corporations remain virtually unaccountable for their activities outside the United States. When a congressional subcommittee investigated Amazon development policy in 1978, it found more information on the kinship patterns of the Bororo than on the multimillion-dollar investments and loans of Volkswagen, D. K. Ludwig, or the Ex-Im Bank.

In 1975, we decided to find out what these organizations were up to in the Amazon. Using government reports and business journals, we found that the same institutions that were concerned with "the poorest of the poor" were financing large-scale infrastructural projects that were uprooting Indians and peasants. The highways, ports, hydroelectric plants, and settlement schemes were of little use to indigenous peoples but proved convenient for corporations interested in the region's oil, minerals, timber, and agricultural wealth.

We next undertook field research at the offices of USAID and the World Bank in Washington. The officials we interviewed were surprised to find that they, rather than Indians, were the subjects of research. They were parsimonious with information but remarkably generous with offers of employment; as we turned on our tape recorder, one official suggested that we might like a job with USAID studying colonists in the Peruvian jungle.

In November 1976, we published our findings in a report called *The Geological Imperative*. We knew the report was successful when Hanna Mining Company protested our exposure of its activities in Brazil and when *National Geographic* wrote to defend one of their authors whose work among the Yanomamo Indians we had criticized.

The Geological Imperative has gone through three printings, and ARC has presented its findings to the United Nations, a congressional subcommittee, and native, environmental, and human-rights groups. Although many people are now aware of the relationships among development policy, multinational corporations, and indigenous peoples, there is much work to be done in agricultural, health, and environmental policies. Anthropologists who take a broad and critical view of development can demonstrate the links among these issues and educate American citizens about the causes of underdevelopment in the Third World.

Native Americans and Energy Development

Following the publication of our Amazon research, we began to investigate the effects of national energy policy on local communities. Leslie White made anthropologists aware of the importance of understanding energy use in its social context. Anthropologists are nevertheless more familiar with the uses of energy in tribal and peasant communities than in modern industrial states. Only a handful of anthropologists have written on energy policy or discussed the implications of the "energy crisis" in the United States.

This lack of concern is particularly noteworthy in view of the impact that energy developments are having on Indian and Anglo communities in the West. Indian tribes are estimated to own one-third of the country's low-sulfur, strippable coal, over half the nation's uranium reserves, and 3 to 10 percent of U.S. petroleum and gas reserves. Although newspapers have noted the increasing exploitation of these reserves and plans for new coal-gasification and electrical-generating plants, few social scientists have researched the effects of these developments on reservation economies, governments, environments, cultures, and health.

ARC has recently published a report, titled *Native Americans and Energy Development*, that documents the effects of energy projects on Indian and non-Indian populations in the West. This report contains articles by five anthropologists who for several years have been studying energy and economic-development issues alongside Western Indian tribes. Harris Arthur, a Navajo working in the U.S. Department of the Interior, has written a preface to the report.

This study differs from other social-impact assessments in several ways. First, the authors use information gathered from anthropological field work, rather than standard cost-benefit analyses, to assess the local effects of energy projects. They consider not only economic variables but also the effects of development on family and community structure, tribal politics, religion, and personal values. Second, they do not take for granted the presence, motivations, and desirability of energy corporations, but analyze the interactions between corporate strategies and local responses. Finally, as independent researchers, they are making their findings available to tribal leaders, native organizations, and local communities.

There is clearly a need for similar public-interest energy research by anthropologists in other areas of the country. Here in New England, we are conducting an investigation of community response to the Pilgrim nuclear power plant in Plymouth, Massachusetts. This study is considering the Pilgrim case within the context of the history of regional electrical planning. One of our goals is to conceptualize the social implications of alternative strategies for electrical generation based on solar rather than nuclear power.

Schooling and Urban Politics

In their emphasis on the learning of tradition and social norms, anthropologists have always been concerned with education; Eric Wolf once characterized the Boasian view of culture as a "large schoolhouse." The modern anthropological study of education grew out of a similar view of educational institutions as transmitters of cultural values. While some anthropologists remain interested in education as a socializing agent, ethnomethodologists have turned their attention to the structure of ever-briefer segments of classroom interaction. When public and college education was torn by conflict in the 1960s, anthropology was caught unawares. Neither the functionalist school nor ethnomethodology provided the tools for understanding the relationship between education and politics in the United States.

Yet, in the 1970s, more and more anthropologists have undertaken educational research particularly in evaluation. As administrators have sought information about program processes in addition to outcomes, they have turned away from statistical analyses of test results and toward the naturalistic methods of anthropology. Although anthropologists may be giving administrators more elaborate data with which to make decisions, they seldom analyze the decision-making process itself or the political and economic context in which decisions are made. Conflict is to be resolved rather than understood.

Researchers at ARC are attempting to come to grips with these problems by investigating educational change in Boston. School desegregation has been a stage on which urban politics have been acted out; the bitter protests against the urban renewal of the 1960s have been replaced by the desegregation struggle of the 1970s. Urban renewal, demographic shifts, and fiscal problems profoundly influence the changes taking place in the Boston public schools. At the same time, parents and other citizens are demanding a greater role in making decisions about education. How, we may ask, can anthropologists contribute to understanding these changes?

ARC is beginning to formulate a research program to answer this question. Current research includes the collection of documentation on the history, finance, and administrative structure of the Boston public schools; participant observation of parent and citizen organizations created by the 1974 court order; and ethnographic study of classroom interaction. The project has two broad aims: to develop anthropological theory and methods to encompass the complexity of urban educational change, and to make research results available to citizens and parents concerned with the schools.

Prospects for Public-Interest Anthropology

Although public-interest anthropology provides a vigorous challenge to the traditions of applied anthropology, this new approach is not without its own problems. Anthropological theory, derived from the study of "isolated" tribal groups, is inadequate for understanding complex political economies and industrial states. Anthropologists are not trained to study corporations and bureaucracies, and ethnographic methods alone provide insufficient data about the structure and distribution of power. Further, we are far more accustomed to putting our research at the disposal of academic journals or administrators than in the hands of citizen groups.

At ARC, we are attempting to confront these problems by organizing informal seminars, intern programs, postdoctoral training, and a public-interest data center. Nonetheless, these programs suffer from a lack of institutional support for public-interest research. Although the National Science Foundation has taken a small step toward increasing funding through its Science for the Citizen Program, the professional associations have yet to bring enough pressure to bear on foundations and government agencies to cause a substantial shift in funding priorities.

On balance, the future of public-interest anthropology will depend on whether or not those who enter the discipline are willing to commit themselves to careers in social change. Faced by declining prospects for academic employment, too many anthropologists are seeking jobs outside the university without considering their social implications or the possibility of alternative anthropological careers. The cultural relativism of anthropology is being replaced by the ethical relativism of the marketplace. But the question is not whether one works inside or outside the university; it is whether or not one brings to one's work a sense of intellectual and social responsibility.

How to Look Like an Anthropologist Without Really Being One

HARRY F. WOLCOTT

By 1980, when this article was first published, ethnographic research was becoming faddish in various fields of social research, especially education. After cleverly teasing out surface similarities between ethnography and other kinds of activities, Harry Wolcott argues that genuine ethnography is distinguished not by its research techniques but by reliance on a cultural framework for interpretation. The latter, he believes, is the most significant contribution anthropology can make to the applied social sciences. Wolcott linked his argument to then-new developments that were to become ever more important in anthropology and far beyond, such as Geertz' ideas on the "interpretation of cultures" and Goodenough's pioneering observations on "multiculturalism."

J. A. P.

In the past decade educators have shown increasing interest in ethnographic research but an alarming tendency to regard ethnography as just another synonym for descriptive (or even "nonquantitative") research. Anthropologists working in other settings assure me that interest in descriptive approaches is rather widespread in other areas of applied social research as well. There, too, it has been accompanied by a "diffusion" of ethnography similar to what I have observed among educational researchers.

For "looking like an anthropologist," I have in mind something other than Alfred Kroeber being photographed next to Ishi or members of the Leakey family appearing in *National Geographic*. I am thinking about the "pose" of the cultural anthropologist when engaged in ethnographic research and "doing fieldwork."

One could be swept away writing a parody advising novices how to achieve this fieldworker pose. My title, "How to look like an anthropologist without really being one," seems to beg for such a script. I have resisted the temptation to

Harry F. Wolcott is Professor Emeritus of Anthropology at the University of Oregon (Eugene, OR 97403; (541) 346-5102; <hwolcott@oregon.uoregon.edu>).

Originally published in *Practicing Anthropology* 3,1(1980):6-7,56-59, this article has been abridged for republication here. An earlier version of the paper was presented during the meeting of the American Educational Research Association in Boston, April 11, 1980. For an update on some of the issues discussed in this article, see Harry F. Wolcott, *Ethnography: A Way of Seeing* (Walnut Creek, Calif: AltaMira Press, 1999).

be facetious. Instead of a parody, I will begin by proposing several essential ingredients of the fieldwork pose. The list serves as a starting point for addressing the purpose of these comments: to help explain (and perhaps even to help reestablish) the differences between what I consider to be an *authentic ethnographic* approach and a more broadly based *descriptive approach*.

Without ignoring the important fact that each field setting poses its own peculiar circumstances and limitations, let me suggest how easy it is to *look* like an anthropologist.

First, you arrive in person on the scene where you expect to conduct your work. (There's nothing special about that: meter readers, house painters, youth workers, firemen, teachers do it every day.)

Second, you self-consciously (and, these days, explicitly) establish yourself as the *research instrument*, a role you typically punctuate with appropriate note taking, augmented perhaps with camera or tape recorder. (Nothing special about that: real estate salespersons, reporters and news photographers, police or insurance investigators, appraisers and estimators do it all the time.)

Third, you announce that you intend to be on hand for an inordinately long time—even if that means only one full day, as it sometimes has in educational research—and that you are inordinately interested in everything. Nothing is to be regarded as trivial that is not trivial to the host or hosts. (Note that we expect similar commitment and an initial period of total immersion from newcomers in many occupations: hospitals and schools have their interns; law offices and many trades have apprenticeships; freshmen have Orientation Week; inductees into the armed forces have the golden opportunity of the intense experience called basic training.)

Fourth, you make conscious, even conspicuous use of multiple sources and multiple research techniques: observing in varied settings, using questionnaires or structured interviews, holding casual conversation, making film and tape recordings. (But so do the CIA, bill collectors, family service agencies, detectives, university search committees, customs and immigrations officers, even some sociologists.)

Fifth, you wear heavily—but willingly—a yoke of ethical and professional obligations: to confidentiality, to objectivity, to fairness and accuracy, to the best traditions of scientific inquiry coupled with the utmost concern for humanity. (I assume that psychiatrists and clinical psychologists, investigative journalists, parole officers, and morticians observe similar tenets.)

Sixth, you recognize a commitment to do something with the information being gathered. Your presence serves some larger purpose than a visit. Though your behavior as a guest at the time of your fieldwork may be exemplary, your intent goes beyond simply making other people aware of what a tolerant, sympathetic, and interested person you are. Since you are obliged to present a report stating your findings, you take the opportunity to explain the kind of report you are making, perhaps even exaggerating a bit on the potential social significance of your work if the end result is not obvious to your respondents. (The census or opinion poll taker, the inventory-control officer, the reporter, the accident investigator, or high school students who have conducted interviews for a class project also need to complete their reports. And they, too, have to be able to give—and recognize—reasonable explanations of why they "need" certain information.)

Cultural anthropologists "doing fieldwork" by engaging in everyday activities of the kind I have mentioned may feel self-conscious, not only about relying on such commonplace techniques for gathering information but also about the possibility of being mistaken for somebody in any one of the numerous other roles of information gatherers. During my own introduction to fieldwork, for example, I was greatly distressed to be accused of being both spy and cop. I have subsequently come to realize how those accusations served as a sort of "Red Badge of Courage," allowing me to take my place among veteran fieldworkers.

The fact that there is nothing outwardly distinguishing about this pose can create problems for anyone wanting to look like an anthropologist, including anthropologists themselves. If so renowned an anthropologist as Margaret Mead found it necessary to include cape and walking stick, small wonder that less well-known anthropologists often signal their professional identity through the conspicuous display of native dress abroad or turquoise jewelry at home. But neither shawls on the women nor the characteristic "field beards" on the men can guarantee the image of the researcher-scholar they wish to create. In the long run, fieldworkers depend on words and labels to convey messages about how they perceive themselves and how they would like others to perceive them. When cultural anthropologists are conducting descriptive research on how some identifiable group of humans believe and behave, they are engaging in the basic work of their discipline. Both the process of doing it and the completed account they expect to render are known as *ethnography*.

Even without the romantic appeal of the exotic tropical island or jungle village, a certain fascination with the image of the anthropologist at work "in the field" and a growing recognition for the value (at least up to a point) of descriptive research have been evident in the applied social sciences in recent years. Among educational researchers one is hard pressed to think of a term that achieved any greater notoriety during the 1970s than the term ethnography. But today the purposes which ethnography was originally intended to serve, and the commitments one traditionally made in laying claim either to conducting an ethnographic inquiry or to writing an ethnographic account, remain in danger of being lost or crushed by that overly enthusiastic educator embrace.

Perhaps too much like a knight in shining armor, my purpose here is to try to "rescue" the term ethnography. If it is not already too late, I want to keep ethnography from becoming confused with and even lost among a group of related terms and purposes that are gaining popularity among educational researchers and other applied researchers as well. I want to set ethnography apart from a host of terms with which it is often confused, terms such as onsite research, naturalistic research, participant observation, qualitative observation, case study, or field study.

Even as I set out to rescue the term ethnography and to reserve it forevermore for referring only to *one particular type* of descriptive work, I applaud the spirit that has nurtured a considerable interest in "descriptive" or "qualitative" or even, if you must, "alternative" approaches to research. In terms of the narrow psychometric orientation that has long dominated educational research, a so-called "ethnographic approach," combining (1) the self as instrument, (2) multiple techniques and (3) ample time, continues to offer needed antidote to educator preoccupation with pigeons and probabilities and a tendency to ignore problems unless they are quantifiable. When I offer my seminar on Ethnographic Method in Educational Research each fall, when I am invited to speak on the topic of ethnography in education, and when I prepared a talk on "ethnographic method" for the series of taped lectures on Alternative Research Methodologies recently released by the American Educational Research Association, the ideas of the self as instrument, the multiplicity of techniques, and adequate time for fieldwork (and the subsequent write-up) are the ideas I stress.

Researchers often seem glad to hear the encouraging message I bring: What better way to keep in touch with reality than by conducting research in real settings? What better way to achieve validity than by using multiple sources and multiple field techniques? What meanings more powerful than those assigned by the actors in any particular cultural scene? What questions more fundamental than how things are and how they got that way? What instrument more powerful than a human being for understanding other humans?

Unfortunately, in the enthusiasm for adding "ethnography" to an already ample set of labels for qualitative approaches, educational researchers are in danger of losing sight of what the term has meant, who has used it, and what the special features of "ethnography" are that distinguish it from other terms either equally distinguishable (e.g., Zelditch's useful explication of the term "field study" in "Some Methodological Problems of Field Studies," *American Journal of Sociology* 67,5[1962]:566-576) or comfortingly broad (e.g., case study; naturalistic research). Today one hears ethnography suggested as a synonym for case study, as an adjective describing a special kind of educational evaluation, and even as the label for a research broadside where investigators insist they haven't a clue about what they are going to be looking "for" or "at." Whatever ethnography is, a considerable number of educational researchers today claim to be ready and able to do it.

Our evangelical efforts in "anthropology and education" to extol the virtues of descriptive research in general and ethnographic research in particular have, I am afraid, produced evangelical results. We have been converting people who *look* like anthropologists but who do not *think* like them.

After prattling on for years about ethnographic methods, I have finally realized that, by and large, anthropologists are not, never have been, and never will be preoccupied with method *per se*. For them, the test lies in the adequacy of their explanations (or their "interpretations," if one prefers Clifford Geertz' more modest phrase). "Multiplicity of techniques" and "length of time in the field" dissolve as satisfactory criteria in the face of the basic question: "How adequate are our explanations of what is going on?" And, to push anthropological interpretations and explanations to their very limits, how good are they for helping interpret data other than those from which they were originally derived?

In his preface to *Islam Observed* (University of Chicago Press, 1971) Clifford Geertz makes important observations about both the origins and the ultimate uses of anthropological interpretations:

> Like all scientific propositions, anthropological interpretations must be tested against the material they are designed to interpret; it is not their origins that recommend them (p. vii).... The validity of both my empirical conclusions and my theoretical premises rests, in the end, on how effective they are in so making sense out of data from which they were neither derived nor for which they were originally designed (p. viii).

When introducing graduate students to ethnographic research, my immediate objective is still to have them learn how to *look* like anthropologists. Among students only recently introduced to the tyranny of number magic, a fleeting glimpse of a "soft and fuzzy" approach invariably sends some of them scurrying back to venerated formulas that can do such things as contradict observed frequencies with expected ones. For other students, renewed faith in their own powers of observation is lesson aplenty; they go forth resolved not to ignore the responses of their own good senses.

A few of the more daring—joined, I suspect, by some of the statistically awed—seriously consider the possibility of taking roles as "observers" or "participant observers" in the scenes that are of research interest to them. Of this group of "semi-converts" to descriptive research I extract but one promise: that although they avail themselves freely of several or many of the fieldwork techniques used by ethnographers, they will never, never, never claim to be doing ethnography as long as their basis for that claim derives only from their use of fieldwork techniques. One could do a participant observer study from now till doomsday and never come up with a sliver of ethnography. As a participant observer one ought, indeed, to come up with the stuff out of which ethnography is made, but that is not much of a claim when ethnography is made of such everyday stuff.

48

(My intent in belaboring the fact that ethnographic techniques are necessary but not sufficient for producing ethnographic results is by no means an effort to keep other researchers from using them. Quite the contrary, I warmly endorse and actively support the prevailing mood that encourages educational and other researchers to employ alternative methods and a variety of techniques. I insist only on a clear distinction between *borrowing the research tools* so readily available and *producing the results* of those who ordinarily use them professionally. In my hands, the scalpel of the most skilled heart surgeon is, after all, only a dangerous knife.)

A few students planning careers in educational research are willing to make a serious commitment to the ethnographic endeavor, something like Zorba the Greek's notion of "the full catastrophe." They want to become ethnographers. They declare their intention not only to use ethnographic tools in their research but to produce accounts that are ethnographic. The necessary next step for them is easy to identify but complex to achieve: they must learn to *think* like anthropologists rather than simply *look* like them.

The fact is, ethnographers are not the empty-headed observers that researchers of other persuasions sometimes take them to be. They have preconceptions that insist some facts are more important than others. Call those preconceived ideas "conceptual frameworks" if you need a euphemism, but I doubt if any harm is done describing them candidly as "prior commitments."

Examining the notion of observer bias in his own field of ethology (and borrowing a phrase from Nietzsche), the insightful "bird watcher" C. G. Beer refers to the doctrine of empty-headed or "pure" observation as the "doctrine of immaculate perception."

There is a view of science that sees the bird watcher's kind of activity as the necessary first step in any field of scientific endeavor. According to Lorenz, "It is an inviolable law of inductive natural science that it has to begin with pure observation, totally devoid of any preconceived theory and even working hypotheses." This view has come under attack from philosophers of science such as Karl Popper, who have argued that preconceived theories or working hypotheses must always be involved in scientific observation to enable the scientist to decide what is to count as a fact of relevance to his investigation. I myself have been a critic of this "doctrine of immaculate perception." Each year my students hear why, for both logical and practical reason, there can be no such thing as pure observation, even for a bird watcher (*Minnesota Symposia in Child Psychology*, Volume 7 [1973], p. 49, University of Minnesota Press).

Beer rejects "pure" observation for ethology; ethnographers must reject it as well. Those who call themselves ethnographers or lay claim to "doing ethnography" are neither engaged in immaculate perception nor free to "do their own thing." Ethnographers are, in fact, *duty bound* to look at the world through a cultural frame of reference. Their proper commitment is to "culture." Their task is not to investigate whether or not culture is "already there" in the scenes they observe, but *to put it there*. Their responsibility is to *impose* a cultural framework for interpreting what is taking place.

Anthropologist Ward Goodenough's perspective has helped me to stop looking for culture "on the ground" or "in the minds of informants" and to realize that explicit culture, at the level where it can be stated, footnoted and argued about, is a construct of the ethnographer. We all know how to behave appropriately in a multitude of microcultural settings within our own society, but only an ethnographer would torment herself or himself trying to make explicit the myriad rules and customs that members of a particular social group practice but cannot state. As Goodenough describes it:

> In anthropological practice, the culture of any society is made up of the concepts, beliefs, and principles of action and organization that an ethnographer has found could be attributed successfully to the members of that society in the context of his dealings with them ("Multiculturalism as the Normal Human Experience," *Anthropology and Education Quarterly* 7,4[1976]:4-7).

What each ethnographer selects as the best sources of data upon which to build an interpretation (e.g., spoken words, informant explanations, observed action); whether to highlight concepts or beliefs or principles of action when one cannot do everything at once; how to accommodate current theoretical predilections; what purposes and audiences a particular study is to serve— including even ethnography as a means of doing evaluation—all tend to give a disheveled look to the ethnographic enterprise. But genuine ethnography is always embedded in and ultimately concerned with cultural interpretation! When you make that singular purpose your own, then you are thinking like an anthropologist, and regardless of how incomplete you know (or later come to realize) your final account is, you have a right—and, for the sake of professional critique, perhaps an obligation—to label it as ethnography.

In these times when educational and other applied researchers seem especially receptive to alternative ways of looking, but still need to be convinced that descriptive research can be rigorous as well as relevant, I would like to see us restrict our use of the label ethnography to those efforts that reflect a genuine ethnographic intent. When in doubt, do not apply the label; the work will not be diminished merely because of modesty or caution.

And if ethnographic purity is retained, what does that get us? For me, the answer lies in the understanding of human behavior that can only be achieved from the cultural perspective. To stay close to the field of education, that perspective serves to remind us that our fellow professionals—and we researchers

50

ourselves—are culture-bearing humans. The special language of education research (of "pophams," "scrivens," "cronbachs," "summative evaluation," and "the NIE"), the particular days of the week on which it is customarily used, the very problems identified as suitable, and the ways individuals use research in order to acquire personal power and status, all give evidence of a set of mutually understood, tacitly approved ways of behaving that signify "culture at work." A pan-human need to make sense of the world in which we live is epitomized in researchers' commitments to research: they try harder in order to make more sense than anyone else.

The new use of "ethnography" as an evaluative tool in education (and in program evaluation more generally) is ample evidence that human groups adapt external elements to their own needs for "making sense" rather than worry about the ways those elements were originally intended for use. Ethnography, a descriptive and calculatedly nonjudgemental approach, has recently been pressed into service to help educators make sense out of one of their most pervasive problems: judging their own effectiveness. (I have developed this topic more fully in a paper titled "Mirrors, Models, and Monitors: Educator Adaptations of the Ethnographic Innovation" in G. Spindler's *Doing the Ethnography of Schooling*, pp. 68-95. [New York: Holt, Rinehart, & Winston, 1982].)

Specific ethnographic techniques are freely available to any researcher who wants to approach a problem or setting descriptively. It is the essential anthropological concern for cultural context that distinguishes ethnographic method from fieldwork techniques and makes genuine ethnography distinct from other "on-site-observer" approaches. And when cultural interpretation is the goal, the ethnographer must be thinking like an anthropologist, not just looking like one.

The qualities that make ethnographic studies ethnographic are worth cherishing, just as the very question of what it is that makes them ethnographic is worth our continual agonizing about among ourselves. I am not suggesting that other researchers and applied social scientists purge the term ethnography from their professional vocabularies, but I do urge them to restrict its use to inquiries in which cultural interpretation is paramount. We are fast losing sight of the fact that the essential ethnographic contribution is interpretative rather than methodological. I think it is not yet too late to reinvest ethnography with its unique property—the commitment to cultural interpretation. Otherwise it is doomed to dissolve into a sea of synonyms for descriptive research.

The Use of Social Scientists in the United States Foreign Aid Program: A Retrospective

GRACE LANGLEY

With few exceptions (largely clustered around World War II), the practice of anthropology has been typified by individual efforts that have had minimal impact in the world's problem-solving arenas. At the United States Agency for International Development (AID), however, there were fifty anthropologists working as full-time career professionals in 1980, and many more served as part-time consultants. Achieving this critical mass made possible a higher level of anthropological practice—a level at which technical knowledge, administrative capability, and disciplinary confidence were sufficient for anthropological thinking to consistently influence high-level national decision making. This transformation of anthropological practice was not achieved automatically, nor altogether smoothly or completely. One issue that AID anthropologists, like others working in large bureaucracies, faced was how best to distribute their energies, individually and collectively, between research and administration. Reflecting on an earlier era during which anthropologists and other social scientists had attained significant numbers in foreign assistance programs, Grace Langley argues that anthropologists' contributions are greatest when they function primarily as researchers and cultural experts. The issues Langley raises are as timely in the 1990s as they were in the 1980s.   R. M. W.

The predecessor of AID, the Community Development Division of the International Cooperation Administration (ICA), was once the nation's largest employer of anthropologists. I will briefly trace how that situation developed and what resulted from it.

Several changes brought about by World War II contributed to the formulation of an American foreign aid program. European productive capacity had

Grace Langley retired as Chief of Sector Planning and Rural Development in AID's Near East Bureau shortly before publishing this article in 1980. She can be contacted at 10450 Lottsford Road, Unit 3105, Mitchellville, MD 20721-2749; (301) 925-7320.

Originally published as part of a special section on "Anthropology in the United States Agency for International Development," guest edited by William H. Jansen II, in *Practicing Anthropology* 3,2(1980-81):9-10,54-55, this article has been edited and abridged for republication here.

been largely destroyed by the war, while United States productive capacity had expanded manyfold. A political aftermath of the war was the newly won independence of many nations. In the United States a major effect of the war was enhanced social awareness, as millions of young Americans had been exposed to poverty abroad. Reflecting this situation, United States foreign aid goals were then described in the idealistic terms of exporting democracy and eradicating poverty. The aid program was intended to share United States largesse and technical know-how.

Paralleling the early days of foreign aid, the social sciences in the United States were experiencing a postwar boom. The GI bill widened opportunities for undergraduate and postgraduate training. The Fulbright exchange program, followed by Ford Foundation programs and others, greatly expanded opportunities for study and fieldwork abroad. Where previously two or three United States anthropologists had done fieldwork in India, suddenly there were approximately thirty-five such researchers a year being sponsored by Fulbright and Ford. Thus, there was a dramatic increase in the number of United States social scientists with overseas experience. Some of these people were the products of long-term research programs such as the Cornell Peru and India village projects. Their experiences were documented in rich case material which highlighted the role of values and social organization in development.

During this early period, United States foreign aid representatives began to learn that they were in the business of social change as well as technical change. I remember vividly the anger of a famous United States agricultural engineer working in a developing country at the time, who discovered that a known amount of improved seed plus a known amount of fertilizer did not produce a known amount of cereal grains. Such experiences were commonplace. Agricultural extension agents transferred overseas had to recognize, for example, that a farmer's capital might come from his wife's dowry and that using that capital required her permission. Likewise, it became apparent to the range management advisor that the technology of improving pastures and improving stock might have to be grounded upon socially defined rules for water rights and land tenure.

In response to these experiences, a team of distinguished United States social scientists recommended in 1951 that a social scientist be attached to each of this country's foreign aid missions. Little came of the recommendation initially. The late Louis Miniclier, in an issue of *Human Organization* devoted to the role of anthropologists in the foreign aid program, offered the following explanation: "As the social scientists could not define their roles or agree amongst themselves which of several disciplines could contribute most directly to operations, only two or three behavioural scientists were placed in overseas missions" ("The Use of Anthropologists in the Foreign Aid Program," *Human Organization* 23,3[1964]:187-189).

Nevertheless, the United States foreign aid program began to recruit anthropologists and sociologists mainly for positions as program evaluation officers and community development advisors. A few mission directors insisted on having a mission anthropologist. I was one of those early appointees, going to India in 1954 with the United States Technical Mission as an evaluation officer. I was placed in an operational role in the mission community development division.

Since a commonality of interest had been building between foreign aid programs and the social science community and a need for social scientists had been identified and dramatized within foreign aid programs, this should have been the beginning of a creative partnership. Instead, the role of social scientists as community development specialists in United States foreign aid programs was criticized by both the foreign aid and social science establishments. Besides the inability to define our roles, we were accused of being too narrowly trained and interested only in long-term research. The social scientists, in turn, expressed irritability at working within a bureaucracy.

Given this prickly beginning, and even given the heavy use of anthropologists by the Bureau of Indian Affairs and the Administration of the Pacific Trust Territories, it is noteworthy that the Community Development Division of ICA was by 1964 the nation's largest single employer of anthropologists. We were "in the door" in sufficient numbers to make an impression and to do a job. I am afraid that we squandered the opportunity.

Social scientists in the United States foreign aid program tended to move into one of two totally opposite roles: They either retained a social science identity and contributed little to policy, or they adopted the role of administrator and contributed little in the way of social science. In the first instance, as program evaluation officers, anthropologists ran orientation courses, participated in host country seminars, drafted country background sections of program documents, commented (often negatively) on everything which came their way, and put out "brush fires." They did little major fieldwork and little actual planning or management of research programs. They kept their social science skirts and shirts clear of the bureaucracy of operations, but they did little that mattered.

At the other role extreme, some community development advisors were fully drawn into operations and policy making. These social scientists became so engaged in program documentation, project management, and advisory and training tasks that some of them became marginal as social scientists. So engaged were they in learning this year's documentation requirements, filling in the gaps in their own management skills and meeting today's deadlines, that many of them became foreign aid *administrators* with social science *backgrounds*. Responsible people who had seen needs within the context of the foreign aid program, these officers had moved to cover those needs. But temporary diversions from their original assignments ceased to be temporary. Busy,

54

committed people may not always have recognized how much of a diversion was taking place.

In neither role expression did these actors help define and legitimize the role of the social scientist in international development. The failure was in not forcing the issue of the need for more social science research in foreign assistance efforts. If we had clearly demonstrated the potential, the personnel requirements to do the job might have been more easily expanded.

There were some notable exceptions. People like James W. Green insisted on doing major fieldwork at the beginning of each assignment. There were men like John Cool and Ferdinand Okada, whose research contributed to the development of the *panchayati raj* program in Nepal. There were people like Gerald Hickey, on whose study of Vietnamese village life others built programs for years to come. We were joined at times by noteworthy research institutions such as the Planning, Research and Action Institute at Lucknow, or the University of the Philippines.

But why did we allow ourselves to try to fill roles for which we were not prepared and to abandon the roles and skills at which we excelled? The United States foreign assistance program needed social scientists. That need did not stem from an altruistic desire to create employment opportunities for anthropologists and sociologists. The point was, and still is, that foreign aid programs would have connected with the lives of people in developing countries more productively if projects were designed and implemented with the social environment and social processes in mind. The foreign assistance program was a society of its own. Either its forces of assimilation were strong indeed, or we were insufficient advocates or inadequate as change agents.

Now again, the United States foreign assistance program has turned to social science and anthropology for help. It is one of the paradoxes of the post-Vietnam retreat from taking on all causes and all international problems that Congress passed legislation in 1973 directing AID to work with the majority of the poor in ways in which the poor will see the effects on their lives directly. The filtered benefits of the so-called "top-down" development approaches are no longer considered adequate. To fulfill these new directives, AID finds itself addressing the problems of other nations in such areas as land tenure, credit systems, food distribution networks, off-farm employment, agricultural inputs, water resources, population, and alternative energy sources, to name but a few.

This "New Directions" legislation, as it became known, has involved us in some very real issues of social reform. It is an enormous and complicated task which requires country-specific knowledge and a deep understanding of rural institutions. To be less than specialized is to be ineffective, meddlesome, even dangerous.

With this new emphasis on work with the rural poor majority has come the additional recognition of the need to involve social analysis in the design of development projects. Now the cycle has been completed. Once more, AID has experienced a crest in the recruitment of social scientists and, again, this recruitment trend is already waning. Are we once again trying to be all things to all who ask, or are we specialists who have an important but fairly narrow function within the agency? Are our skills easily transferable from country to country, or should we, of all professions, insist that social scientists be assigned within the area of their cultural expertise?

I have observed contract anthropologists working a week in Afghanistan and then flying to work in Bolivia, routing themselves through Africa to make a contact there. Surely this is not responsible of AID or the anthropologists. I see social soundness units asked to comment on every project in every country which receives assistance. When we do so, surely, we are operating at the thin edge of our capabilities and run the risk of encountering some of the same problems which plagued the earlier involvement of anthropology in United States foreign assistance efforts.

With the reflection of one who has newly retired after twenty-six years with AID, I believe that the most effective way to discharge our professional responsibilities to programs of social change is to participate as anthropologists, not as project managers. I know there are others in AID who might say that if the anthropologist is to be pragmatically and well used in overseas programs, then we must move beyond analysis and prescription. They would suggest that we must become operational and occupy pre-existing roles within the bureaucracy which carry legitimacy with them. I do not agree. With hindsight and some regret, my recommendation to my colleagues is that we propose narrowly defined social science job functions. To do so may require that we accept a limited career ladder for the periods we spend with government. But let us also be bolder in insisting that United States foreign aid programs be genuinely based on an understanding of the societies which programs are intended to assist. That still remains the purpose of the effort.

A Fable:
The Anthropologist and the Bear

Michael K. Orbach

In this satirical tale, Michael Orbach contrasts the pressures facing anthropologists in the 1970s with a putative golden age—when ethnographers could focus on basic research, position themselves as advocates for native peoples, and criticize government actions from the safety of their university posts. In the 1970s, the discipline was being accused of implicit collaboration in cultural imperialism, and academic employment was becoming scarce. New employment opportunities were materializing in applied fields, from which anthropologists could influence decision making more directly. Such positions required anthropologists to take unaccustomed responsibility for the impact of their advice, however, and to consider its effects on all peoples. Speaking through the voice of the bear, Orbach urges anthropologists to embrace those opportunities and accept those responsibilities. While historians of anthropology may find fault with Orbach's portrayal of the field (many early anthropologists were directly involved in applied work, for example), and applied anthropologists of the 1990s may be less ambivalent about their work, his fable struck a chord at the time, and it touches issues of perennial importance in the discipline. P. J. H.

Some time ago, in Tuolumne Meadows at the upper end of Yosemite Valley, an anthropologist was sitting down to his campfire at the end of a long day of hiking and fishing. He had caught a few trout and was cooking them when a bear sat down beside him. Since this is a fable, bears are allowed to talk, and the two struck up a conversation. After a short while, the anthropologist noticed that the bear had a large concentric target painted on his backside. Being naturally curious, he asked the bear about the target.

"Oh yes," the bear said, "I acquired that some years ago. You see, many of us bears used to live down on the valley floor, long before man began to visit there. We were the indigenous inhabitants, and even after man discovered the valley we existed together for a long while in relative harmony. As more and

Michael K. Orbach is Professor of Marine Affairs and Policy and Director of the Marine Laboratory at Duke University's Nicholas School of the Environment (135 Duke Marine Lab Road, Beaufort, NC 28516-9721; (252) 504-7606/7655; fax: (252) 504-7648; <mko@duke.edu>).

Originally published in *Practicing Anthropology* 5,4(1983):4-5.

more people came, we were soon perceived to be troublesome on account of helping ourselves to people's stores, overturning trash cans, and so on. The rangers began to capture the more active of our numbers and deport us up here to the Meadows, or somewhere else out of the way. They were very annoyed when we found our way back down again, and after repeated offenses they painted these targets on our backs as sort of a strong hint that we should stay where they put us."

"Ah," said the anthropologist, "How well I know how it is to be a target."

"Really?" said the bear. "You mean that those Native Americans you anthropologists have been studying all these years have also been targets of the spread of the white man, is that it?"

"Oh no," said the anthropologist. "I mean that we anthropologists have of late also been the target of scorn and ridicule!"

"How so?" said the bear. With that, the anthropologist began the long tale of applied anthropology and natural resources management.

"It used to be," began the anthropologist, "that anthropologists spent the majority of their time recording in vast detail the rapidly disappearing 'primitive' people of the world, and more particularly those of the North American continent. We wrote lengthy works on everything from the economics and religion to the physical type of these people. We saw it as our duty to not only record these societies and cultures, but we most often made it our business to let everyone know that these people whose cultures were slowly being eradicated were somehow noble, and that it was very bad that they were being destroyed and absorbed by the larger United States society and culture. We spent untold hours living with these peoples, as what we called participant observers, to ensure that we gained the depth of knowledge that would make others understand the culture of these Native Americans."

"That must have been very lonely for you," said the bear, "and it must have been difficult to convince anyone that what you were doing was scientific activity. You seem to have a strong identification with your research subjects."

"That is quite true," said the anthropologist. "It took a certain type of person to spend so much time in the field, often alone, in the midst of harsh conditions and foreign cultures. We were as careful as any scientist with our data and information, and we did not have any more of an advocacy position than, say, a conservation-oriented natural scientist might have. Almost everyone has some form of basic occupational ethic. A game warden's bias is usually game; as anthropologists, ours was the conservation of people.

"We were quite happy during those years. Even though we made continual recommendations and criticisms concerning the government's handling of native peoples, we were rarely if ever in the position of having to make the practical decisions which affected those people. There were lots of teaching jobs for anthropologists in universities in the '50s and '60s, and we published the results of our work in our own journals. We were in a good position to criticize the government, the corporations, and all of those organizations whose activities had some impact on our research subjects. Our place in the universities enabled us to do this at very little risk, and with no actual responsibility for implementing the substance of our criticisms.

"At the same time, we formed a distinct group among our social scientific colleagues. Our work was most often qualitative rather than quantitative, and it was extremely difficult to replicate a given researcher's findings. We performed our research in intimate relationship with our informants, and since we were dealing directly with the human side of many different issues we were sometimes perceived as either being very political ourselves, or as in general being involved with the political aspect of situations. This did not often make us very popular with people in positions of authority and responsibility who were trying to bring these situations to resolution, and it also fed our reputation as advocates rather than scientists."

"That sounds like a very difficult position, " said the bear.

"No," said the anthropologist. "It didn't actually become a problem until the middle '60s when Vine DeLoria, a Native American, wrote a popular book called *Custer Died for Your Sins*. In this book, he criticized the general handling of Native American affairs by the United States. He also, to our very great chagrin, took anthropologists to task. He said that by using Native Americans for research subjects we were in fact exploiting them. Further, he said that by encouraging the preservation of their traditional cultures we were in fact standing in the way of the very progress that would help Native Americans in their plights. Here was one of the people to whom we had devoted our lives and careers, all of a sudden turning against us. We were devastated."

"Well," replied the bear, "there certainly are plenty of other people in the world left for anthropologists to study."

"That would seem to be true. But we anthropologists had taken as our great cause the primitive, small-scale, native people of the world, and of all these people the Native American had always held a special place with us. Our colleagues, the archaeologists and physical anthropologists, largely avoided the throes of this dilemma, and their work went on as usual and gradually expanded. Besides their natural advantage of looking and acting more like scientists because they used numerical methods, dealt with physical processes, and could actually assemble collections of the things they studied for people to look at in museums and the like, they were less directly identified with cultural imperialism than were we cultural anthropologists. We had put ourselves in a double bind. Because we emphasized research with cultures which were very different, we lost our awareness that everyone has a culture, and that it may be important to avoid the advocacy of one culture over another. On top of all of this, while graduate schools had continued to produce anthropologists, enrollments in universities had begun to peak and decline. A lot of us were looking for work."

60

"That seems to be an oversimplification of the actions and motives of a very large number of anthropologists," said the bear.

"Oh yes, it is," said the anthropologist, "but in the end it did not matter anyway. In the late '60s and early '70s, a series of federal laws were passed which gave us the opportunity for new avenues of employment, especially in situations related to natural resource management. The National Environmental Policy Act, the Marine Sanctuaries Act, the Endangered Species Act, the Marine Mammal Protection Act, the Alaska Native Land Claims Settlement Act, the American Indian Religious Freedom Act—all of these laws stipulated that the impacts of federal actions on the economic, social and cultural framework of the affected public must be formally considered. Here was our opportunity to ply our trade once again, albeit in a different manner and for different clients than we had in the past."

"How nice," said the bear.

"Ah, but there was a catch," frowned the anthropologist. "These laws stipulated that we consider the economic, social, and cultural concerns of all affected people. No longer could we simply do research on our Native American friends. Now we had to consider as research subjects recreational hunters and fishermen, factory workers, environmentalists, commercial fishermen, truckers, bureaucrats, backpackers, and who knows what else. Once you realize that everyone has a culture that is important to them, you can really get into a muddle. The provisions in these new laws generally addressed multiple-use approaches to such things as natural resources management, rather than allowing one to advocate one specific use or another. When you added these considerations to the mandates under which we anthropologists had done work for years, such as the antiquities statutes administered by the National Park Service, there is a perplexing array of things to consider and very little guidance on how to go about it."

"How distressing for you, " sympathized the bear.

"To make matters worse," continued the anthropologist, "the world itself had gotten so much more complicated, especially with respect to Native Americans. People who claimed native ancestry began attempting to revive religious rituals they had not used in quite some time, claiming that these cultural activities gave them special privilege, for example, in the trespass of certain fish and game conservation laws in Alaska and other places. The traditions of the Native Americans had eroded and changed due to overwhelming culture contact and intermarriage. The dispersal of tribal peoples made it very difficult to even decide who was and who was not a Native American, or for which legal purposes.

"Since we were now in the position of considering the multiple, sustained use of both physical and cultural resources, we were sometimes even put in the position of recommending which among many of these resources was the most expendable. Marine archaeologists, for example, were asked to recommend which underwater sites were necessary to protect entirely, and which could be used for recreational diving where a certain amount of resource alteration was to be expected. Cultural anthropologists were asked to assess the critical aspects of Native American dependence on certain whale species, in the face of the transformation of the native peoples who hunted them to cash economies and increasingly sophisticated technologies. We were actually asked to help make decisions on these matters. A lot of these questions come up in the management of national parks, in everything from how park lands are selected to decisions about what kinds of activities and uses are permitted on park land."

"What is wrong with that?" asked the bear.

"Oh, I suppose nothing really," sighed the anthropologist. "One does have to be careful that one's position as an objective and disinterested scientist does not become compromised by participation in decision making. But much of the anthropologist's problem lies in the fact that, after all those years of making outgroups of government, corporations, and the like, we now find ourselves on the outside looking in. In 1975, for example, there were only 32 people employed as cultural anthropologists in the entire federal government. Psychologists, who had taken a considerably different direction in their profession, had on the order of 6,000 of their profession employed in the government. We anthropologists were used to being professors and researchers, not applied problem solvers. And, we were still gunshy. In 1979, when the American Indian Religious Freedom Act was being implemented, anthropologists who were approached for help in this task were noticeably reticent to become involved, and often brought up the name of the fellow who had written the book in the '60s which I mentioned earlier. Now that we have a broad statutory mandate to do our science, our past stance as a profession is still haunting us."

At this point the bear, who had grown quite hungry listening to the anthropologist's story and smelling his cooking fish, walked over to the frying pan and flipped the trout into his mouth, swallowing it at a single gulp. The anthropologist, seeing his dinner disappear, became quite angry.

"I have a good mind to report you to the ranger, and have them remind you again what that target on your back is for!" stormed the anthropologist.

"There is something I should tell you," said the bear. "This target on my back is very old. People's values change, as you yourself have pointed out, and we bears and the other natural creatures of the seas and forests are back in good favor right now. People have realized that we are an integral part of the natural environment, and that there is considerable value to your human society in keeping us happy and healthy. No, my time as a target is over for the time being. You, on the other hand, are the one who has a tenuous position. That is too bad, because your profession seems to have much to offer in the analysis of the human aspect of multiple-use problems in resource management."

The anthropologist buried his head in his hands. "Oh bear, you are so right. Sometimes I just don't know what to do."

"Allow me," said the bear, "to make a few humble recommendations. First, in your work as a social analyst, make sure that you study all sides of an issue—that is, all the human perspectives through the eyes of all of the people and groups who are involved. This may help quell your reputation as advocate rather than scientist, and in any case it will enable your work to be used with much more confidence by, for example, those who must make final decisions on resource management. Don't let go of your opinions, but clearly separate them from your work.

"Second, it seems that you need to learn how to put the terms of your research and your findings into others' frames of reference. One way to do this is to learn to use quantitative techniques a bit more. I hear (in fables, bears can be very well connected) that some members of your profession have been quite successful with quantitative techniques, but that they are only a small minority. In concert with this, learn to pay more attention to the needs of others— Native Americans, bureaucrats, corporations, and park rangers alike—rather than always framing your research based on your needs and interests as an academic. These things will bring you closer to many people who might be very interested in your work, but who heretofore could neither understand nor use it.

"Third, it seems that you must have a more open mind concerning your work situation and your place in the real-world processes which you are studying. People need your help in solving their problems, but you must place yourself among them to learn how their system works and what their real needs are. This will mean breaking down some of your parochialism about your mode of employment. Get out of the university, and into positions in the government and other places where professionals actually have to do something about the issues of our time. It is only in that way that you will ever have the results of your work truly translated into useful new directions in the human activities which you study. You don't have to change the course of history; simply put yourself in a position where your work can be informed and used by others outside of your profession. If you do these three things, cultural anthropology as a profession may be of very great use to the likes of the people who run the park we are sitting in right now."

The anthropologist was silent. The bear slowly got up, and as he walked away he turned and said, "You see, although public favor has turned in my own direction, I still wear my target. I must pay attention to both the general public who visit the park, to whom I owe much of my salvation, and to the rangers and other government people who make it possible for that same public to implement the values and choices it makes in the matter of the use of natural resources and environments.

"You still have your own target, anthropologist. I hope you do as well as I have in understanding who might have been doing the shooting, and why."

An Anti-Fable:
The Anthropologist and the Snake

MERRILL SINGER

In a reaction to Orbach's fable of the anthropologist and the bear (this volume), Merrill Singer tells a story with a different message. Anthropologists have been correct, he suggests, to be wary of opportunities to work for the rich and powerful. Not only are anthropologists likely, in accepting such employment, to betray the less powerful populations whose interest they have traditionally defended, they also expose themselves to betrayal by their new masters. Many anthropologists—academicians, practitioners, and students—continue to struggle with ethical issues raised by applied work. Whether an anthropologist can effectively represent the interests of individuals or groups other than those who commission the work and pay the bills is certainly one of the most basic of these issues. P. J. H.

The anthropologist sat at his desk in a dimly lit university office proudly turning the crisp pages of a brand new hardcover book. Periodically, he flipped to the inside dust cover to admire his photograph and the brief but impressive bibliography printed there. Lost in fantasy about the accolades this new publication would bring him from colleagues, he failed to lock his overstuffed briefcase properly as he prepared to head out for suburbia at the end of the school day.

A few minutes later, as the anthropologist walked across the tree-lined campus to his car, his briefcase suddenly popped open, spilling his many notebooks, journals and papers, and his new book onto the ground. Shaken from his musings, he hurriedly tried to retrieve his possessions. But as he reached for his book, he was shocked to realize it had landed squarely on the head of a dark green snake curled up by the edge of the pathway.

"Nice shot," said the snake in a sarcastic tone, "just what I'd expect from one such as you."

"Such as me?" questioned the startled anthropologist. "What do you mean?"

"Come now," the snake said, "you anthropologists have long been enemies of snakes. You are forever and always defending rabbits and mice, telling

Merrill Singer is Associate Director and Chief of Research at the Hispanic Health Center (175 Main Street, Hartford, CT 06106; (860) 527-0856; <anthro8566@aol.com>) and Assistant Clinical Professor at the University of Connecticut.

Originally published in *Practicing Anthropology* 6,3-4(1984):3.

everyone about the world from their perspective, showing everyone that they have unique cultures and what not. We know you hate snakes because we eat rabbits and mice."

"That's not true," responded the anthropologist. "It's not that we're anti-snake. It's just that you snakes are rich and powerful; you hire press agents and media representatives to tell your side of the story. You own the newspapers and television stations. But who speaks for the poor rabbits and mice? They have been pushed to the margins by the snakes. They are even forced to live underground. But look in my new book on rabbit culture," said the anthropologist, holding up his new book. "On page 43 I even put in a good word about snakes, about how they help keep the rabbit population down."

"Big deal," fired back the snake, rising up on his muscular body until he was eye to eye with the anthropologist. "You're an anthropologist. Your job is to study culture. You have to recognize that everyone has a culture. But you should study the world through the eyes of all the groups in the forest. You have to recognize that we snakes, however rich and powerful we might be, have a culture too!"

"Well, I guess that's true," said the anthropologist. "I've always striven to be a value-free scientist rather than a rabble-rousing advocate."

"Good to hear that," clipped the snake. "By the way, did you know that the Snake Protection Agency has some openings for anthropological consultants?"

"Oh really?" responded the anthropologist with growing interest.

"I'll be sure to have an application sent to your office," said the snake as he uncurled his tail and prepared to slither off.

The anthropologist bent down to shake hands with the snake, forgetting in his enthusiasm that snakes have no hands. Undaunted, he grabbed the snake's head and gave it a hearty jerk. Startled, the snake instinctively sunk his fangs into the anthropologist's hand. Instantly, the anthropologist fell to the ground, dead. His new book fell too, its pages flipping slowly in the evening breeze.

A Social Anthropologist Looks at Job Survival

Barbara J. Sibley

The late Barbara Sibley wrote of a time when many anthropologists had to go "undercover" to get a job in the business world. Disguised as generic social scientists, anthropologists like Sibley paved the way for greater appreciation of the anthropological perspective in government and industry—even if sometimes that perspective lay in no more than pointing out that an intended audience is likely to read newspapers different from those typically read by members of one's firm. Despite some changes in the years since Sibley wrote her advice to anthropologists on finding—and holding—a spot in the workplace outside the Halls of Ivy, her admonitions are still timely and sage. In her refined ability to retain a detached ethnographic perspective on disagreeable attitudes and behaviors in corporate office culture, Sibley proved herself a truly saintly practitioner of anthropology.   J. A. P.

As social anthropologists, we are trained to study cultures and to observe and describe the behavior of others. Traditionally, we have worked in other countries or among distinct subcultures here in the United States. However, anthropological and related training also serves well in "mainstream" American society, especially when it comes to recognizing where jobs can be found, then acquiring and keeping them.

I have been employed almost six years as an environmental planner with a large consulting architecture, engineering, and planning firm. The Planning and Environmental Systems Division is a multidisciplinary group of about twenty persons with such academic backgrounds as geology, urban planning, economics, biology, landscape architecture, hydrology, chemistry, history, and library science. The professional staff in the two other divisions are primarily engineers and architects. Like the rest of the firm, our division competes in the open market for jobs in both the public and private

Barbara J. Sibley (1932-1998) was employed by Dalton Dalton Newport in Cleveland, Ohio, at the time this article was written. After completing a doctorate in nursing she worked in hospital-based acute psychiatric care. In the 1970s and 1980s she was active in assisting younger anthropologists to appreciate the possibilities of nonconventional work careers.

Originally published as part of a special section on "Women Practicing Anthropology," guest edited by Carole Browner, in *Practicing Anthropology* 6,1(1983):8,10, this article has been edited for republication here.

sectors. When a job contract is secured, individuals are assigned to the job team according to the nature of the work and their skills, experience, and availability.

My own assignments have been primarily in four major categories: writing social impact assessments; arranging community involvement programs for proposed federal, state, or city governmental projects such as highways; designing management systems to help federal agencies comply with the National Environmental Policy Act; and incorporating social and behavioral factors into the architectural design of such facilities as hospitals.

Adaptation to Avoid Extinction

In developing the means to survive and grow in my profession, I have relied upon training as an anthropologist (and such additional sources as my academic work in psychology and biology, the women's movement, and child rearing experience) to identify and adapt to several key elements within "mainstream" culture.

The first element has to do with academic training, fields of study, and one's own perception of that training. In nonacademic employment, the label "anthropologist" seldom brings a quick job interview and a good salary offer. I think the reason is that the word is usually associated with far-off peoples and places and digging up artifacts, Margaret Mead's example of anthropology's relevance to contemporary society notwithstanding. Linkages between these traditional word associations and the modern business world are not immediately apparent to most employers. Many work situations which could use a good social anthropologist, and where anthropology could make valuable contributions, are places where people have little idea of what anthropology is, or how it can be useful to contemporary society. The uniqueness the discipline has to offer is subtle and hard to describe, especially when dealing with people untrained in the social sciences. The value of anthropology is much easier to comprehend once experienced within an organization.

The way I have gotten around this perceptual and semantic difficulty is to call myself something that is more easily recognized and understood, namely a "social scientist." This label—certainly an accurate one—denotes the ability to gather data; analyze and evaluate it; make predictions; write reports; interview people; use calculators, libraries, and computers; read maps; know demographic sources; and meet with the public and the press. True, with this label my training may be initially confused with the related disciplines of sociology, psychology, history, political science, or economics. But I do not mind the blurring of distinctions between these related fields, because I believe being in the right place is more important than the fine-tuning of the label. On the job, I have found at least as many different kinds of engineers or architects or medical doctors as there are kinds of social scientists.

Once in the right place, an anthropologist can make a distinct contribution. For example, I was assigned to help prepare a citizens' involvement program for a proposed segment of interstate highway in an urban area. We were to hold a series of public meetings within the study area. One of the means of publicizing the meetings was to place advertisements in the two major metropolitan daily newspapers. Since part of the study area was in an inner-city black community and another in a white suburb, I suggested that advertisements also be placed in the metropolitan black-owned newspaper and the local suburban weekly. Most of my team members had never heard of the other papers, but agreed it was a good idea. The ads brought word of the meetings into many more homes in the area. This was a simple suggestion and certainly required no special training in anthropology. But such lack of awareness of other cultural groups is not uncommon.

On the same assignment, some of my colleagues were reluctant to go into the inner-city neighborhoods where some of the meetings were held. My offer of a ride, plus some good-natured cajoling, helped bring the white middle-class engineers face to face with the inner-city people whom their highway design might be displacing. The engineer learned why they should change some lines on the map a little and the people in the community learned how complicated transportation planning and highway design really are. Thus, my contributions as an anthropologist increased my colleagues' awareness of other cultural groups and helped bridge the gap between the social issues raised by the community and the technical issues raised by the highway engineers.

Acquire Skills in More than One Area

Survival, in my job and others like it, is greater when there is a knowledge of several different academic subjects, and the willingness to continually expand this background. Versatility and flexibility have been valuable for me in finding and keeping a job. For instance, my undergraduate and master's degrees in biology recently won me a place on a summer project when there were few assignments for the staff social scientists. In order to have a better background for some studies in industrial and municipal water pollution and hazardous and toxic waste storage and disposal, I recently completed an evening course in organic chemistry. Although I believe many of the issues relating to these topics are as much social and political as chemical and mechanical, my position lacks credibility among the technical staff unless accompanied by "scientific" knowledge.

I have noticed that maintaining a job often follows the organic evolution principle that variety and adaptation lead to survival, and its corollary, over-specialization leads to extinction. In times of political, social and environmental change, those with a variety of skills, training, and experience are more

68

likely to be able to adapt and remain employed in a related field than those on a single, specialized track. The outlook for environmental planners under President Carter was very encouraging, in contrast to the policies of the Reagan administration. To adapt to this political change, I am expanding my knowledge base and experience by learning more about the health care industry, with an emphasis on the way design and engineering of health facilities can be made to fit the needs and expectations of users. The role of bridging a gap remains the same, but the subject matter changes.

Ethnography of the Workplace

The second element of "mainstream" culture which requires adaptation for job survival is awareness of self. I owe much of my own consciousness of this dimension to the women's movement and its precursor, the black movement. In my case, it has meant surviving as a woman in a predominantly man's world. Along the way I had to acquire a basic attitude toward myself and my job.

My career and advancement had to be regarded as carefully and as seriously as I had treated my previous academic progression towards a degree. I could not assume that because I had been hired, got my work done on time, did a good job, and built up a broad experience base, that I would get additional responsibilities, promotions, and advances. Some of this has happened. But when the chips were down, my company decided to save a little money (my salary) by laying me off for a while until a new job assignment came through. In marshalling my response, I realized that I had to be more alert than I had been to the political and social milieu of my job setting. After a series of negotiations which I initiated, I ended up not getting laid off.

This incident taught me to be more aware of the policies and directions the company and my division are interested in pursuing. I am also more alert to the marketplace, and where I would like to be one year and five and ten years from now and how I can get there. Career planning is now offered as a course in many high schools and colleges, and I am sure many other women are more aware than I was. Now, I too know that I need to take almost total responsibility for my own growth and progress. No one else should be expected to do this for me.

Part of the above awareness can come by doing an "ethnography" of your own work setting. It means understanding the little cultures of the immediate office, the division, and the corporation. It means being aware of who has power and who doesn't. It means trying to anticipate where the changes are going to occur, and then growing so as to be ready to meet those changes. This is far better than being taken by surprise when a shift occurs in a system that is really in a constant state of flux.

Cultural Sensitivity to Different Values

A third element in our culture that relates to job survival is something that we as anthropologists are sometimes better in applying to other cultures than to our own. In preparing for fieldwork, we are taught to observe nonjudgmentally customs, attitudes, and behaviors—even those we might not relish. We note them as products of the culture, time, and place of that group. We neither get angry at people for holding certain beliefs, nor do we adopt such beliefs for ourselves.

In reference to the contemporary workplace, I suggest that each period of time (such as a decade) has also generated a culture of its own. Each decade has left its mark on those who lived through it. Therefore, one's own age and stage of life during each period affect not only how one viewed the events that took place then, but how one views what is taking place today as well. Thus, people of different generations are most likely to feel differently about the role of women at work. I notice that some of my older male colleagues are uncomfortable and rush to help me when they see me carrying a big box of supplies. But my younger colleagues know I am capable of carrying my own supplies, and let me do it myself unless I ask for help. Some of the older males are still learning how to relate to women as fellow professionals, in addition to their previous experience with women as mothers, wives, daughters, and secretaries. The younger ones, some of whom have rather independent wives, are used to the more varied roles of contemporary women.

In terms of job survival, it helps to think of the job setting as fieldwork, where we are not supposed to get angry when we see an attitude or belief with which we do not agree. Nor do we need to adopt these same attitudes or beliefs for ourselves. Therefore, when I am confronted with a traditional stance toward women from an older person (usually male), instead of taking offense I try to remember what generation he is from. Realizing that his experience with professional women may be limited, I take it upon myself to increase his experience by my own persistent, but nonbelligerent example of professionalism. It has taken time and patience to develop this attitude, but after a few years of mutual association, some of my older co-workers and I have become quite comfortable with each other. So much so, in fact, that sometimes when we go out on a job to another location, I am startled to meet men who assume I am the secretary, or who wonder who is minding the children at home. Yet, we need to recognize the values held by others in our own culture, even if they may not always still be appropriate, and then learn to bridge the gaps between them. Employers value staff members who can work harmoniously with a wide variety of people. This kind of cooperative attitude, and a sense of humor, can certainly help one survive in the workplace.

Problems in Pocatello: A Study in Linguistic Misunderstanding

Barbara Joans

Barbara Joans recounts a successful case of advocacy anthropology in which professional skills are used to speak or intercede on behalf of others. Joans served as an expert defense witness in a court case in which six Indian women were charged with welfare fraud. Her task was to determine whether these women could have understood the instructions given to them about eligibility rules and reporting requirements. Following a set of anthropological hunches, she constructed an ingenious set of cultural and linguistic tests to determine the women's competence. Her approach showed that the women, though they spoke some English, could not have understood the regulations as presented to them. Joans then used her anthropological skills to package her findings, and herself, in a way that was compatible with court custom. Joans's work is rare in that the positive outcome of her work was unequivocal, and it led to a substantial change in policy. A. M. E.

In November 1978, the Pocatello Social Service Agency accused six older Bannock-Shoshoni women from the Fort Hall reservation of withholding financial information while receiving supplemental security income (SSI). The women were charged with fraud and ordered to repay the SSI payments. With the help of an Idaho legal aid office, the women contested the agency ruling on repayment. Legal Aid contended that the women were misinformed of SSI rules and of their individual responsibilities. The social service agency claimed the women knew the rules and chose to ignore them. When the disagreement ended up in court, I was asked to help out. The issue seemed clear. *Did the Indian women understand what was expected of them?*

Background

In December 1978, a lawyer for the Idaho Legal Aid Services requested my aid on behalf of the Bannock-Shoshoni women. As a cultural anthropolo-

Barbara Joans is Director of the Merritt Museum of Anthropology and a faculty member at Merritt College (12500 Campus Drive, Oakland, CA 94619; (510) 436-2607).

Originally published in *Practicing Anthropology* 6,3-4(1984):6,8. For a recent example of Joans's work in this area, see Barbara Joans, "Infighting in San Francisco: Anthropology in Family Court," *Practicing Anthropology* 19,4(1997):10-13.

gist and Director of Women's Re-Entry at Idaho State University, I was the logical person to contact. This was a fortunate meeting all around, as I had been trying, unsuccessfully, to make contact with Fort Hall Indians all year. Fort Hall and Pocatello are two ends of a wide spectrum. Pocatello is a poor railroad town situated in the southeast portion of Idaho. Major employment comes from the fertilizer plant and other heavy industry and marginal ranch and farm lands. In spite of the poverty and general hardness of people's lives, there are prevailing attitudes of rugged individualism and pride in the pioneering spirit of town ancestors. There is also a small state university of surprising vitality. Pocatello is a town of extremes.

Situated about ten miles out of town is the Fort Hall Indian Reservation. Over 1,000 Bannock-Shoshoni live, farm, and work at Fort Hall. While the reservation is large, most of it is desert. Few Indians do more than scrape a meager living from the soil. For supplemental income they make pottery and jewelry which they sell to the local townspeople. Some of the Indians rent part of their lands to local Anglos for a small yearly income. Fort Hall is an Indian cultural center hosting intertribal feasts, dances, sweat lodges, powwows, initiations, and meetings all summer long. The Bannock-Shoshoni maintain a vital political/cultural role in the western Indian community. They provide meeting places for many tribes.

The close proximity of Fort Hall and Pocatello assures continuous contact between the two populations. Unfortunately, frequent meetings are not often beneficial to either group. Typical culture contact takes place in such non-neutral spaces as local bars, unemployment and welfare lines, and hospital clinics. Old antagonisms fanned by years of mutual prejudice reinforce debilitating stereotypes. The two communities may live side-by-side, but there is little positive cultural exchange and even less mutual understanding.

The Problem

The lack of understanding between the two communities crystallized around the issue of SSI payments. Six older (all past sixty) Bannock-Shoshoni women were having trouble with the Pocatello social service agency that handled their SSI accounts. The women were accused of withholding information from the agency and receiving unreported monies. Several of the women had small parcels of land at Fort Hall which they were able to rent to neighboring Anglos. They received between one and two thousand dollars in rental income. They rented the land in January, but did not receive payment on the land until the following December.

Under SSI regulations, the women were required to report all income. The Pocatello SSI explained, in English, at reservation community lunches that all monies had to be accounted for. The women did report the rental of their lands in December when they received payment. SSI claimed that the income should have been reported as soon as the land was rented. Because it was not immediately reported, the SSI people stopped all checks and demanded that the women pay back the monies they had received during the year. To compound the problem, several women were sent extra checks which they assumed they could keep. They reasoned that if the government sent them money, the government knew what it was doing. SSI wanted all the monies returned. The payments in question amounted to around $2,000, and the women had no way of repaying it. They went to see the legal aid lawyer and he came to see me.

Problem Solving: The Methodology

The SSI workers claimed that the rules and regulations had been fully explained. The legal aid lawyer wanted to know if, in my estimation, this was so. *Did the Indian women understand what was expected of them?*

I used language as the criterion for cultural understanding. Since all the verbal exchanges between SSI staff and Bannock-Shoshoni were in English, I decided to use the women's comprehension of English as the index for general cultural understanding. If the women sufficiently understood English, then the SSI staff would have justification in their claims. If on the other hand, the women's comprehension of English was minimal, a case for misunderstanding SSI rules could be made. Drawing from my general knowledge of language (anthropological training but not specific training in linguistics), I created a three-part system to test the English language sophistication of the Indian women. Levels 1, 2, and 3 were the categories in the system.

Level 1: This consisted of everyday common speech. For example: "How are you?" "I am fine." "Are you cold?" "Do you need a coat?" "Are you hungry?" Each of the women understood and was able to communicate on Level 1 English.

Level 2: This consisted of language joking behavior. Could the women understand nonliteral sentences? Could they share in joke-making behavior about local Pocatello officials? We had spoken often about their contempt for Pocatello officials and I knew that they disapproved of town politics. But could they understand the double-entendres, the mixed meanings, the puns, and the jokes? At this level, only one woman was able to follow my conversation and understand the linguistic ambiguities and joking statements. The one Indian woman who understood English Level 2 participated in joking behavior and made outrageous comments about the nature of the Pocatello political system. With her alone, I tested for Level 3.

Level 3: This consisted of understanding the rules and regulations governing Indian lives and the ability to articulate these rules. I tested for Level 3 by first inquiring about Indian laws. Did the woman understand how the Indian police operated on the reservation? She did. Could she articulate an understanding of tribal policies, laws, and rules? She could. Did she understand

74

how Pocatello police operated? She did not. Could she understand Indian councils? Yes. Did she understand Pocatello town councils? No. I saw that she was not able to translate rules from Indian society to Pocatello society on Level 3 using English as the language of communication. I concluded from her lack of Level 3 understanding that there were severe cultural misunderstandings between her and the Pocatello SSI people. The SSI people thought that the Bannock-Shoshoni women knew what they were talking about when they described procedures in English. I was in a position to demonstrate that they did not.

Since it was my job to determine how much English the Bannock-Shoshoni women actually understood, I devised methods to keep me in frequent communication. I visited the women at their homes, at the lawyer's office, at my office, and at the reservation trading post. Using the traditional methodologies of participant observation, I stayed with the Indian women about three months. At the end of that time I was able to conclude that while they were all talking English, the Indian women and the agency people used English with very different meanings. The Indian women did not understand what was expected of them.

Problem Solving: The Process

The next problem was how to make my knowledge acceptable to the judge. I had to prove culture conflict and cultural misunderstanding. These women looked like they talked English, but, in reality, they didn't have a clear idea of what the SSI people were telling them. The women were all in their late '60s and early '70s, and had lived most of their lives on the Indian reservation where they had very little voluntary contact with English. Their normal, everyday language was either Bannock or Shoshoni.

I set about preparing for the court appearance. I researched information about the judge and discovered that he was not sympathetic to feminist causes. That left a problem because I had a seven-page vitae filled with feminist activities. I decided it was best to take out all of my activities that centered around women. By the time my vitae got into the Idaho court system, it was a page and a half. The other thing I researched for my court appearance was how a middle-aged Anglo woman was supposed to look when she went to an Idaho court. I went out and bought what I now call my "court dress." I pulled my hair back, put on a lot of bright red lipstick, and a pair of '50's glasses. I don't mean this disrespectfully; this is the cultural norm there and I didn't want to violate it.

I had another problem. My skirt ended at my knees and my cowboy boots ended three inches below my skirt. I don't shave my legs. For my court appearance, I shaved just that three-inch area between the tops of the boots and the bottom of the skirt. For the next two months I'd look down and see on my legs a three-inch ring of hairlessness.

The Results

For my court appearance it was necessary to prepare an anthropological brief documenting the linguistic and cultural misunderstanding. I had to supply a bibliography dealing with other cases of cultural misunderstanding. I also had to submit my much shortened vitae as evidence of credentials enabling me to research contact situations. Then I was permitted to testify. The legal aid lawyer and I chose to use the evidence from the Bannock-Shoshoni woman who was most proficient in English (Level 2) for our first test case. We stated:

- that the SSI people always came to the reservation on busy days when many things were happening.
- that the SSI people always spoke to a large number of people during a community lunch and never gave individuals specific attention.
- that the SSI people always spoke English and the Indian women did not understand English sufficiently to comply with their demands. The Indian women never understood Level 3, the level of laws and rules.
- Therefore, the Bannock-Shoshoni women should not lose their SSI benefits, nor should they have to pay any monies back.

After considering our evidence, the judge ruled that the women did not have to return any money. He decided that there was too great a possibility that the women did not understand the SSI instructions and, therefore, could not be held responsible for either failing to report rent monies before they received them or failing to return checks that should not have been sent. The judge added that in the future the SSI would have to use a Bannock-Shoshoni interpreter when they went to the reservation to describe program requirements.

By using linguistic patterns as criteria for cultural understanding, I was able to initiate a program of action anthropology in Idaho. Interpreters are now used in all contact situations between town agencies and reservation peoples. For the first time in Idaho, variant cultural patterns were accepted in court as determinants of behavior. Through these actions the Bannock-Shoshoni women have gained some control over their economic resources.

If Only They Would Listen: The Anthropology of Business and the Business of Anthropology

S. Brian Burkhalter

In this lively parable, Brian Burkhalter juxtaposes the "headhunters" of Amazonia and of Madison Avenue. He grippingly shows us how anthropology "works" in now not-so-exotic faraway places. He helps us see how anthropological methods that made new sense of the distant and strange world of tribal peoples can now help to do the same for the near and familiar world of business, even as the two worlds become more and more alike. And, perhaps anthropology, as well as some anthropologists, can profit from it. In what might seem a surprising turn, Burkhalter brings the reader back to the very roots of academic anthropology in laying his case for business anthropology as basic anthropology. In his few words on "labor problems," Burkhalter conjures up the work of some of those in the 1930s who were to be the founders of modern applied anthropology and the Society for Applied Anthropology.

J. A. P.

The air of the small town was laden with red dust that felt gritty against the eyes. But what I felt most were the heat of the early afternoon and the relentless glare of the tropical sun. Outside there was no shade, for the citizens of Itaituba, perhaps to prove their mastery over the nearby jungle, had hewn down almost every tree, and buildings baked beside the broad, glittering Tapajos River, a tributary of the Amazon. I had come to town to buy supplies before returning upstream to the villages of the Mundurucu Indians, and on this, the 24th of May, 1980, I stood by a cash register and counted my change.

S. Brian Burkhalter was Assistant Professor of Anthropology at the University of South Florida when this article was first published. Serious illness interrupted his academic career in 1988. He is now a certified senior trainer in Evangelism Explosion and can be contacted at 2404 Seabreeze Court, Orlando, FL 32805; (407) 423-9709; <sbrian@gdi.net>.

Originally published in *Practicing Anthropology* 7,4(1986):18-20, this article has been edited for republication here. For an update on some of the issues disucssed here, see S. Brian Burkhalter and Robert F. Murphy, "Tappers and Sappers: Rubber, Gold and Money among the Mundurucú," *Amercian Ethnologist* 16,1(1989):100-116. The research on which this article is based was funded by a Fulbright Hays Training Fellowship (1979-80), The Organization of American States (1989-81), and Columbia University.

"That's the thief!" shouted a stout, young man in a red tee-shirt as he pointed at me. He spoke quickly, and I could not understand his excited Portuguese. But I could not miss the fifteen or so armed soldiers who surrounded me or the polite, cautious man in plain clothes who identified himself as the Capitão of the police.

It is at times like these that one hopes one can answer the most important questions or, at the very least, understand what they are. And it is the search to determine these questions that directs sensitive ethnography. You may wonder, for example, just what my fieldwork among the Mundurucu Indians of Central Brazil has to do with business and commerce, and thereby to the anthropology of business and the business of anthropology.

Mundurucu Commerce

Consider the wristwatches, the portable shortwave radios, the battery-powered record players, the new clothes. Mundurucu no longer make pottery; they use aluminum pots and pans. Only old women occasionally weave hammocks; others always buy theirs from riverboat traders, missionaries, government Indian agents, or merchants in town. Small boys stalk lizards with bows and arrows, but their fathers hunt with shotguns and rifles. Face and body tattoos of elders are not seen on men and women middle-aged and younger, who also forgo perforating their earlobes in traditional fashion. To anyone sporting novelties, they ask a question not heard a few decades ago: "How much does it cost?" Mundurucu know money and love it.

But it was not the love of money so much as the desire for goods that induced village after village to move to distant riverbanks where riverboat merchants plied their trade. Diets changed as people relied more on fish and less on game. Tools, dress, and housing types became indistinguishable from those of Brazilian peasant neighbors. And there were cheap perfumes, plastic icons, and peroxide to bleach their children's hair. Travel to regional towns became easier, and there men could buy cigarettes, liquor, and the embraces of local prostitutes.

Mundurucu history reflects their growing reliance on trade. Dense jungle and row after row of rapids on the Tapajos River made reaching the territory difficult for outsiders, but Mundurucu attacks on the Portuguese prompted a punitive expedition against them in 1795, and they were soundly defeated. The Portuguese victors, however, offered them machetes, axes, cloth, and other goods to act as mercenaries against other tribes of the region, and this the Mundurucu did, taking heads as trophies and spreading terror among their enemies.

Their Indian neighbors subdued, they sought other ways to gain access to these goods, bartering manioc flour to Brazilian rubber tappers, then learning to tap rubber themselves. Merchants advanced credit and kept their books, so that these Indians, like many of their Brazilian peasant neighbors, were kept in perpetual debt. Their land was demarcated as a reservation, and missionaries, government Indian agents, and itinerant merchants all became active in trading with the Mundurucu. In the mid 1950s gold was discovered to the north of their reservation, and from Brazilian miners Mundurucu learned to dig alluvial deposits, run the dirt through sluices, and pan the sediment for gold dust. These techniques were applied to streams within their reservation, and output was rewarding enough to make it worthwhile, but not so great as to attract miners from more productive sites downstream to the north.

In 1952 and 1953 when Robert and Yolanda Murphy studied these same people, they found them ignorant of bank notes and eager to catch a glimpse of the tiny people hiding within the Murphys' radio (Robert Murphy, personal communication). But now radios are common, and *cruzeiros* quickly spent. Gone are the days of relying on credit and barter alone; now Mundurucu deal in cash.

Their transformation is far from unique; it mimics the experience of tribe after tribe in Amazonia and throughout the world. To lose sight of the impact of money, of trade with the outside world, or of the wealth of introduced goods would seriously distort our understanding of them as a people and a culture undergoing change.

This leads us to business and commerce, but I should add one note before exploring our roles as anthropologists in these enterprises. Business is inevitable; our food, clothing, and shelter depend upon transactions carried out within a capitalist system. To observe that this is so is neither to condemn nor to condone this economic arrangement. Business is not so much immoral as it is amoral, and it appears to me that we would do well to study it as we would any other social phenomenon. In applying our skills to the business world, we must take care to exercise due concern for those affected by our actions, but this should not inhibit our interest.

The Anthropology of Business

Beads of perspiration ran down my forehead, stinging my eyes, and the air seemed thick and heavy as I faced the local militia and tried to make sense out of what my accuser was saying. How I loved Brazil, truly—the lively strains of the samba, friendships warmed by cachaca, children laughing on the wharves, stoic peasants fishing from canoes. Fieldwork had demanded patience above all things, patience with malaria, patience with inevitable delay, patience with bureaucracy. And so, resolved to be patient and calm, to maintain my poise, I began to understand the charges against me. I was being accused of having helped sell my red-shirted antagonist a stolen car some four months earlier, when, in fact, I had been deep within the jungle. If only they would listen...

My role of late has been a double one, encouraging my friends in anthropology to consider options in business, where I feel they have much to contribute, and encouraging business scholars to concern themselves with what anthropology has to offer to them. If only they would listen to each other, there could be a fruitful meshing of interests.

Anthropologists have contributed little to the growing volume of scholarly work on the conduct and scope of business, although, clearly, we should have much to say about it. Consider, for example, corporate culture, a notion in vogue among business scholars. Surely this is a subject which we should feel comfortable exploring. Furthermore, closer links to business offer the very real prospect of employment for trained anthropologists able and willing to help solve particular problems. Corporate managers beset with hosts of opportunities, costs, and questions need to know such things as how their corporations actually function and how this differs from its organizational chart and how its operations could be streamlined, made more effective, broadened or narrowed in scope, or otherwise "improved." Participant observers may offer insights that others may neither be in a position nor have the training to offer. How are business decisions made? Who influences these decisions, how do they do so, and why? Some answers may be obvious—and thus less interesting—but some may not be immediately evident at all. How does such decision-making behavior affect a corporation's response to its outside environments? How does it enhance or reduce the firm's ability to compete?

Personnel and labor problems also invite anthropological contributions. If management is considered aloof and uncaring by its employees, what can be done to improve labor relations and to offer a higher quality work-life? Here, the anthropologist as a consultant working with unions and management could play the role of a disinterested third party, providing an understanding of the social context in which such problems arise. Teams of anthropologists could achieve an even more holistic view in such situations.

Consulting anthropologists could also offer services to small businesses, especially those that are "starting up." What sort of store is or is not appropriate for a particular neighborhood? What appeal will a shop have and to which ethnic group or social class? These may seem obvious questions and clients may be reluctant to consult us on them—but they should not be underestimated. A pizza shop may not prosper in a Chinese neighborhood, and a Greek community may or may not frequent a boutique selling imported French fashions. Such preferences however, can, to a certain degree, be assessed in advance using ethnographic methods, and results could be valuable not only to small business, but also to the communities involved, which might need goods or services that a small business would be glad to provide.

Our contributions need not be limited to these considerations. The interactions between government and business in the guise of federal, state, or even municipal efforts to encourage business growth, to foster the establishment of minority-owned businesses, or to stimulate business activity in economically depressed areas are further examples of projects in which anthropological consultants could be of tremendous service. What steps a local government should follow to encourage the development of business in decaying urban neighborhoods and how residents would be likely to respond to various measures are matters that anthropologists are well-equipped to research and for which they could provide feasible policy guidelines.

In brief, in any business or public situation requiring extensive knowledge about how a local community, ethnic group, or group of businessmen think, feel, believe, and act, there is an opportunity for applied anthropologists to make policy suggestions based on ethnographic research.

Problems, of course, abound. To research a question, we need to know what the question is, and clients may not be quite sure what they need or desire from us. It is not enough to agree that "things aren't working here." Problems should be stated in such a way that they are manageable. Often the formulation of questions and the search for solutions will be a team effort, so applied anthropologists should get used to working with engineers, city planners, government officials, and businessmen.

Again, there are ethical problems. Anthropologists conducting research for businesses or for public agencies must be sensitive to any restrictions imposed on subsequent scholarly publications based on this research. Even more importantly, we must try to ensure that our findings are not used to harm the interests of the communities we study. These and like concerns will appear and reappear in consulting work in business, and we must anticipate areas of conflict in advance and become skillful in using contracts to protect our interests and those of the people studied.

The Anthropology of Marketing

All eyes in the store turned toward me, and passers-by stopped to gawk and listen. I was bigger than any one of the soldiers, and that, I was sure, did not make them happy. One had his hand on his hip, and, as I watched him out of the corner of my eye, I wondered if it rested on his pistol. My shirt was tucked in, and I was glad of it, for this proved that I did not carry a gun. The Capitão asked for my identity card, and, calmly and deliberately, I fished my passport from my right front trouser pocket. The passport was wrapped in plastic, and as I unwrapped it I joked about it, saying that this protected it from water, for I had already been clumsy enough to fall in the river once. No one laughed, and I felt very nervous.

I said that I had other documents in a bag that I had checked when entering the store and offered to get them. The Capitão showed no interest.

The face of one soldier seemed restless, bored, eager for action, and I did not want to provoke him.

Thought after thought vied for my attention during the first brief moments of this confrontation, and I contemplated spending weeks or months in the town jail, which I imagined was filthy, ill-equipped, and dangerous. I realized, with a shudder, that I did not know what my rights were or whether or not they would be respected. Curiously, I did not feel fear. But, as voices rose in argument, I considered the prospect of jail, incarceration in the Amazon, being trapped behind iron bars in the tropics...

We can imprison ourselves in paradigms that are too restrictive, definitions of what anthropology is that are too inflexible to allow us to explore promising avenues of research. In a moment, I will sketch some work I believe anthropologists can do in marketing and international business, two of my particular interests.

Let us begin by noting that studying exchange has long interested anthropologists. Boas's work among the Indians of the North Pacific Coast, Malinowski's study of the kula ring of the Trobriand Islands, and Marcel Mauss's "Essai sur le don" are early examples. The anthropological literature is replete with discussions of exchange as can be seen in the work of Claude Levi-Strauss, Melville Herskovits, Edward Spicer, Robert F. Murphy, Marvin Harris, Clifford Geertz, Manning Nash, and Marshall Sahlins, to name but a few.

With this in mind, consider the definition of marketing proposed by Philip Kotler in his classic text *Principles of Marketing* (Englewood Cliffs, N.J.: Prentice Hall International, Inc., 1980): "Marketing is human activity directed at satisfying needs and wants through exchange process." Were we to adopt a normative view of definitions, we could claim that this encompasses much of anthropology and might well be surprised to learn we had been studying marketing all along.

In its focus on consumers and on marketing behavior, however, the literature has largely taken either a data-analytical, modeling approach or a psychological approach. Scant attention has been accorded to cultural influences. But, although psychological aspects are important, exchange is primarily a social and cultural phenomenon intended to satisfy economic ends. Anthropologists have much to say concerning the cultural dimensions of marketing, and we have scarcely been heard.

This is not to say that anthropologists have ignored marketing altogether; it is instructive to consider some titles that bridge the gap between the two fields. Examples are George M. Foster's "The Folk Economy of Rural Mexico with Special Reference to Marketing" (*Journal of Marketing* 13[1949]:153-162), Charles Winick's "Anthropology's Contribution to Marketing" (*Journal of Marketing* 25[1961]:53-60), David E. Allen's "Anthropological Insights into Customer Behaviour" (*European Journal of Marketing* 5[1971]:45-57), Alan S.

Marcus's "How Agencies Can Use Anthropology in Advertising" (*Advertising Age Magazine*, 14 September 1956, pp. 87-91), John F. Sherry, Jr.'s "Gift Giving in Anthropological Perspective" (*Journal of Consumer Research* 10,2[1983]:157-168), and Norbert Dannhaeuser's *Contemporary Trade Strategies in the Philippines: A Study in Marketing Anthropology* (New Brunswick, NJ: Rutgers University Press, 1983). My own *Amazon Gold Rush: Markets and the Mundurucu Indians* (Ann Arbor: University Microfilms International, 1983) explored how an Indian group behaved as consumers. Since 1978, the American Anthropological Association has co-sponsored one of the major marketing journals, *The Journal of Consumer Research*. Other cultural anthropologists, like Walter J. Dickie of Creative Research, Inc. (*Anthropology Newsletter*, December 1982, p. 7), and Steve Barnett of Planmetrics, Inc. (*The Wall Street Journal*, 7 July 1983, p. 25), both University of Chicago Ph.D.s, have put their ethnographic skills to use doing marketing research for consulting firms.

Conducting international business in general and international marketing in particular demands sensitivity to cultural differences in behavior and expectations, and the scope for practical advice from applied anthropologists is tremendous. Vast differences in cultural norms determine what is considered proper and tasteful advertising, what are appropriate colors for packaging, what are the most appealing sizes of units offered for sale, and what are the most effective means of promoting a product. Practices vary greatly. What is a token of regard in one country may be deemed a bribe in another. Customs regulations may be designed to encourage exports and to discourage imports, while appealing to concerns like consumer safety or fairness in advertising. This contrast between latent and manifest intentions should be familiar to consulting anthropologists.

Knowing the importance of credit and how credit is managed could be of help to marketers wanting to increase sales. Such information could influence, for instance, the type of outlet chosen or the advertising media used. My observations of purchasing in an Amazonian peasant village provide a pertinent example. Here, the shopkeeper is seen as a patron, and goods are often bought on credit. This is sometimes advantageous to the buyer, as when medicines or food are needed and money is unavailable. More often, it is to his disadvantage, for the shopkeeper minds the books, not always fairly, and does not fear losing customers if prices are high because they cannot afford to risk losing his patronage by buying elsewhere. The norms governing this patron-client relation relate to the customer's need for security in times of want and to the shopkeeper's willingness to profit from this.

The social context of purchasing should not be ignored. Thus, besides noting that a farmer buys an item in a country general store situated at the intersection of two state roads, we should seek to learn what social relations permeate interactions between the farmer and the merchant. Are they relatives

84

or old friends? How long have they known each other? What activities do they pursue in common, such as hunting and fishing, attending church picnics, or promoting the county fair? Are purchases made on credit or with cash? Are acts of purchasing often just an excuse for the buyer to socialize by joining the men hanging about the general store?

What could such information on the social context mean to management? In some cases, marketing strategies could be affected considerably. If the relations between the buyer and seller exclusive of the act of purchasing are more important than product attributes, then it might be wise to retail one's product in a greater number of smaller stores than in fewer larger ones, where prices may be lower but customer-merchant relations more attenuated. Such decisions would depend upon the market segment targeted and upon the product's appeal to those of various social classes, ethnic groups, age categories, and regions.

Anthropological guidance may also help avoid tragic mistakes. Recall the marketing of Nestle's powdered infant formula to areas where water sources were contaminated. Nestle's later efforts to defend itself from international reproach are reprehensible, but the initial decision to launch the product in such areas was at base an error that anthropologists could have prevented. Anyone with extensive knowledge of these regions would have been familiar with the threat diarrhea poses to infants and known that it was induced by contaminated water. Had this advice been sought and heeded, possibly millions of infant lives could have been spared.

The Marketing of Anthropology

The voices that rose in argument were voices in my defense. Two friends from the government Indian agency, FUNAI, had accompanied me to the store, and one, Francisco, argued furiously. He showed his identity card to prove that he worked with FUNAI and claimed that I had been with him in the jungle four months earlier. When my accuser declared that the thief had been from São Paulo, Francisco retorted that my accent and passport clearly showed that I was an American and that the only reason I was suspected was because I had blonde hair like the thief.

The debate was so quickly paced that I could not get a word in; this, I suspect, was an advantage. But, as Francisco confided to me, the two of them had beards, and, in rural Brazil, bearded ones were often considered sympathizers with Fidel Castro and, hence, not to be trusted. Perhaps they were not the best people to press my case.

When we reflect upon how we, as anthropologists, can best press our case to market our skills, it is evident that we should strive to enhance our credibility with the clients we seek to serve. Physicians in white lab coats, jealous of their title "doctor," do so; investment bankers on Wall Street do so when they dress up in their dark blue pinstriped suits and carry attaché cases. When I began my fieldwork among the Mundurucu, I confess that the style of dress adopted by the men—pastel-colored slacks (often patched or dirty) and tight-fitting short-sleeve shirts worn unbuttoned in front—seemed a bit uncouth. It is droll to think that, at the end of my fieldwork two years later, I dressed that way and thought nothing of it. Further, I became accustomed to walking some-what as they did, to holding my shoulders as they did, and to having conversa-tions without looking at the person with whom I was speaking just as they did. We must adapt ourselves to our social environment.

This is but an illustration of a frame of mind. To succeed as applied anthro-pologists in commerce, we need to be mindful of what we can do to attract customers. It is this sort of talk, I know, that sends shudders down the spines of anthropologists, for we value intensely our status as "marginals" and our critical, "gadfly" tradition. It is far more comfortable to ponder aloud the ethi-cal dilemmas we may face as consultants, than to reorient ourselves toward seeking to satisfy clients. But both, alas, are important.

Consider what we have to overcome. One has only to recall the opening paragraph of Boas's *Anthropology and Modern Life*, first published in 1928 (New York: W. W. Norton & Co.), to realize how relevant his words are today: "Anthropology is often considered a collection of curious facts, telling about the peculiar appearance of exotic people and describing their strange customs and beliefs. It is looked upon as an entertaining diversion, apparently without any bearing upon the conduct of life of civilized communities." Boas sought to challenge this conception, as did other anthropologists during and since World War II, especially during the last decade, but, nonetheless, it remains.

An internship program is a clever way to market our services. From the viewpoint of the candidate for the master's or Ph.D. degree, the internship establishes his or her credentials as an applied anthropologist while he or she gathers data for the thesis. But it is the appreciation that the host agency or business has for what the intern has accomplished once the internship has been completed that makes for good marketing. It creates a demand for these services, just as manufacturers try to do when they give out samples of their product.

The internship offers a further advantage in that it encourages the student to adapt to meet the demands of the host agency or business. If you will ex-cuse my behaviorism, applied anthropology is what applied anthropologists do when they apply their skills. If there is no call for those skills, they will not be applied. The successful practitioner, then, must be market-oriented. This should remind us to ask: "what is our product?" and "what is our business?" Too narrow or inflexible a response to these questions may eventually mean, as the makers of horse-drawn carriages, wooden barrels, and oil-burning lamps at length discovered about themselves, that we have no product and no busi-ness at all.

Prospects for the Future

Perhaps it was my passport, perhaps my accent, perhaps the spirited defense by my friend Francisco. My accuser began to stammer and blush, having discovered his mistake. He first asked my pardon and that of Francisco and shook my hand. He apologized to the Capitão, to all of us again, and appeared embarrassed and defeated. In his haste to get even with those who had cheated him, he had pointed his finger at the wrong man. The Capitão indicated that I could go. The soldiers seemed disappointed, but, what could they do? It was clear that I was innocent.

Just then a small white car screeched to a halt outside the store and raised a thick cloud of red dust. Out jumped a thin man in shorts and a striped shirt—the chefe of FUNAI headquarters. Word spreads quickly in small towns, and an unknown passer-by had warned him of my plight. He ran up to us, declaring that it was absolutely ridiculous to have accused me of selling the stolen car. The Capitão must have felt a bit sheepish, for they were good friends. The case against me was closed.

As the crowd dispersed and the soldiers wandered reluctantly away, Francisco, my other friend, and I gathered our purchases and caught a ride back to FUNAI headquarters with the chefe. Francisco urged me to get a lawyer and prosecute for false arrest. The chefe laughed and declared that he would chide the Capitão with "what kind of monkey was this?" the next time they sat down to play cards. I felt that tempered uncertainty one experiences after a narrow escape. Strangely enough, I was neither angry nor offended, just greatly relieved. I mused about how I loved doing anthropology and delighted in the thought of what a novel entry this incident would make in my field notes. Working as an ethnographer in Brazil seemed, in some indescribable sense, a charmed existence. I welcomed the next challenge and wondered, "what is in store…next?"

The Study of Chronic Disease in Samoan Populations

Joel M. Hanna and Paul T. Baker

In the late 1970s, biomedical anthropology, the interface between physical anthropology and the health sciences, emerged as a distinct area of inquiry with profound applied implications. The multidisciplinary Samoan study described here was unique in the mid-1980s, and it served as a model for subsequent research on Turkanans in Africa and Tibetans in Asia. The Samoan case is particularly well-suited to scientific inquiry because of its "natural laboratory" situation. Samoans live in a quantifiable continuum of cultural environments ranging from distinctly rural and non-Western in the South Pacific to highly urban and Westernized in California. This research demonstrates perfectly the value of the perspectives and methods of physical anthropology in attempting to understand such contemporary health problems as obesity and cardiovascular disease, as well as the detrimental health effects of modernization on non-Western populations. The authors' biocultural, anthropological perspective leads them to consider both specific cultural practices and prior environmental conditions in explaining the Samoan patterns. C. W. W.

As human populations become modernized through migration or by *in situ* Westernization, they experience a change in their patterns of morbidity and mortality. Infectious disease, gastrointestinal disorders and traumatic injury generally decline, while heart disease, stroke, diabetes, gout, and carcinoma increase in prevalence. These chronic diseases are accompanied by a number of observable risk factors such as obesity, hypertension, hypercholesterolemia, and lack of physical activity. As these populations begin to resemble modern nations in their morbidity and mortality profiles, there is also an increased life expectancy; but chronic diseases are characteristic of mature adults, so the increased life span is not necessarily a healthy one.

Joel M. Hanna is Professor of Anthropology at the University of Hawaii at Manoa (Honolulu, HI 96822).
Paul T. Baker is Evan Pugh Professor Emeritus of Anthropology at Pennsylvania State University.

Originally published as part of a special section on "Applied Directions and Dimensions in Biomedical Anthropology," guest edited by Curtis W. Wienker, in *Practicing Anthropology* 8,1-2(1986):8-9, this article has been edited and abridged for republication here.

Human biologists and physical anthropologists traditionally have been interested in changing patterns of morbidity and mortality, which have considerable importance as parts of the evolutionary process that can be studied in contemporary human populations. Our understanding of adaptive processes in human populations also aids in identification of the causes and consequences of risk and disease. As health professionals become more aware of the complex causality involved in the chronic diseases of modernization, they more often turn to anthropologists for assistance in investigating the underlying conditions of disease.

Human biologists and physical anthropologists bring several tools to the study of chronic disease: an evolutionary perspective, a cross-cultural approach, and an assortment of tools for studying human morphology and physiology in the field. From the evolutionary viewpoint, a disease is part of an adaptive process resulting from the interaction of a population with its constantly changing environment. In this paradigm some chronic diseases are seen as adaptations to past conditions which no longer persist. In a changed environment the metabolic results of underlying genetic adaptations may become maladaptive and are subject to selective processes. This adaptive paradigm has provided anthropological explanations of such diseases as diabetes and sickle cell anemia.

Accompanying the adaptive model of disease is the concept of population, which is central to evolutionary theory, but often missing from clinical thinking. Normal variation in human population can be exploited to clarify patterns and development of disease. The host population can be demographically subdivided and relative risks assigned to different segments. Demographic division allows us to pinpoint those at risk for a variety of diseases and provides clues as to etiology. Population analysis has shown, for example, that diabetes, previously a single disease category, can be divided into Type 1, which is of viral origin and seems to attack a given genotype, and Type 2, a different disease, which occurs mostly in adults. Each segment of the population is subject to its own particular risks and requires different types of cure and prevention.

The cross-cultural approach has also furnished valuable insights into chronic disease. The discovery that incidence of chronic diseases varies among human populations exposed to different environments has increased our understanding of the process of disease development. For example, human biologists have demonstrated that blood pressure does not increase with age in some populations; this finding casts doubt on hypertension as an integral part of the aging process. Likewise, studies of nonmodernized human populations have shown that large amounts of dietary salt and cholesterol are not necessarily causes of hypertension and hypercholesterolemia. Cross-cultural research has led to a replacement of such universal explanations with an appreciation of the importance of biocultural interactions. The cross-cultural perspective has also been employed to clarify genetic correlates of disease through the study of isolates and island populations with relatively homogeneous gene pools.

Finally, physical anthropologists have developed a number of field techniques suitable for describing human variation which are also useful in the description of the risks for chronic disease. Morphological measurements can be used individually or combined into more complex measures such as the body mass index (BMI= weight/height^2) which differentiates between body size and obesity. The measurement of skinfold thickness has been of particular importance and is a current worldwide standard for the assessment of obesity and nutritional status.

Physical anthropologists have frequently pioneered in taking laboratory techniques into the field to study naturally occurring, widespread health problems. Blood typing and measurement of blood pressure were early applications; more recently techniques such as glucose tolerance, blood lipid analysis, and exercise testing have been used in the field. This kind of fieldwork has provided comparative data for Western populations as well as clarification of the environmental, cultural, and behavioral components which influence risk.

During the last fifteen years we have been studying the effects of modernization and migration on the health and well-being of Samoans. This joint study by the University of Hawaii, the Pennsylvania State University, and the University of California at San Francisco has employed the tools of physical anthropology within a broad multidisciplinary program. We have collected and analyzed a wealth of data on demography, physical fitness, nutrition, anthropometry, stress response, growth and development, hematology, coping behavior, and a variety of associated areas. These investigations have been described in detail in *The Changing Samoans: Behavior and Health in Transition,* edited by Paul T. Baker, Joel M. Hanna, and Thelma S. Baker (New York: Oxford University Press, 1986). Here we summarize some of the major points which are of interest to applied biomedical anthropologists.

The Samoan archipelago lies south of the equator about one thousand miles from Hawaii. The indigenous Samoan population is of Polynesian ancestry and has inhabited the islands for at least one thousand years. The islands are currently divided into two political units: Western Samoa, an independent country, and American Samoa, a territory of the United States. Western Samoa has a population of about 160,000 and is largely rural and traditional, although its capital, Apia, is clearly a modern center with electricity, paved roads, television and other expressions of the modern world. American Samoa is composed of the island of Tutuila and the outlying Manuan Islands. Tutuila, the largest island and the population center, has been the site of a major U.S. Navy base for most of this century. A blend of Samoan and American cultures is evident, but there are some rural villages with a traditional Samoan ambiance. The outlying Manua islands are geographically isolated from Tutuila by one hundred miles of open sea. The Manuan group is also rural and traditional in nature, but modernization is now having an impact in the form of new roads, trucks, television, and imported foods.

Within the last fifty years there has been a major migration of Samoans from the islands to the United States and now New Zealand. This was precipitated by the closing of the naval base in 1950 and has continued at an accelerating pace since then. Western Samoans have gone to New Zealand where some 30,000 are now resident; about 18,000 American Samoans have migrated to Hawaii and 30,000 to other parts of the United States. Although many Samoans have settled permanently abroad, the migration has had a circular component. Many migrants return to Samoa after being abroad for several years; in some cases children are sent abroad for an education and return at a later date. Thus, the contemporary Samoan population, which is genetically homogeneous, lives in a variety of environments ranging from the rural and traditional Western Samoan villages, to modernized Apia and Tutuila, to migrant enclaves in Hawaii and California.

We have undertaken several surveys which sampled most of the major populations. These have been supplemented by existing public records and intensive investigation of special problems. We now know something of the characteristics of each population and of the changes in health and well-being which have accompanied migration and modernization.

The most obvious result of modernization seems to have been an increase in body mass. The lightest populations are found in the rural areas of Western Samoa. Modernized populations are heavier, and migrant populations are the heaviest. Because these populations do not differ in stature, an increase in body fat is implicated. This has been verified by measurements of skinfold thickness. High body weight characterizes all ages including infants and children, but is most evident in adults. Even though adult Samoans are equal in stature to U.S. Whites, they average between the 75th and 90th percentiles in weight. While an increase in body weight is a frequent consequence of modernization, the Samoan population is unique in its high prevalence and magnitude.

The health consequences of such a massive increase in body weight are evident from various aspects of our data. Young Samoan men have high prevalence of hypertension, up to four times that of U.S. Whites of the same age, while the prevalence in Samoan women exceeds U.S. White women in later years. That obesity is a major factor in the development of hypertension is shown in our analysis of anthropometric data. The best predictors for elevated blood pressure are measures of body fatness. The prevalence of diabetes, a frequent consequence of obesity, also parallels modernization. As measured by fasting glucose, the prevalence of diabetes is very low in rural Western

Samoa; it is higher in modernized Apia, American Samoa, and among migrants to Hawaii.

Given the high prevalence of obesity and its potential pathological effect on the population, we have attempted to discover its origins. In Polynesian society, status and body size are directly related; chiefs and their wives typically weigh more than commoners. Using interviews, somatotype sorting, and story-telling techniques borrowed from psychology, we have investigated status seeking as a possible cause for obesity. The results clearly show that Samoans do not view obesity as either desirable or healthy. There is a clear preference for normal body build in any role except chief. Obese individuals are seen as more sickly and less able to provide for the community. It is also clear that obesity must follow the attainment of status, not precede it. Informants suggest that an obese commoner would be less likely to receive a chiefly title than his normal counterpart because he would be viewed as lazy.

We have also explored a nutritional explanation with surveys in Western Samoa, American Samoa, and Hawaii. All studied subpopulations consumed a large number of calories each day (compared to levels recommended for the U.S. population), but the level of consumption was lower in modernized subpopulations. The highest caloric consumption was among rural villagers and urban residents with physically demanding jobs, while the lowest consumption was among urban, modernized sedentary workers. There were no major differences in the quality of the respective diets.

David Pelletier simultaneously studied daily physical activity and diet in several areas of Western Samoa, including villagers, urban residents with physically active jobs, and urban residents with sedentary occupations. Food consumption and energy expenditure are closely associated, but the urban sedentary workers may not completely balance their daily food intake with physical activity. Sedentary workers, who consume the least, also have the greatest skinfold thickness. Pelletier found that the traditional Samoan pattern of Sunday feasting may play some role. Large amounts of food were consumed on Sunday by all subpopulations. While the normally vigorous activity of villagers and active workers expended the excess calories during the work week, a gradual accumulation of excess calories from Sunday feasting could account for the greater fatness of sedentary workers. Although additional study is required, the level of daily activity is probably an important contributor to the degree of obesity.

We have also found major changes in patterns of morbidity and mortality, but not exactly as anticipated from the study of other populations. As expected, diabetes seems to follow modernization. Cardiovascular disease (CVD), the major killer in modern countries, does not follow so clearly. The rate of CVD mortality from 1950 through the present has increased, but the increase has been slow and levels are not high in any of the Samoan populations studied. Moreover, much of the observed increase may be the delayed effects of an epidemic of rheumatic heart disease rather than artherosclerosis. Our mortality data are derived from analysis of death records from the Samoas, Hawaii, and California, and there are questions as to their completeness; but the Samoans do not appear to be experiencing the high degree of heart disease anticipated.

Another anomaly is the association of risk factors with heart disease. Epidemiological studies have identified risk factors such as obesity, hypertension, diabetes, hypercholesterolemia, and suppressed levels of high density lipoprotein cholesterol (HDL). Our surveys have shown that the first three are present in Samoans but that the level of heart disease does not appear to be elevated. Given the Western diet enjoyed by most modernized and migrant Samoans, we also expected high levels of blood cholesterol; however, several studies have shown that blood cholesterol of Samoans is lower than in comparable U.S. populations. Since an elevated level of plasma cholesterol is implicated in artherosclerosis, the prevalence of that disease may also be reduced in Samoans.

A related problem is seen with HDL cholesterol. HDL bears an inverse relationship to heart disease; those with high HDL levels are at lower risk. Physical activity leads to increases in HDL, and women have higher levels than men. Our studies of modernized and migrant Samoans show some of the lowest HDL levels ever recorded, for both sexes. This would suggest that modernized Samoans are at high risk for CVD. In the Manua Islands levels of HDL are higher in men than women which is a reversal of the normal relationship. Conrad Hornick thinks that this results from changes in physical activity which accompany modernization. Men continue to engage in agriculture and fishing while women become more sedentary. The greater physical fitness of men offsets the biological advantage of women and leads to reversal of the ratio.

To summarize our investigation of CVD and risk, Samoans seem to be at high risk due to their obesity, hypertension, high prevalence of diabetes and suppressed levels of HDL, yet mortality from CVD seems low. The reduced levels of total cholesterol may provide a clue. Elevated cholesterol occasions artherosclerosis, which in turn precipitates most heart problems. We know that Samoans are consuming amounts of fat equivalent to that consumed by modern Americans, yet have lower cholesterol. We also know that Polynesians have traditionally consumed large amounts of fat derived from the coconut. Perhaps these populations have become adapted to high lipid intake in a manner which has lowered circulating cholesterol.

Another important finding concerns migration. Our research has clearly shown that migration is less important in effect than is modernization. While there are differences between residents of Samoa and the migrants to California and Hawaii, the major health risks seem to change between village and urban life in modernized Samoa. It is this transition which is associated with the major changes in body size, prevalence of diabetes, hypertension, reduced physical activity, and a variety of other variables. It would be inappropriate to generalize to other modernizing and migrating populations, but this pattern is worthy of additional investigation.

The massive obesity which seems to characterize the modernized Samoans may be of some evolutionary significance. Its prevalence and magnitude seem unsurpassed in other populations studied. One of us (PTB) has argued that selection may have favored a genotype which produces an exaggerated weight gain under certain conditions. Some of the major problems encountered by Polynesian voyagers in the open ocean would have been cold stress (because of technological limitations) and potential food shortages. Likewise, the inhabitants of small islands and atolls would have been subject to periods of feast or famine. In each case selection would have favored survival of the individual with more body fat. This would have been a selective sieve for a larger body mass which repeatedly occurred in small populations. These are the ideal conditions for rapid evolution.

We have also investigated aspects of modernization including physical fitness, diet, growth, stress and coping behavior, and demography. In each case modernization has had a clear influence with changes generally in the direction of a Western profile. Continued study of groups such as the Samoans will enable us to understand the process of continuing adaptation to a modern environment. Such studies benefit the Western world as well as assisting peoples such as the Samoans to enjoy some of the benefits of modernization while avoiding some of the pitfalls.

Anthropology and Multicultural Teacher Education

Carol Chapnick Mukhopadhyay

The 1980s witnessed a growing awareness among anthropologists that the country's increasingly diverse population offered them an opportunity to address pressing social problems, including education. A former social studies teacher, Carol Mukhopadhyay calls on anthropologists to create strategies for infusing anthropology into teacher training to enhance teachers' effectiveness in multicultural settings. Mukhopadhyay describes four factors that led to the success of her approach within the California State University system: the university's recognition that teachers needed multicultural training, the paucity of education faculty to offer it, the state's teacher credential program that encouraged noneducation faculty to contribute to teacher education, and personal ties among faculty members. In the years since, the popularity of multiculturalism seems to have crested in some places. The recent backlash against affirmative action, bilingual education, and open-door immigration policies—a backlash largely led by people in Mukhopadhyay's state of California—suggests that there is even more need now to "practice anthropology" by crossing disciplinary boundaries and by seizing opportunities to further genuine intercultural understanding.

R. O. S.

In decades to come, anthropologists and educators will face an enormous and exciting challenge. Virtually all demographic projections suggest that anthropology students will no longer travel long distances to experience the fascinating variety of human cultures. Instead, our own cultural landscape will be transformed from the metaphorical salad bowl into a gigantic salad bar.

Educators will face new challenges as the projected ethnic demography manifests itself in the classroom. In California, for example, so-called

Carol Chapnick Mukhopadhyay is Professor of Anthropology at San Jose State University (One Washington Square, San Jose, CA 95129-0113; (408) 924-5732; <mukh@email.sjsu.edu>). She was Associate Professor of Anthropology at California State University, Chico, when this article was published.

Originally published as part of a special section on "Anthropology in Pre-College Education," guest edited by Ruth O. Selig and Patricia J. Higgins, in *Practicing Anthropology* 8,3-4(1986):27-28, this article has been edited and abridged for republication here.

"minorities"—i.e., children from non-European ethnic backgrounds—currently [1986] constitute 42 percent of the school age population. By the year 2000, this figure will be 52 percent and Anglos themselves will be one of California's many ethnic minorities.

Given these realities, institutions of higher learning will be asked to produce teachers who can teach effectively in multicultural settings and who can teach their students to function in and appreciate a culturally diverse world. No longer will teacher educators be able to argue that multicultural education is a competency needed only by the few in "inner-city" schools. Instead, all educators will have to become multiculturalists.

These circumstances offer anthropologists the opportunity to form mutually advantageous partnerships with teacher educators. Educators generally have not been trained to deal with or even appreciate cultural and linguistic diversity in the classroom. Historically, schools have tried to assimilate nonmainstream ethnic groups to the dominant northwestern European cultural tradition. This has produced a cultural bias in the educational system which most educators can neither recognize nor correct. The need for anthropological input into teacher preparation programs certainly exists.

In order for alliances to be created, however, anthropologists must first convince educators that their theories, data, and approaches have relevance for teacher education. Anthropologists must then identify and actively pursue strategies to infuse our approaches and insights into teacher preparation programs.

The Relevance of Anthropology for Teacher Preparation Programs

Of the two tasks noted above, the first is perhaps the easiest. Anthropologists have long argued that our discipline provides the broad perspective and conceptual framework necessary to function effectively in a multicultural society—or classroom. Ethnic studies courses, although valuable, tend to focus on the history and culture of specific ethnic groups. Anthropology provides concepts and describes cultural processes which enable prospective teachers to understand and deal effectively with any and all ethnic groups.

Yet anthropologists must explicitly indicate how their discipline can aid prospective teachers in multicultural classrooms. For example, the idea that culture consists of social, behavioral, and mental/ideological products, as well as material/tangible items, can alert prospective teachers to the subtle cultural differences that may exist between students and the school. These differences might include appropriate student-teacher, parent-teacher, or student-student behavior; communication rules, such as direct eye contact; cultural values contrary to the individualistic, competitive, hierarchical nature of most American classrooms; and culturally specific systems of classifying reality (e.g., colors, relatives) or differentiating items (e.g., shape vs. use).

The notion of smaller microcultures within larger cultures can be used to prepare prospective teachers for student diversity arising out of regional, class, religious, gender, and occupational, as well as ethnic, microcultures. The school itself can be analyzed as a microculture—a process which will sensitize prospective teachers not only to the school environment but also to the culture shock their future students may experience when first encountering it.

The basic properties of culture—that it is symbolic, integrated, shared, pervasive, and learned, and that it structures our perception and emotional response to reality—can also be applied to the classroom setting and to problems which prospective teachers will encounter. The notion of cultural adaptation can be useful for understanding variation in student behavior and for predicting how students will respond to various classroom structures or teaching styles.

The impact of culture and language on our perceptions, including hearing, can sensitize prospective teachers to the difficulty non-native speakers of English may have with the English phonemic system. Such insights can help teachers understand their own problems and feelings when trying to understand these same students and their parents. Appreciating the culturally specific nature of systems of classification can help teachers see cultural biases in school-administered tests and can reveal the cultural basis for our geographic categories (East vs. West); temporal categories (B.C.—before "Christ"); and maps (the centrality and size of the U.S.).

Fundamental, also, are the concepts of ethnocentrism, cultural relativism, and the "emic" (native-insider) vs. "etic" (observer-outsider) perspectives. These concepts engender respect for cultural diversity within the classroom and an obligation and desire to understand the perspectives which children and their parents bring to their school experience.

Other relevant processes include the nature of prejudice and ethnic conflict; acculturation and assimilation; "race," culture, and learning; language acquisition, bilingualism, and code-switching; and the formal and informal mechanisms through which culture is transmitted and learned. The latter is important if teachers are to be aware of the "hidden curriculum."

Also relevant is the vast ethnographic literature on social organization and ideology/belief systems of non-European cultures. The ethnographic literature is an invaluable resource for understanding the sociocultural context which shapes the lives of first and second generation immigrant children.

Ethnographic and ethnolinguistic methods can help new teachers learn about the microculture of the school and that of their students. In simplified form, such methods can also be incorporated into social studies projects examining cultural diversity in the local community.

Finally, there is the growing body of educational anthropological research, particularly that dealing with language, cognition, and schooling. Too often, colleagues in schools of education are not aware of our efforts in this area, the

98

Council on Anthropology and Education or *Anthropology and Education Quarterly*. We should familiarize our colleagues and their students with anthropology's contributions.

Clearly, there are numerous potential links between anthropology and teacher preparation. We must, however, connect our knowledge to the specific concerns and competencies of teacher preparation programs in our own states and institutions. For many anthropologists, this may require informal field experiences in the K-12 setting as well as familiarizing oneself with the local teacher credentialing program.

Involving oneself in the microculture of teacher education and learning to articulate the pragmatic links between anthropological knowledge and the needs of prospective teachers is not sufficient, however. Anthropologists must also discover strategies and vehicles for incorporating their materials and approaches into the teacher preparation program.

Adding Anthropology to Teacher Preparation

My own experience in the California State University (CSU) system provides one case study of how anthropology can work within the present system of teacher preparation. I became involved initially by developing personal links with like-minded colleagues within the School of Education. This led to several co-authored grant proposals on multicultural teacher education, including workshops for education faculty, and a multicultural curriculum resource guide focused around the specific components of our teacher credential program; membership on the campuswide Teacher Education Council; developing anthropology courses relevant to future credential candidates (e.g., a seminar on language and schooling); and encouraging our anthropology students to pursue K-12 teaching as a vehicle for their own anthropological and multicultural interests. I have also established links with multicultural teacher education programs at other California State University campuses, partially, through chairing a systemwide conference on Effective Teacher Preparation for a Multicultural California.

In retrospect, these strategies have emerged from the fortuitous combination of four factors: (1) the perceived need for multicultural teacher education; (2) the relative lack of personnel in schools of education who can fulfill this need; (3) the nature of our state and local teacher credential programs; and (4) the pre-existing personal links between faculty in education and anthropology.

1. Need for Multicultural Training

As previously noted, California is currently and will become increasingly a multicultural state. The California State University system, as the major producer of California's teachers, is concerned that teachers be adequately prepared to teach effectively in multicultural settings, particularly given current low levels of school achievement by non-Asian ethnic groups.

Apart from a genuine commitment to educational equity, the potential impact of both demographics and achievement levels on future college enrollments has alarmed university officials. In brief, given the current high drop-out rate and low achievement levels of Hispanics and Blacks, the state university of the future will find itself in dire need of students. Similarly, without intervention, the future supply of teachers will become even more overwhelmingly Anglo than at present.

Such concerns have prompted the state university system and the California State Legislature to promote multicultural education on campuses and through effective teacher preparation for multicultural settings. Monies have been made available through the Chancellor's Office, and several major funding proposals are under consideration by the State Legislature. Hence, in the State of California the time is ripe for multiculturalism.

2. Lack of Personnel

Faculty of "color" or with substantive exposure to non-European cultures are relatively rare in schools of education. While there are some outstanding multicultural/bilingual programs in the system (e.g., San Diego State), such programs are small, isolated, or absent at most campuses. Moreover, bilingual programs tend to be oriented towards the local predominant linguistic groups (e.g., Spanish at one campus, Cantonese at another) and are often neither prepared nor funded to deal with the full range of ethnolinguistic groups in California.

Under these circumstances, educationally oriented anthropologists can fill an existing void in the educational program and augment its staff. Our field experience—whether in the U.S. or abroad—gives us, unlike our colleagues in education, concrete knowledge of languages and cultures and a sensitivity to the kinds of problems non-Anglo children experience in the classroom. Our academic training provides the broad perspective needed to deal with multiplicity of cultural groups. Politically, we are unaligned with any single ethnic group and hence able to mediate between ethnic groups, a clear advantage in the world of ethnic politics.

3. The Teacher Credential Program

California has no undergraduate major in education. Instead, prospective teachers are required first to major in an academic discipline and then to apply for the credential program. Any bachelor's degree is sufficient for entry into the credential program, if the candidate can pass the National Teacher Education exam (NTE). This exam is waived, however, for candidates who have completed a so-called "waiver" program. Since NTE passing rates are extremely low, most prospective teachers elect the waiver program. Waiver programs are developed by each campus to conform to state guidelines and the type of credential being sought. The Liberal Studies major is generally the approved multiple subjects waiver for elementary school teaching. For prospective secondary school teachers there are "single subject waiver programs" that reflect the subjects taught in secondary school. Regrettably, anthropology is not included. Anthropologists and educators agree, however, that basic multicultural concepts and sensitivities should be acquired at the undergraduate level, prior to entering the methods-oriented credential program.

In California teacher education is not solely in the hands of schools of education. Rather, education faculty are primarily involved in the credential program while the undergraduate educational experience tends to be in the hands of noneducation faculty. Thus, a basis for partnerships in multiculturalism already exists along with a formal structure in the form of the campuswide Teacher Education Councils and the waiver programs. Campus administrators and the Chancellor's Office are encouraging greater involvement of noneducation faculty in teacher preparation in part to strengthen the academic background of prospective teachers. The field is thus wide open for anthropologists to become involved in teacher education, thereby affecting the type of competencies that will constitute "multicultural" elements of this program.

4. Personal Ties

Whatever the structural opportunities, the actual impetus for action often depends on personal ties with educators. In my own case, a chance conversation with Hilda Hernandez, a personable colleague in the School of Education, led to the discovery of common interests. We initiated a collaboration which is in its fourth year and has produced a teacher preparation guide, *Integrating Multicultural Perspectives into Teacher Education: A Curriculum Resource Guide* (Chico: California State University, 1985). This is probably the only such guide co-authored by an anthropologist and an educator.

This friendship introduced me to other educators and to the microculture of the School of Education. The partnership also exposed each of us to previously unfamiliar bodies of literature and to areas not within our previous expertise. At times, I have been concerned about overstepping disciplinary boundaries and intruding upon others' presumed areas of expertise. Nonetheless, I have learned to trust my own discipline's ability to provide a set of analytical tools, as well as a substantial body of data on learning processes; and I realize that my particular perspective is useful and appreciated by my colleagues in education.

In summary, anthropologists must not miss this opportunity to apply our knowledge and insights to the area of multicultural teacher preparation. Certainly some of the circumstances described above are present at other institutions, such as the need to train teachers for multicultural settings and the relative lack of multicultural expertise within schools of education. Ironically, by involving ourselves in teacher education we will not only perform a needed public service; we will also increase our own visibility and anthropology's viability as a discipline.

An Anthropologist on the Anchor Desk

JAMES LETT

Lights! Camera! Action! Many anthropologists pride themselves on being star-quality classroom teachers. And the subject matter of anthropology almost guarantees high audience appeal. Yet, with but a few outstanding exceptions—Margaret Mead and Oscar Lewis at the top of the list—anthropologists (especially those who study the living rather than the dead!) have been lousy at getting themselves into the mass media and promoting their value for understanding the here and now. (True, the media often do seem to want to keep their anthropologists in the past and among the "primitives." But it doesn't have to be that way. Witness the way the business world has lately embraced the sexy phrase "corporate culture.") Anthropologists—even applied ones—don't seem to know how to deal with the media. Who better to guide anthropologists into the heart of TV-studio culture than one of their own kind. In this punchy piece, anthropologist-journalist James Lett provides a quick ethnographic sketch of the work culture of television production and gives us the equivalent of the traveler's vest pocket phrase book for media-speak. The need for anthropological perspectives in the media is still with us, and Lett's tips are as timely as ever.   J. A. P.

Since the spring of 1983, when I completed my doctorate in anthropology at the University of Florida, I have been working as a broadcast journalist. I currently anchor and produce forty minutes of local, state, and national news every day of the week at the CBS television affiliate in Ft. Pierce, Florida. To my knowledge, I am the only professionally trained cultural anthropologist in the country who's working full-time as a television journalist. As far as I'm concerned, however, I'm doing what I was trained to do: observe, record, describe, and explain human behavior. I'm just doing it in what is, for anthropologists, a nontraditional medium.

Most of us, as anthropologists, communicate our findings, perspectives, and insights to a very narrow audience—our students, our colleagues, our clients, or our agencies. We have not been trained or encouraged to communi-

James Lett worked as a television newscaster from 1983 to 1986 before returning to academe. He is presently Professor of Anthropology at Indian River Community College (3209 Virginia Avenue, Ft. Pierce, FL 34981-5596; (561) 462-4523; <jlett@ircc.cc.fl.us>).

Originally published in *Practicing Anthropology* 9,1(1987):2,22, this article has been edited and abridged for republication here.

cate with the general public; yet, the general public needs us desperately. Myth, superstition, irrationality, prejudice, and pseudo-science are flourishing in our society today. If we're going to reach the general public, we need to take advantage of the most powerful and pervasive medium of mass communication in the history of the world: namely, of course, television. That's what I'm trying to do, and not just for what I perceive to be the good of the general population, but for the good of the discipline as well—and, for that matter, for the good of the media, who lack the kind of informed, comparative, and holistic perspective we could provide. Anthropology is facing declining enrollments, shrinking job markets, and a public image that borders on the ridiculous. We need the media, and the media needs us.

A decade ago, in a special issue of *Human Organization* (35,2[1976]) E. B. Eiselein and Martin Topper surveyed the field of "media anthropology" and concluded, among other things, that television news provides one of the most accessible and most effective opportunities for anthropologists to make use of the media. I agree wholeheartedly. I want to share an insider's perspective on the world of television journalism and to encourage anthropologists to become newsmakers (not newscasters!). I have some suggestions and information that may prove helpful toward that end.

First, it is important to understand the barriers that keep anthropologists off the news and out of America's living rooms. One obstacle is that anthropologists and journalists know very little about one another. Most journalists, like most members of the general public, have never been exposed to anthropology (beyond a bones-and-stones stereotype), and most anthropologists know relatively little about the world view and working assumptions of journalists. Further, most anthropologists work in either academic or bureaucratic settings, and journalists have a well-founded antipathy towards academicians and bureaucrats—which academicians and bureaucrats reciprocate, on equally good grounds. Journalists are afraid that people not accustomed to speaking before a camera will be dull, dry, colorless, cryptic, and self-conscious; and people who are not accustomed to speaking in front of cameras are afraid that journalists will be shallow and manipulative and will distort, misrepresent, or at least misunderstand what they are trying to say.

As anthropologists trained to recognize and understand the cultural assumptions of other groups of people, we can be aware of all this, and we can teach journalists to recognize the value of the anthropological perspective and to seek our opinions. But we have to approach them. Journalists are not going to make the first move.

Contacting Television Journalists

As an anthropologist, you are likely to appear on television news in one of two roles: as the focus and subject of a news story or as an expert commentator on another news story. If you have a research conclusion or a project result that is worth a scholarly article or a contract report, chances are you have something that is worth a news story. Contact your local television newsroom and tell them about it. Filling the "news hole" is a daily challenge in the newsroom, and your idea is likely to be filed away and saved for that day soon when the challenge seems insurmountable. Anthropologists and journalists share the same subject matter—the adventures and misadventures of the human experience—and getting journalists to recognize the similarity of our endeavors is simply a matter of effective translation.

A role that an anthropologist can play more often in television newscasts is as an expert commentator—and there are very few stories in any television newscast upon which some anthropologist somewhere could not offer an informed perspective. Journalists regularly seek out expert opinions, although, unfortunately, the experts to whom they turn to explain social issues are usually psychologists. Anthropologists should establish contact with their local television newsrooms and establish themselves as authorities who can put confusing or controversial questions in context. As anthropologists, we are generalists, so we have meaningful things to say on a very wide range of social issues—and that talent can serve the journalist's purpose very nicely.

Before you make that call (which you should do as soon as possible—before an issue hits the news that you're qualified to comment on), you should know a little about how a newsroom is organized; it is important that your call get through to the right person. In television, newsroom personnel are identified by a set of terms peculiar to the medium. Asking to speak to the "editor," for example, will not give you the person in overall charge of the news product, as at a newspaper, or even a person who proofreads scripts; instead, you'll find yourself talking to one of several technicians responsible for the electronic assembly of the audio and video in each news story.

So which member of the newsroom should you contact? It depends. In large markets, the television newsroom may have specialized reporters, such as science reporters or health reporters, who would make the best initial contacts, especially if you want to propose and discuss a particular story idea. A reporter is the person who goes out "in the field," conducts the interview, writes the story, and narrates the report for broadcast. (Such a prerecorded report is called a "package." It contains the reporter's narration covered visually by appropriate video shot in the field and interspersed with "soundbites"—brief audio-visual segments of the interviews conducted in the field. A soundbite, or simply "bite," is sometimes referred to as a "talking head.")

Not all television news stories are presented by reporters, of course. The anchor may read the story while the viewer watches video illustrating it (a "voice-over" or "v.o." which may be combined with a bite to be read as a "v.o.-bite"); or a "reader" without accompanying video may be presented by the anchor "on camera."

In most cases when you call the newsroom to offer your services, however, you won't ask for the reporter but for the assignment editor—the person responsible for deciding which reporters and which camera crews will cover which stories on any given day. The assignment editor maintains a file of names and phone numbers. When a reporter is looking for an expert on the gay subculture or illegal immigration or bilingual education, he or she will ask the assignment editor.

You may have contact with other newsroom personnel, particularly once you have established yourself as an articulate and accessible authority. The producer is the person who decides which of the available stories will appear in the newscast, how much time will be given to each story, and where each story will appear in the "line-up" or the "run-down." The "lead" story is always the first story, analogous to the headline story on the front page of a newspaper, and it is the producer who decides which story merits that honor. If you approach the producer with your story idea first, however, you are likely to be referred to the assignment editor.

Finally, the news director is the person responsible for the overall management of the newsroom. Depending on the size of the market, he or she may or may not be intimately involved in the day-to-day decisions about the form and content of the newscast. A cover letter to the news director couldn't hurt: keep it simple, enclose a one-page resume listing your credentials and your principal areas of knowledge and expertise, and indicate your willingness to be interviewed on topics in your field.

Tips on Being Interviewed

Now we come to the most important advice I can offer—things I wish I could have taught the academicians and bureaucrats I've had to interview as a journalist. The advice is simple, although putting it into practice will take a little thought and a little work, much like learning another language. This is it: when being interviewed, speak concisely, confidently, concretely, and colorfully.

Be concise. A commercial television newscast must be fast-paced if it is to survive; the medium dictates that. Every viewer must be persuaded to sit through every story in a television newscast. (Unlike a newspaper, viewers can't skip past the stories that don't interest them.) Television stories must be kept short. If you are being interviewed for a v.o.-bite, you may have as much as fifteen to twenty seconds to make your point; but if your comments will appear in a package, you may have only eight seconds. The reporter will ask you several questions, and chances are only one of your answers will be used. You won't know which one until the report is broadcast. So speak in simple, complete sentences, and answer every question *briefly*. Be precise, but be pithy. Think about the essence of the point you are trying to make, and then distill that essence and present it in its purest form. That's the process the reporter will follow when writing the story; you should use the same method.

Be confident. You are being interviewed as an authority; speak like one. Remember too that you are not speaking to your colleagues who share your specialized knowledge. Instead, you are speaking to members of the general public who know little or nothing about the topic. Therefore, you should not qualify your observations, or explain your methodology (unless you are asked, and that's not likely), or identify your paradigmatic commitment. You are being asked for information: the interviewer wants basic truths and general conclusions, and you should answer on that level. Do not exaggerate or misrepresent the limits of your knowledge, but by the same token, do not retreat from the obvious implications of what you know.

Be concrete. Television is a visual medium, and television journalists are especially uncomfortable with abstractions. This means that you should use specific illustrations whenever possible. Don't talk about ethnological theory; talk about ethnographic facts. Particularize, don't generalize; humanize, don't objectify; and don't leave it to the reporter to draw the conclusion or discern the relevance.

Be colorful. Television reporters and producers are always looking for the "human" element. It is true that journalists often forego intellectual content in favor of emotional impact, but most anthropologists (to be fair, most academicians) generally neglect emotional impact for intellectual content. The two need not be mutually exclusive. It is possible to share your knowledge while being warm, witty, personable, relaxed, unguarded, and uninhibited—and if you do so, you have a much better chance of being aired. (Dr. Neil Frank of the National Hurricane Center in Coral Gables, Florida, has practically achieved national celebrity as an authority on hurricanes, not because of his professional accomplishments—which are solid, but by no report spectacular—but by his enthusiastic on-camera demeanor.) If you can find a colorful turn of phrase, use it; if you can't find one, keep looking.

In conclusion, I am well aware that many anthropologists regard the media as shallow and superficial and unworthy of serious consideration or investment. As well-deserved as those criticisms may be, the media play an enormously influential role in our society—as agents of enculturation and as virtually exclusive sources of information about the world at large for vast numbers of people. They are going to continue to fulfill that role whether anthropologists offer any input or not. I don't think we can afford not to share our perspective.

.

Staying Out of the Bottom Drawer

LINDA M. WHITEFORD

Linda Whiteford addresses a crucial question for applied scientists—how do they make sure their research directly influences what clients do? She offers six criteria of utility—relevance, credibility, attention to process, access, knowledge of constraints, and perspective—which she illustrates by analyzing three studies of child welfare and health care delivery. Ideally, plans for meeting these criteria should be built into applied research projects from the very beginning. This means understanding in advance what can and cannot be done, and it means comprehending the bigger picture and the short- and long-term implications of the research. Applied anthropologists have sometimes been at fault for not addressing these criteria. They may also have to take a more active role in seeing that the criteria are addressed by clients as well. This article demonstrates the utility of retrospective examination of applied research to learn from past mistakes and improve future project planning with clients. A. M. E.

Horror stories abound: findings of carefully designed and executed research projects ignored; good programs lost because decision makers failed to see their relevance; problems not solved because key people lacked access to information; critical data not collected or not presented in usable form. Each of us knows of research reports that, once read, are filed away in "the bottom drawer," never to be read again.

One of the aims of applied research is to provide the user with appropriate information; successful applied research must incorporate into its design potential utilization of the results. Thus, our concept of research design should be broadened to encompass utilization, an element clearly facilitated by constant, collaborative communication between researcher and potential user.

I present six criteria of utility by which applied anthropological research can be evaluated and discussed. Three case studies illustrate the importance of these six criteria and discuss the differential success and failure of each project in light of the criteria.

Linda M. Whiteford is Chair and Professor of Anthropology at the University of South Florida (4202 E. Fowler Avenue, Tampa, FL 33620-9900; (813) 974-0818; <lindaw@chuma1.cas.usf.edu>).

Originally published as part of a special section on "Utilizing Applied Research," guest edited by Daniel R. Scheinfeld, in *Practicing Anthropology* 9,1(1987):9-11, this article has been edited and abridged for republication here.

Criteria of Utility

Each of the six criteria of research utility needs to be incorporated into the design process. None have priority over the others. The six will occur in different sequences, however, depending upon the particular project.

1. Relevance: Does the formulation of research issues relate to the potential user's concerns? The research needs to address the user's needs and focus on issues and goals important to the user. In addition, the researcher must translate the content and style of presentation of research findings into language, concerns, and products with which the user is comfortable and familiar.
2. Credibility: Are the findings credible to the user? The collaborative process includes sharing ideas about appropriate categories of research and the types of data needed. The researcher should adopt units of measurement and standards of validity and reliability that are acceptable to both researcher and user.
3. Process: How are the research findings disseminated? The research design should include a discussion of how the research findings will be used and how the results will be made available.
4. Access: Who is the audience for this research? The researcher needs to know which people are important to reach, what channels are available to reach them, and what types of information they will consider significant.
5. Constraints: Are the recommendations formulated with an understanding of the kinds of changes that are possible? A realistic view of the kinds of changes that can be made within the limitations extant should result in recommendations that are feasible. This in turn increases the likelihood that the findings will be used.
6. Perspective: Do the recommendations address both immediate applications of the research findings and long-term planning? The scientific, anthropological perspective permits researchers to plan for obtaining information needed in long-term policy making while gathering information for immediate application.

Case Study I: Pediatric Emergency Room

A cooperative endeavor of individuals in the pediatric emergency room (ER) of an urban county hospital, the anthropology department, and the pediatrics department of the local medical school, this project was designed to evaluate the relationship between:

1. child's age and patterns of use of emergency room services,
2. child's behavior during illness episode and caretaker's decision to seek health care, and

3. compliance with recommended follow-up visits and child's subsequent health status.

Data were collected from both a retrospective sample of 524 cases from hospital records and a prospective sample of 57 current cases in which the caretakers were interviewed.

Analysis showed that:

1. younger children were brought into the pediatric ER more often than were older children;
2. children were brought into the ER when the caretaker felt that the child's condition had deteriorated and the child was not responding to the caretaker's remedies; and
3. bringing the child to the prescribed follow-up clinic visit apparently made little or no difference in the child's health.

While not startling, these findings provided the first documentation of these issues for the participating hospital.

Research results were shared by the three cooperating departments. The medical school faculty person used the materials for Grand Rounds; the anthropologist presented a paper at a conference on international health and published an article on the research. As far as I know, the Director of Emergency Room Services, who originally asked to have the research conducted, has not used the findings at all.

In terms of the six criteria for research utilization outlined earlier, what went wrong with this project?

1. Relevance: Members of the research team worked together on the project without a strongly defined issue and without a clearly defined "client" for the research results. Although this was never acknowledged, all the team members shared was a research population. The pediatrician was interested in whether compliance with routinely prescribed follow-up examinations was correlated with child's health status. The anthropologist was interested in how caretakers decided to bring a child to the ER. The Director of ER Services wanted to know how to make his department more effective. The two members of the research team from pediatrics and anthropology were most involved in the design and actual research, and research findings were of interest to them. But the findings were of little relevance, and therefore of little use, to the Director of ER Services. The research topics did not address his concerns, nor were findings presented in a style relevant to his normal ways of accepting new information.

2. Credibility: Among the members of the research team, there was no shared sense of units of measurement or standards of reliability and validity. Thus, credibility was never established. This was in part a result of the researchers' differing interests, the lack of clearly defined responsibilities among researchers, and the lack of a clearly articulated common agenda of research priorities.

3. Process: There was no plan to disseminate the results of the project. Each of the participants used the data for his or her own ends. Clearly, for this project to have succeeded as useful applied research, the research design should have included a process for sharing the information.

4. Access: The questions of access—who were the important people to reach and what channels were available for reaching them—were never asked. While copies of the final data analysis were given to the chairs of the cooperating departments, the information was not translated into materials that ER staff could use, nor were executive summaries provided for hospital administrators.

5. Constraints: Realistic evaluation of what could and could not be changed was never made. As a result, some of the recommendations were impossible to implement. For example, the recommendations which entailed changing hospital record keeping and procedures fell outside of the administrator's purview, so they were ignored.

6. Perspective: In the Pediatric Emergency Room study, problems of case flow, management, and follow-up should have been put in the larger framework of population projections, consequences of regional and international migration, subsidiary qualified care givers, and anticipated problems of a provider overly dependent on Medicaid reimbursement.

In summary, this case shows the effects of insufficient attention to defining goals, providing for communication among researchers, and planning how research findings might be used. This case further illustrates how the two academic members of the research triad failed to understand the practical research needed in order for the results to be useful for the client.

Case Study II: Child Watch

The Child Watch project was designed to measure the effect of reductions in the federal budget on the delivery of social services to poor children. It was sponsored by the Children's Defense Fund (CDF), a public, nonprofit, research and lobbying group with thirteen years experience as a national advocate for children's rights. I was asked to direct the local county-wide project, one of twenty such studies conducted across the nation. It was an eighteen-month voluntary project (1981-83) without paid staff.

To document the effect of federal budget cuts on child welfare in the local community, we conducted a series of interviews (250) at three-month intervals. Four topics were researched: child health, child welfare, day care, and Aid to Families with Dependent Children (AFDC). For each topical area, we interviewed individuals at four levels of the delivery system: administrators, advocates, providers, and users of social services. We also collected volumes of data in the form of reports showing changes in programs and services, budgetary restrictions, waiting lists, and statistics on infant mortality and morbidity and child abuse.

In addition to the content goals of the research, two implementation goals were added locally: to inform the local public of the situation, and to create a grassroots infrastructure either to continue the research or to serve as an ongoing monitoring group.

Applying the six criteria of utility highlights some of the successes and failures of the project.

1. Relevance: Because CDF designed the project and developed the questionnaire, there was strong continuity between the formulation of research questions and the user's concerns. CDF anticipated the structuring of information by predetermining the categories of analysis we were to use.

Relevance was more difficult to establish on the local level. Because we were not sure who the audience should be (discussed more fully as "access"), it was difficult to find the topics and categories they would value. The style of presenting information took the form of a public information campaign, augmented by CDF. News releases provided a style of data presentation familiar to community leaders.

2. Credibility: While the findings were built on units of measurement with which the user (CDF) was comfortable, lack of reliability of the data disturbed me, the researcher. CDF wanted case studies, anecdotal materials, and documentation of program changes, but a consistent format for analyzing these data was lacking. A second problem was that the overwhelming amount of "soft" data needed painstaking and time-consuming analysis. The overall project maintained credibility because of the strengths of supporting organizations such as CDF; but had other kinds of measurement been used (such as cost-benefit analysis), the project would have had greater impact on local administrators.

3. Process: Raw data and summary reports were sent to CDF in Washington, D.C., every three to four months, and a major analysis occurred before President Reagan sent his budget to Congress. Locally, information was disseminated through the local media and presentations to community groups. On a statewide and regional basis, information was shared through communication channels established by CDF and through a statewide conference. In addition, the director of the local project presented findings to state legislators, to physicians' associations, at regional conferences with administrators of Health and Rehabilitation Services, and at conferences in Washington, D.C. Nationally, information was made available to the news media through CDF offices. The process for disseminating the research results was established in the research design and was used effectively at both local and national levels.

4. Access: The audience for this research was clearly identified during the initial planning. CDF provided access to members of Congress and their aides, advocacy and lobbying groups, and the news media. Locally, the intended audience for the research included the public at large, local politicians and state legislators, and providers of services to children. To reach the general public we relied on print and television media. Access to politicians and legislators was developed through personal contacts, letter writing, and the creation of policy papers for their use. To reach providers of services to children, we created a grassroots coalition of organizations.

5. *Constraints*: Recommendations based on the research were carefully framed in terms of what might be possible to accomplish, given a realistic appraisal of the political situation, the federal budget, laws affecting the disbursement of funds, and affected programs. Locally, recommendations focused on issues of child health care and lack of access to care for children of the indigent. During the research we became aware that no private practice pediatrician would see a Medicaid child in his or her office. That information helped us focus on the need for better reimbursement policies, more accessible care, and maintenance of block grant funded programs. At both national and local levels, many of the recommendations were accepted and some even developed into programs.

6. *Perspective*: Child Watch combined a variety of perspectives from lawyers, lobbyists, and social scientists in Washington and from people at the local level. As a result, research findings were applied to develop a grassroots base for advocacy for children's rights, to create public awareness of lack of provisions on the local level, and to provide support in the form of documentation for any concerned group seeking to rectify the situation. Furthermore, because this project was generated from a national office and was one of a number of such projects, its application extended beyond the local setting. Several projects in Florida combined their results to present state and local elected representatives with information, recommendations for practical applications, and suggestions for policy making.

In sum, the Child Watch project is an example of research put to use. One reason for its success was the cooperative relationship developed between the sponsor-user (CDF) and the researchers. Discussion of research aims and ways to use the information, and support in the form of media awareness ("how to deal with the press"), were part of a process of constant interaction between researcher and user groups. Credibility could have been enhanced locally through scientific sample selection and greater use of statistics and quantitative analysis. But the research design cannot be faulted for lack of plans for utilization. The audience was recognized in advance. Channels of access to the audience were identified, and data were gathered for those purposes.

While the most visible effect of the research has been changes in budgetary restrictions from Washington, local aims also were met. As a direct result of the project, two pediatricians and several nurses set up free clinics to treat children of migrant farm laborers, children who otherwise were without medical care. A number of private practice physicians became willing to see Medicaid children in their offices. Findings from the Child Watch project were publicized and made available at a time when there was a local initiative to create both a children's hospital and a free-standing children's clinic (especially designed to care for children of the indigent). The children's hospital opened in 1998.

Case Study III: Reproductive Health Care Clinic

A needs assessment conducted under the auspices of Planned Parenthood demonstrated that the need for low-cost reproductive health care was not being met locally, in Tampa, Florida. I was approached to become a member of the organizing board of directors for a local chapter of Planned Parenthood. Simultaneously, I began teaching a course designed to familiarize graduate students in applied medical anthropology with the theory and techniques of evaluation research. As a result, I initiated a cooperative endeavor between anthropology students and the Planned Parenthood Board.

Planned Parenthood's target population was women between the ages of 19 and 34 whose households had an annual income close to the 1980 median for Tampa. These women were ineligible for low-cost reproductive health care and also unable to afford private gynecological care. As researchers we were asked to find a suitable location for a clinic, close to the target population but also in a setting that would draw paying clients. Students also conducted a formative evaluation of clinic operation and a summative evaluation of several Planned Parenthood programs in nearby locales.

In evaluating the research project in terms of the six criteria of utility, special focus was paid to the proposed location of the clinic.

1. Relevance: Issues that were important to the user were the focus of the research—where to locate the clinic. For boardroom presentations, content and style were formulated in terms familiar to the user, while issues of theoretical interest to the researchers but not to the user were confined to classroom discussion.

2. Credibility: Guidelines from the National Federation of Planned Parenthood, adopted by the local Board of Directors, were similar to the criteria of reliability and validity used by the researchers. Constant interaction and communication between the local Planned Parenthood director and the research project director apprised each party of the other's thinking and helped maintain shared categories of what constituted appropriate and useful research.

3. Process: Every few weeks, the researchers met with the user, usually to present a prepared document. We prepared flip-charts, multicolored transparencies, and other graphic demonstrations of the ideas to "sell" our knowledge. Reports were mailed to Board members not present at that meeting. Because the local clinic would be an affiliate of another Planned Parenthood chapter,

116

both the regional office in Atlanta, Georgia, and the "parent" clinic were sent copies of the reports.

4. Access: The audience for this research was the Board of Directors of the local Planned Parenthood; however, the process of establishing a clinic was also tied closely to the regional and national offices of Planned Parenthood and to another affiliate local chapter. Access to these various offices was accomplished through direct mail, in-person presentations, and written documents.

5. Constraints: The clinic needed to be located within city limits, and it was designed to be self-supporting (not dependent on government funds) and yet available to low-income women. A number of sites were recommended to the Board, each consistent with the parameters laid out by the Board. The Board selected one of the sites, and the clinic was built.

6. Perspective: The anthropological perspective provided knowledge of the community, ranging from interviews with potential users to "cognitive maps" of neighborhoods. It was even more useful in the summative evaluation which resulted in simplified protocols and information presentation to reflect user terminology. Knowledge of how different ethnic groups perceive care givers informed suggestions for clinic procedures, and culturally sensitive sociomedical indicators were developed and employed in designing mechanisms for program evaluation.

In short, the various skills of the researchers and careful attention to the six criteria of research utility resulted in a research design which focused on user needs and applications of the research; research results were translated into recommendations for immediate use and for long-term planning.

Conclusion

The three case studies differ in many ways, including the kinds of applications the research engendered. The hospital study brought to light valuable information about patient decision making and noninstitutional health care practices, but it did not change hospital procedures. Child Watch prompted individuals to provide intermittent health care for children of migrant farm workers and provided documentation of need for health care delivery to poor children. As a result of the study, local health care providers and advocates were able to develop plans for a children's hospital and a free-standing clinic for the children of indigents. In the case of the reproductive health care center, utilization of research information was immediate; the clinic is presently in operation, serving the population it was designed to reach.

Insight provided by applying the six criteria of utility to these case studies can contribute to improved future research. The hospital study shows the results of the lack of clearly defined goals, focus, and responsibilities, evidenced by the hospital administrator's not using the research. Child Watch had far greater impact because the research was relevant to the users and because awareness of access and process were built into the design. Child Watch could have had greater long-term effects on the local community had the researchers been more aware of the criteria of constraints and perspective, and had the original design incorporated more controls on credibility. Research for the reproductive health care facility was most successful because a design incorporating the utility criteria and interactive communication between researcher and user were established early in the research process.

Anthropologists must acknowledge the difficulty and importance of learning to render research results useful. We do so in part by conceptualizing the process, in part by providing lexical domains for discussion, and in part by evaluating our own work within a utility framework. It would be no mean achievement if fewer research reports ended up forgotten, in the bottom drawer.

Working with Japanese: U.S.-Japanese Joint Venture Contract

TOMOKO HAMADA

Despite early interest among applied anthropologists in the transfer of methods used in the study of tribal communities to studies of the workplace and the corporate boardroom, industrial and business anthropology languished in the post World War II era, only to be reborn in the 1980s. The realm of business, domestic and international, has attracted increasing interest among anthropologists in the past decade, and the corporate world is an expanding venue for practicing anthropologists. Experts in business and management have also become more conscious of culture, as it pertains to the microculture of the company and the macroculture of nation-states. They have also become more sensitive to the possibility of cultural differences, especially in an international context. Nevertheless, the likelihood of cross-cultural misunderstanding when two companies from two nation-states attempt to work together has hardly diminished since the mid-1980s when Tomoko Hamada analyzed the U.S.-Japanese joint venture described here. She uses disagreements in the interpretation and implementation of clauses in a carefully stipulated joint contract to probe distinctive features in the two parties' underlying philosophies of business and social organization. Anthropological insight applied early in the process could prevent future complications in joint ventures of any type, but especially those in international business. P. J. H.

Foreign direct investment in Japan has tripled over the last decade to reach five billion dollars (based upon investment approvals), of which 46.6 percent has been American. Tokyo's continuing liberalization of the goods and services market is beginning to affect the level of foreign direct investment in Japan. My research focuses upon problems related to cross-cultural decision making experienced by American corporations in Japan. This article high-

Tomoko Hamada is Margaret Hamilton Professor of Anthropology at College of William and Mary (P.O. Box 8795, College of William and Mary, Williamsburg, VA 23187-8795; (757) 221-1060; fax: (757) 221-1066; <thamad@wm.edu>).

Originally published as part of a special section on "Anthropology and International Business," guest edited by Elizabeth K. Briody and Marietta L. Baba, in *Practicing Anthropology* 10,1(1988):4-5.

120

lights cultural differences between American and Japanese business organizations, using the case of a U.S.-Japanese joint venture contract. Any foreign firm wishing to establish an operation in Japan has to begin by making a contract. I shall illustrate that anthropological insight is essential at this initial stage in order to avoid future complications.

In the past, scholars compared and contrasted U.S. and Japanese business organizations in their respective environments. (See, for example, Rodney Clark, *The Japanese Company* [New Haven: Yale University Press,1979]; Ronald Dore, *British Factory, Japanese Factory* [Berkeley: University of California Press, 1973]; Thomas Rohlen, *For Harmony and Strength* [Berkeley: University of California Press, 1974].) Instead of listing similarities and differences between the two systems, however, I shall discuss what happens to one system when it meets the other in a 50-50 joint company.

United America and Nippon Kaisha

In the early 1970s, an American multinational corporation, which I call United America, signed a basic joint venture agreement with a large Japanese company, Nippon Kaisha, in Tokyo.

When Nippon Kaisha was preparing the draft of the technical agreement and the joint venture agreement, the chief of the legal document section had constant contact with all the managers within Nippon Kaisha who would be even slightly involved in the new joint venture operation—other plant managers, chief engineers, personnel managers, R&D managers, and international division personnel, as well as the senior directors and president. The absence of an inside lawyer in Nippon Kaisha is typical of a Japanese company. On the other hand, the major American persons involved in writing the draft were the general manager of the Japan office, the area president, and a lawyer from the Legal Department of the International Division. They also hired a Japanese lawyer in Japan to check on their decisions.

It took many months to reach an agreement, partly because of the slow consensus-seeking Japanese decision-making process, and partly because of each party's attention to detail. The Japanese staff of the corporate legal department were very familiar with the everyday operations of Nippon Kaisha, while the lawyer from New York and the Japanese consulting lawyer had little access to practical field operations in Japan. United America's general manager had been in Japan for only one year and had no previous training or experience concerning Japanese business practices. (Such mobility of American professionals in Japan is typical.)

With sections on Definitions, Organization of the *New Company*, Capital, Transfer or Sale of Shares, Directors and Management, Management of the *New Company*, Production and Sale, Technical Assistance, Notices, Effect of Invalidity, Government Approval, Integration, Arbitration, and Interpretation, the joint venture basic agreement appeared to be comprehensive. Nevertheless, some clauses permitted different interpretations by the two parties. For example, the section on management read: "*New Company* shall use its utmost effort to maintain good financial condition and achieve, as promptly as practicable, independent management."

Because of the lack of an independent distribution network for the company, the Sales Division and the Marketing Division of Nippon Kaisha were to provide services to the new joint venture company in terms of the delivery of the product, sales, and distribution. The American side nevertheless insisted on the future independence of the joint venture company from Nippon Kaisha. But what the term "as promptly as practicable" meant was that the Japanese side could maintain its control over the new joint venture as long as it was "practicable." An American manager stated: "Because of the vagueness of the terms of the contract, we could not act to pursue the perceived best interest of the joint venture company which may have been in conflict with Nippon Kaisha's objectives."

If the lawyer had understood the cultural meaning of the term "subsidiary," this mistake might have been avoided. It is important to appreciate that in Japan a subsidiary may be considered by the parent corporation as a manipulable "child" unit within the industrial group.

The Concept of Industrial Grouping

In Japan, the main feature of the overall business hierarchy is the stratification of firms according to size. The top 100 Japanese companies in terms of capital control another 3,000 firms because of the *keiretsu* (literally "alignment") system of industrial "groupism." The capital of these parents, subsidiaries, and affiliated firms altogether account for nearly 40 percent of the nation's total industrial capital. The industrial group, embracing no competitors, nurtures one major firm in each kind of industry. *Keiretsu* is a whole cross-industrial network of major firms and their affiliates and subordinates, fostering business interactions within a group complex. Foreign firms are normally concerned with large firms affiliated with major industrial groups who are either their joint venture partners, clients, or competitors. It is therefore vital for an American investor to understand the dynamism of the Japanese industrial group. The management of the parent company in *keiretsu* may exercise differential decision-making authority in order to produce desired results in various parts of its empire. Unfortunately, this is difficult to see from the outside, due to the highly subtle nature of control and decision making in Japan. However, it is important to appreciate that a Japanese partner of a joint venture may regard its joint venture with foreigners as but one more manipulable or even expendable subsidiary, while Americans are likely to stress the joint venture's autonomy as an independent company.

HAMADA

Managerial Style

According to the United America management, there are other clauses which could have been more precise, if they had known the actions likely to be taken by the Japanese; for example:

> Both United America and Nippon Kaisha shall give reasonable assistance to *New Company* in connection with management administration, personnel affairs, services, etc.

"Reasonable" assistance can be judged subjectively. In some cases, "reasonable" actions by Nippon Kaisha were interpreted by United America Inc. as intervention in the managerial power of the new joint venture.

Another American manager said:

> Because of the lack of a time limit, we could not start or stop the actions taken by the Japanese. Although we have 50 percent ownership, the Japanese side seems to have more control over the new company.

A Japanese manager recalled the situation:

> The new company is organized and exists under the laws of Japan having its office in Japan. Although it is jointly owned by both companies, we believe that the new company should be administered mainly by Nippon Kaisha, because we have more experience in operating a Japanese company. It was difficult to persuade United America's management on this issue. They insisted on 50-50 managerial participation.

Selection of Appropriate Managers

Regarding personnel management, United America gave the authority to assign employees for the new companies to Nippon Kaisha. Since there was no time limit in the contract regarding the term of this responsibility, United America was often frustrated by getting seemingly unqualified personnel.

The contract continues:

> Nippon Kaisha shall provide such possible assistance and guidance as from time to time may be necessary. Until independent management is achieved, Nippon Kaisha shall assign employees to perform the day to day management functions in accordance with the directives and resolutions of the board of directors of the *New Company*.

This clause gives Nippon Kaisha the authority to appoint operators and employees. United America cannot assign employees until "independent management is achieved." United America must rely on hard bargaining and negotiating when the personnel appointed by Nippon Kaisha are not acceptable.

Financial Reporting

Regarding the financial reports, the contract reads:

> *New Company* shall keep all books of accounts and make all financial reports in accordance with the standards prescribed by Japanese laws and regulations and generally accepted accounting principles in Japan...
> *New Company* shall prepare and forward to United America and Nippon Kaisha a balance and profit and loss statements made pursuant to books of account so kept as provided in the above section.

The new company naturally followed the practices of Nippon Kaisha and its industrial group to maintain a uniform financial system among them. For example, the new company followed the accelerated depreciation rate which had been used by the Japanese parent company. At the initial stage of the joint venture operation when they had losses rather than profits, it seemed reasonable (according to the American side) to use the straight line depreciation rate, which is an accepted accounting principle in Japan. The new company, which considered uniformity with the Nippon industrial group more important, refused to do so.

Another problem with financial reporting was that the contract indicated only the requirements of the balance sheet and profit and loss statements. They alone could not provide exact operating data on the new company which would measure strategies or assess progress or efficiency. United America had to struggle to get necessary operating data from the new company, Nippon Kaisha's Sales Division, Marketing Division, etc.

Performance Evaluation

Japanese management puts strong emphasis on group accountability for performance, and on close interpersonal communication rather than written communication among organization members. Unlike the American corporation where job descriptions and formal chains of command and reporting are emphasized for specialization and assignment of individual responsibility, Japanese corporate culture stresses flexible organizational structure based upon human dynamics. Because of the long-range goal orientation and emphasis upon group efforts for goal attainment, Japanese managers, unlike Americans, are not evaluated by short-term performance indicated in monthly or quarterly figures. It is thus difficult for Japanese to appreciate the "bombardment of requests for figures" by the American partner.

124

Concerning the board of directors, the contract reads:

New Company shall have the representative director nominated by Nippon Kaisha, who shall be president. One of the directors nominated by United America shall be the vice president of *New Company*.

The new company was to have six directors at the time of its incorporation, although the number was later amended to eight. The voting power was equally distributed between the two parties. When there were six directors (three from Nippon Kaisha and three from United America), each resolution or action presented to the board of directors for approval required the affirmative vote of a least four directors, including at least two directors nominated by Nippon Kaisha and United America. The concept of majority voting was retained after the number of directors increased.

Power of President
An American executive recalls:

One of the problems was that we did not limit the power of the board of directors against the shareholders. Since we could not use proxy voting at a board of directors' meeting, and we could at a shareholders' meeting under Japanese law, we could have made major decisions at a shareholders' meeting without bringing in all the American directors. Another problem in this contract was that we did not state clearly which issues had to be discussed either at a board of directors' meeting or at a shareholders' meeting. Since the Japanese directors were also the operating managers of the new company, it was implied that many decisions were day-to-day operational decisions without the requirement of a board of directors' meeting.

A brief discussion on the power of a Japanese corporation president will illustrate the relationship between the shareholders' meeting and the operating committee meeting. Theoretically, American management is responsible ultimately to the stockholders and has to strive for profit maximization to produce dividends. In Japan, on the other hand, management and control are fused into one, and they may forego short-term gains in order to achieve important long-range goals. The Japanese board of directors itself is composed of the same corporate hierarchy from president to ordinary directors. Many Japanese companies' shareholders are banks which are interested not so much in dividend payments as in ongoing business with the firms. If need be, the main lending bank may send an executive director into top management to strengthen financial matters, but they do not use the general stockholders' meeting for this purpose.

The real decision-making power of the Japanese president and his operating committee appears indeed to be unlimited. Because the power of the president is so large, and because the influence of ownership is so small, the factor which influences top management most is the desire to maximize the benefit for the total company community. Presidents and the operating committee, representing the company as a whole and needing most of all their consensus and cooperation, will work for long-term goals shared by the majority within the Japanese company. These goals may not be shared by the American partner.

Fundamental differences between the joint venture partners' goals, objectives, and relations with the larger environment may present barriers to successful joint venture negotiation and operation.

Comparison of Business Philosophy

The expectation and interpretation of legal documents, such as the contract, differ between Americans and Japanese as illustrated in this case study. Unlike the vast majority of international business subsidiaries which are wholly owned and controlled by a single corporation, an international joint venture is created by two or more legally independent enterprises, thus containing in its nature a probability of disputes between the partners.

A quick comparison of the following issues may illustrate in a general way how far apart the prospective partners could be in their thinking.

- *The relationship between the parent company and the joint venture.* The Japanese consider the joint venture as a part of the *keiretsu* group and may treat it accordingly, while Americans insist on its independence. The American company as a stockholder of the joint venture justifies the right to carefully monitor the policy making of the joint venture company. The Japanese use more informal or personal channels and prefer an indirect but sometimes more powerful influence on their decision-making policy.

- *The responsibility of the manager.* The Japanese emphasize teamwork and group responsibility, while Americans put emphasis on individual responsibility. The job title of an American manager more or less corresponds to his actual decision-making authority and managerial responsibility. In Japan a title alone does not determine the person's real decision-making power, because the social ranking system is different. For example, the Japanese director of a subsidiary has social prestige and bargaining power roughly equal to that of a manager in the parent company within the industrial group. Unless one is aware of the formal and informal personnel structures of the company and its industrial group, one cannot fully understand the real authority and responsibility of the individual.

- *The managerial role.* American managers are supposed to be independent, pragmatic, goal-oriented, and professionally competent. Japanese managers should be sociable, hard-working, humane, and loyal to the company. These perceptions affect the evaluation of individual competence in the organization. What is more, Americans believe in the right to dismiss incompetent personnel, while the Japanese tend not to dismiss employees.

- *Interpersonal relationships.* Japanese businessmen put greater emphasis on interpersonal relationships. The Japanese emphasize a trustful relationship between negotiating parties and try to avoid formal and legal methods of dispute settlement.
- *The social responsibility of the company.* The most important responsibility of the Japanese top executive is to enhance the prosperity of the company community, i.e. employees, not shareholders.
- *Profit motivation.* American businesses put greater emphasis on immediate profitability, while Japanese tend to hold a longer-term perspective and consider other social and political factors.
- *Reasons for joint ventures.* Americans consider a joint venture as a means for further expansion in the Japanese market, while the Japanese often want only the technology or management know-how of the Americans.
- *The government-business relationship.* Because of economic motivations and historic reasons, the Japanese government and business circles cooperate with each other in a larger area of economic activities. Linguistic and cultural homogeneity make it easier for the Japanese to set national targets and work together toward mutually agreed-on national goals. In the United States, there has been less mutually positive dialogue between policy makers and business people.

Unfortunately, these differences in attitudes and motivations are rarely explored in depth before the two parties sign the contract. What usually happens is that the American partner of a joint venture is confused, shocked, and dismayed when he finally discovers how far apart his basic views and objectives are from those of his Japanese partner. There needs to be a new perspective, in addition to the conventional judicial rationale, which delineates the relationship between cultural values and corporate legal behavior.

With an increasing number of Japanese direct investments in this country, American business people interested in business transactions with the Japanese should study their behavioral patterns and managerial philosophy in depth, since they are considerably different from American business practice.

Risk Perception Shadows: The Superconducting Super Collider in Michigan

Richard W. Stoffle, Michael W. Traugott, Camilla L. Harshbarger, Florence V. Jensen, Michael J. Evans, and Paula Drury

Social impact assessment forecasts future conditions, comparing likely changes from a proposed public policy or development project to changes that might occur without the project. In the 1980s, social impact assessment relied increasingly on anthropology to study "impacts that count," rather than simply those that can be counted easily. This article shows how survey techniques and ethnographic methods can be used in combination to reveal specific circumstances that explain differences in risk perception. Results showed that popular perceptions of environmental hazard may be at odds with the hazards as calculated by risk specialists. The counter-intuitive finding, contrary to the assumptions of many decision makers, that past experience increases rather than decreases risk perception, illustrates the importance of not overgeneralizing from research on one kind of environmental hazard, e.g., hurricanes, to another. Michigan lost out to Texas as host for the enormously complicated Superconducting Super Collider project; construction of this huge research facility was abandoned in 1992. E. B. L.

Richard W. Stoffle is Associate Research Anthropologist at the Bureau of Applied Research in Anthropology (University of Arizona, Tucson, AZ 85721-0001; (520) 621-6282; <rstoffle@u.arizona.edu>).
Michael W. Traugott is at the Institute for Social Research at the University of Michigan.
Camilla L. Harshbarger is with CARE in Atlanta.
Florence V. Jensen is retired and lives in Racine, Wisconsin.
Michael J. Evans is Senior Cultural Anthropologist with the Midwest Region of the National Park Service (175 E. 5th Street, Suite 418, Box 41, Saint Paul, MN 55101; <Michael_J_Evans@nps.gov>).
Paula Drury is a communication specialist.
All the authors worked at the Institute for Social Research, University of Michigan, during the study reported here.

Originally published as part of a special section on "Anthropology in Environmental Risk Studies," guest edited by Amy K. Wolfe, in *Practicing Anthropology* 10,3-4(1988):6-7, this article has been edited and abridged for republication here.

128

The effects of radiation on humans are not clearly understood or agreed upon by scientists. Thus in any situation involving potential risk from radiation, the scientific assessment of facts—"probabilistic risk assessment"—is almost always disputed among experts. The public's assessment of risk—"risk perception"—is made even more complex by the many types of radiation and the fact that radiation is closely associated with controversial issues such as the potential of nuclear war and waste disposal problems. Given this milieu, the public has few firm standards against which to test their own perceptions of what radiation will or will not do to them and what can or cannot be done to protect them from radioactivity. This article is about differences in how people from two areas of southern Michigan perceived the risks from radioactivity that would have been produced by siting the Superconducting Super Collider in their communities.

In 1987, the State of Michigan entered a national competition to host the Superconducting Super Collider (SSC). Using superconducting magnets, the SSC would accelerate two beams of proton particles to nearly the speed of light, rotating them in opposite directions around a fifty-three mile long underground tunnel. The two beams would be made to collide at certain points around the tunnel where scientists would study the resultant spray of particle components and investigate the basic subatomic components of matter. Among technological projects currently planned in the United States, the SSC is spatially one of the largest, financially one of the most expensive, technically one of the most difficult to understand, and perhaps the one that holds the greatest scientific promise. When compared with other federal projects, such as nuclear waste repositories, the SSC project seems benign and even beneficial for the host community.

As part of its effort to site the SSC in Michigan, the state funded researchers at the Institute for Social Research at the University of Michigan to study the potential social impacts and community responses to the SSC. The social assessment research strategy involved ethnographic interviews and public opinion telephone surveys. The core study team was composed of four anthropologists, a political scientist, and a communication specialist.

Two rural, farming areas in southern Michigan were selected by the State of Michigan as potential sites: one located about thirty-five miles southwest of Detroit near the village of Dundee, and the other located about sixty miles west of Detroit near the village of Stockbridge. The two areas are comparable in terms of standard demographic variables. The "study area" included all the people who lived in the two counties surrounding the agricultural villages.

Social assessment studies began in 1986 in the Dundee study area. Stoffle, Traugott, Jensen, and Copeland published the findings as *Social Assessment of High Technology: The Superconducting Super Collider in Southeast Michi-*

gan in 1987 (Ann Arbor: Institute for Social Research, University of Michigan). Findings from the Stockbridge study were published by the six authors of this article as *The Superconducting Super Collider at the Stockbridge, Michigan, Site: Community Support and Land Acquisition* in 1988 (Ann Arbor: Institute for Social Research, University of Michigan).

Telephone Surveys

Telephone surveys were conducted with random samples of local people residing in the two study areas in order to ascertain their perceptions of the SSC project's impacts and their support for siting the project in their area. The methodology involved a panel study so that initial interviews would form a public opinion baseline against which change could be measured through recontacting the original respondents.

The Dundee study area panel consisted of 602 people and the Stockbridge panel consisted of 605 people. Overall, the SSC project received the support of the majority of local people in both areas. However, when asked, "What do you perceive to be the disadvantages of the SSC," 47 percent (n=282) of each sample suggested a total of twelve key issues. (See Table 1.) Dundee and Stockbridge respondents agreed that the SSC presents potential problems with the environment, safety, changes in rural life, population, economics, and the quality of life. Differences between the two samples' perceptions of the potential dangers from SSC-related construction, radioactivity, and damage to farmland were statistically significant ($p < .05$).

Radiation was mentioned as a health threat by almost twice the percentage of people in the Dundee study area (12 percent) as those in the Stockbridge study area (7 percent). Both supporters and opponents of the project perceived radioactivity to be a health-related problem, but opponents were more likely to mention the issue.

The behavioral significance of this difference in risk perception is demonstrated by the fact that radioactivity served as a rallying point for SSC opponents in the Dundee area. In the Stockbridge area, the issue was raised, failed to rally support, and within a few months was replaced by other issues such as land acquisition.

What can explain the measurable differences in radiation risk perception between the two populations when (1) respondents came from two random samples, (2) respondents were from demographically similar study areas, (3) both study areas were located in southern Michigan, (4) interviews occurred during the same time, (5) persons responded to the same SSC project proposal, and (6) an identical survey instrument was used? Because this question emerged after the telephone survey had been conducted, data for the explanation had to derive from subsequent ethnographic interviews.

Table 1. Perceived Disadvantages of the SSC—1987 Responses

Dundee (N = 282)		Issue	Stockbridge (N = 282)	
Rank by Frequency	Percent of Respondents		Rank by Frequency	Percent of Respondents
1	43%	Environment	1	51%
2	40%	Construction*	2	31%
3	24%	Safety	3	24%
4	14%	Change in Rural Life	7	7%
5	12%	Radiation*	10	7%
6	12%	Population	6	12%
7	12%	Economic	5	13%
8	9%	Damage to Farmland*	11	2%
9	9%	Quality of Life	4	13%
10	4%	Fear of Unknown	8	7%
11	4%	Services	10	8%
12	1%	Loss of Private Control	12	<1%

*These differences between the Dundee and Stockbridge sample are statistically significant at the 95% confidence interval.

Ethnographic Interviews

Ethnographic interviews were conducted by anthropologists in the two study areas in 1986 and 1987. Key cultural experts, usually local people in an elected office, were asked to define the types of people most likely to be affected by the program and to select a few knowledgeable persons in each category to serve as respondents. The methodology was guided by recent findings by L. Freeman, A. Romney, and S. Freeman ("Cognitive Structure and Informant Accuracy," *American Anthropologist* 89,2[1987]:310-325). Participant observation, focus groups, and documents provided additional data that were used to triangulate the interview findings.

Essential to the social assessment was the sequential use of survey and ethnographic research methods. Ethnographic interviews were conducted first to help define issues to be measured by the telephone survey. The telephone survey raised new issues, some of which could be further researched by subsequent ethnographic interviews. The telephone survey permitted the estimation of the frequency distributions of perceived SSC project impacts, while the ethnographic interviews provided an in-depth understanding of the impacts and relationships between them. Research findings influenced public policy decisions in part because of the strength of the research design that used both qualitative and quantitative methods.

In the Dundee study area, forty-nine ethnographic interviews were conducted with the three types of persons whom the key cultural experts perceived to be most affected by the project: farmers, townspeople, and professionals. In the Stockbridge study area, fifty-five ethnographic interviews were conducted with the four types of specially affected people: large-scale farmers, small-scale farmers, rural residents, and small-business owners. These interviews documented a pattern of concern for radioactive risks that closely parallels that documented by the telephone survey.

The Public's Rules of Evidence

Most physicists who are knowledgeable about the SSC proposal agree that there are some very remote but quantifiable risks from radioactivity associated with the facility. However, they believe that in the unlikely event of an accident during operation of the facility, radiation risks would be mitigated by the underground design of the tunnel. In addition, they believe that low-level radioactive wastes generated by the SSC are similar in volume and degree of danger to those of a large university hospital and therefore are manageable through normal procedures.

Two other scientific statements—an article published in a popular science magazine and an official report from the Texas low-level waste management office—document higher assessments of risk than other scientists had calculated. The conflicting reports were widely circulated by opponents of the SSC. Evidence of disagreements among scientific experts was sufficient to weaken the role of such data as a factor in the public's assessment of radioactive risks. The ethnographic interviews suggest that two other factors—experience with previous radioactive projects, and trust in the agencies associated with the project—are more significant than scientific studies in the public's formulation of risk perceptions.

Two Michigan Communities and SSC Radiation

The Dundee study area was once a large swamp that has been converted into high-yield farmland through a complex drainage system. People in the area face a variety of social and cultural changes due to the expansion of nearby Detroit and Toledo. The study area has a variety of urban encroachments such as numerous gas pipelines and high voltage electrical power lines, as well as planned projects like those seeking to bring hazardous and domestic wastes to the area. While recognizing the impact of these other projects on their lives, most people attributed their concerns about radiation to their proximity to the Fermi II nuclear powered electrical generating facility. They noted that the facility has a history of being technologically flawed, and its management has a reputation for either deliberately preventing the public from knowing about problems or misrepresenting the potential dangers associated with these problems. Local people expressed little confidence in the ability of state or federal agencies to either monitor or regulate this facility.

The original nuclear generator at the location, Fermi I, almost reached a critical meltdown and thus came dangerously close to causing the first United States Chernobyl-type nuclear accident. After Fermi I was cut into pieces and hauled away to a high-level radioactive waste disposal facility, the utility proposed Fermi II. Construction of the new facility apparently was met with extensive, but scientifically undocumented local public opposition. The facility siting was approved by state and federal agencies despite this opposition. Many people in the area expressed the opinion that they now live in the shadow of another Chernobyl.

The persistence of this perception is attributed, in part, to the poor operational record of the Fermi II facility. In the opinion of many people, these operational problems document the potential for another Fermi I-like meltdown. Compared to the people of the Stockbridge area, the people of the Dundee area are both more fearful of radiation and have a lower level of trust in companies and the agencies who would normally regulate these companies.

The Stockbridge study area, in contrast to the Dundee study area, does not contain a facility that has radioactive, hazardous materials, or even large-scale, domestic waste landfills. Only one high voltage power line crosses the area. The Stockbridge area contains a mixture of farmland, natural woodlots, wetlands, and lakes, all of which are interspersed with small agrarian service centers. The economy and quality of life in the area are not threatened by neighboring urban centers.

Stockbridge area people interact on a regular basis with state agricultural and natural resource agencies, and they generally describe relations with these agencies as involving a high level of trust. The research, however, documented two past project interactions that reduced levels of trust for the people involved. Electrical power transmission lines have been sited in such a way that some farmers perceive that they have experienced more farmland damage than was compensated. Only a few farms, however, have been crossed by power lines.

Perhaps the project that has affected trust in agencies most adversely was the siting of a sour gas plant. The plant processes gas containing the toxic substance hydrogen sulfide so that the gas will meet pipeline quality standards. The plant was approved by the state despite the fact many people in the local area opposed it and that local people had sought an injunction against the siting. When the location of the proposed SSC ring was announced, the strongest initial concern was expressed by the local group who had organized against the sour gas plant.

These two projects cast what is termed here "risk perception shadows," i.e., a predisposition to distrust projects involving potential adverse health or social impacts and to doubt agency or company statements regarding the potential dangers associated with these projects. The risk perception shadows of these two projects are small when compared with that of the Fermi II power plant, so most people in the Stockbridge study area have much higher level of trust in companies and public agencies than do people from the Dundee study area.

Conclusion

The findings of this study run counter to assumptions commonly applied by professionals who site projects. These professionals would argue that people who face risks from radioactivity learn about it, become less fearful of it, and find ways to accommodate to it. Such people, so the logic goes, would provide a better host community than a community lacking experience with radiation.

The findings of the SSC social assessment research, on the other hand, argue that past projects can increase the perception of risks associated with radiation. In this instance, people from an area that had no experience with radioactivity perceived their risk from radioactivity as being much lower than did people from an area that had extensive experience with radioactivity. The study also suggests that the level of trust in the agencies involved in previous projects, including ones that do not involve radioactivity, can become a key risk perception factor, especially when there is a lack of scientific agreement about probabilistic assessments of risk.

Anthropology and Environmental Problems in the U.S.: The Case of Groundwater Contamination

Janet M. Fitchen

Dealing with the consequences of groundwater contamination is a lengthy and expensive process, often fraught with conflicts. Janet Fitchen describes her dual role in a multidisciplinary research project—trying to capture the perspectives of affected citizens and of the technical and agency people, who are the audience for the research, with the aim of improving the effectiveness of institutional response to environmental problems. Although technical and agency personel initially doubted the usefulness of her ethnographic data, understanding the cultural dimensions of community responses did reduce their frustration over apparently random and incomprehensible public behavior. American emphases on individualism and on privacy and local variations in values, community self-image, social relations, and trust in government form key aspects of cultural context that make public behavior more predictable and differences between specialists' and nonspecialists' views of risk and risk management more understandable. E. B. L.

The underground aquifers that supply drinking water to about half of the U.S. population are now known to be vulnerable to contamination from leaking landfills, waste lagoons, underground storage tanks, improper use of agricultural chemicals, and various industrial operations. Manufactured chemical compounds, including industrial degreasers and solvents, as well as gasoline, pesticides, and fertilizers (in all, over 700 synthetic organic chemicals) have been detected in groundwater. Nearly every state has identified cases of contamination serious enough to require closing some public or private supply wells.

Janet M. Fitchen (1936-1995) was Professor and Chair of the Anthropology Department at Ithaca College at the time of her death. Her extensive research in rural America touched on policy domains as diverse as household and family structure, poverty and welfare reform, and environmental management.

Originally published as part of a special section on "Anthropology in Environmental Risk Studies," guest edited by Amy K. Wolfe, in *Practicing Anthropology* 10,3-4(1988):5,18-20, this article has been edited and abridged for republication here. Funding for the project, "Environmental Chemicals and Individual/Community Risk Management," included a National Science Foundation EVIST grant (RII-8409912) and support from The Ford Foundation.

136

This article describes the role of a cultural anthropologist in a multidisciplinary groundwater research project. A team of biologists, toxicologists, chemists, hydrologists, and Extension educators at Cornell University studied what happens in actual situations where groundwater contamination has been discovered and is being addressed. Research was carried out from 1984 through 1987 in over a dozen small and mid-sized communities, mostly in New York State. The "hard science" component of the research team concentrated on the chemical contaminants, investigating their toxic properties, reviewing their potential health effects, and modeling their deposition and transport in the local soils and geological formations. In order to study the institutional and public response in each of these cases, the group added a graduate student toxicologist with training in public policy, and also a cultural anthropologist.

The research team was surprised to learn that after contamination is discovered in a water supply, it may take seven to ten years or more, as well as millions of dollars, to solve the problem. Whether for a whole city or just a few affected homes, resolving a groundwater problem is an extremely complex technical procedure. This technical complexity is further compounded by institutional complexity. Several agencies of state and federal governments and various officials and offices of city and county governments are usually involved. There may also be several private engineering firms and other consultants, each retained by different agencies for different facets and phases of the work. This institutional thicket often involves overlapping or fragmented jurisdictions, different sorts of expertise and responsibilities, disparate funding sources and legal constraints, as well as different procedures, timetables, and mandates. Compounding this complexity still further is the fact that groundwater contamination cases inevitably involve a resident public—the consumers of the water, the people at risk, the payers of taxes and water rates, the onlookers scrutinizing (or ignoring) the whole process.

As we soon learned, the interaction of these institutional and public actors on the local scene is seldom smooth; frustration and dissatisfaction with one another and with the progress of investigation and remediation seem to be the norm. An antagonistic, adversarial atmosphere easily develops which may slow the progress of resolution, undermine public confidence in the agencies and offices charged with resolving the problem, and reduce the opportunity for local publics to learn valuable lessons about protecting their groundwater resource in the future.

One approach to improving response to groundwater problems is through technology: new methods for detection, investigation, and remediation, such as new methods of "stripping" chemicals from contaminated water (without unacceptably polluting the air). Another approach is to enhance the institutional aspects of the response, to create smoother operation and interaction among the multiple institutional actors on the scene. Our multidisciplinary research aimed primarily at improving the institutional response. Towards this end, the research team's findings are being translated into strategies, suggestions, and tools that could be used to improve future institutional response to groundwater contamination—or to any similar local environmental contamination problem. The applied "products" of our research include training sessions and a written guide to help agency "experts" and technical "intervenors" act more smoothly and effectively in communities, and interactive computer software about groundwater and toxicology for use by community groups and agency people.

The Anthropological Research: Two Studies in One

A major part of the anthropological assignment was to discern how local residents perceived, interpreted, and reacted to the groundwater problem. Research included a variety of strategies under the loose rubric of participant-observation: listening to residents' comments and questions at public hearings and information sessions; observing interactions between local residents and government agency representatives; tracking the water issue in local media; holding informal discussions with groups of residents; and especially carrying out unstructured but focused interviews with key informants, including local leaders and officials, as well as affected citizens.

Because of the applied nature of this research, it was also necessary for the anthropologist to learn about the technical and agency people, who were both part of the field being observed and part of the ultimate population of clients we hoped to reach with our research-based materials. To this end I conducted interviews with a variety of specialists from various state and federal agencies, including both field representatives and headquarters personnel; I observed their activities and interactions in the communities; and I participated in their training workshops (initially as observer-trainee, later as trainer). Thus I was involved in a double version of the anthropologist's standard insider-outsider role, for while I was nominally investigating local communities with contamination problems, I was also doing research on and for institutional clients. It was also essential that I learn enough basic technical information about groundwater and toxic chemicals to converse with and gain credibility among practitioners.

Anthropology for Practitioner-Clients:
Culture, Context, and Process

In the process of observing communities as they slowly negotiated the long, tortuous path from discovery to resolution of a groundwater problem, I found that anthropology's standard concept, culture, was a tool of considerable leverage. To make the cultural insights applicable to and by the practitioner-clients, however, it was necessary to translate anthropological observations into their intellectual frameworks. Discovering the intellectual orientations of practitioner-clients thus became a research need in itself.

Despite the diversity of specializations among the officials of state and federal environmental agencies; the health, water, and sanitation specialists; and the practicing engineers; such technical and bureaucratic practitioners all share a world view that emphasizes action. These practitioners are task-oriented and product-minded. Their orientation towards knowledge is instrumental, a "show-me" stance in which data from research have to prove their usefulness. The key questions practitioners ask of research data concern its relevance to the job at hand: "What do we do with the information?" "How do we translate it into action?" "Will it work?" On the whole, these practitioners perceive the contaminants in the groundwater as a technical problem, requiring a technical fix. For them, the "people factor" represents an unwelcome source of difficulty, a block to resolution of a technical problem.

The limited interest these practitioners have in knowledge for its own sake became apparent in an early workshop I did for agency specialists. After I presented them with what I thought were fascinating and relevant ethnographic insights on people's reactions to pollution, one geologist spoke for the crowd when he commented, "That's very interesting, but now could you tell us something useful?" On evaluations of my presentations, a frequent comment was, "What she had to tell us was certainly interesting, but she didn't take the next step; she didn't tell us what we should do about it." It was apparent that I might please these clients most if I skipped all the ethnographic data and just presented a list of *dos* and *don'ts*, thus simplifying rather than complicating their already difficult task. While I could not do that, for there are few hard and fast rules of *do* or *don't*, I subsequently tried harder to meet their perceived need for usefulness.

In fact, a knowledge of the cultural dimensions of community response did turn out to be useful to practitioners in several ways. First, such new understanding helped reduce the frustration practitioners often expressed over "the incomprehensible behavior of the public." In many a public forum, the outside technical specialist or agency official becomes the butt of caustic criticism from local residents. The official, perhaps a sanitary engineer, has probably had little training in how to deal effectively with local publics, and no preparation for encountering a hostile crowd. Cultural insights about public behavior can help insulate technical experts from taking these criticisms personally, and in this respect they are regarded as useful.

The cultural insights may also help counteract the practitioners' belief that public behavior is random and incomprehensible and help to make the behavior predictable. For example, the American cultural emphasis on individualism explains a good deal of public behavior witnessed in these cases, including general distrust of experts. It also underlies a commonly expressed desire for local participation in the process of remediation, such as monitoring the water-testing apparatus and procedures.

Individualism also helps explain a common public reaction that often mystifies the technical specialists, namely that residents tend to be unsatisfied, even hostile, when a state health official answers their anxious questions about the health risk from contamination by presenting a formal risk assessment statement, phrased in the official scientific language of probabilities and aggregates. ("Based on studies of laboratory rats, we estimate that at the level of 50 parts per billion in drinking water, this chemical could cause between one and ten additional cancer deaths per million people, assuming a person of 90 kg. who drinks one liter of the water every day for 70 years.") The crowd's dissatisfaction with such answers is directed at—and stingingly felt by—the health official. There is a cultural mismatch here between the aggregate macro-level nature of the official's scientific probability statement and the lay person's culturally shaped need to have micro-level guidance for individual actions. What each member of that public audience really wants to know is: "Should I drink the water?"

Another relevant cultural value is privacy, particularly in the home. When a contamination problem occurs in a residential area, residents are upset not only about the contamination, but also by the fact that strangers, from state health officials to consulting engineers, come into their yards and their homes to take water samples, do drilling tests, bring water jugs, or adjust filters. While the practitioners perceive these actions as "routine" technical procedures, residents perceive them as an invasion of the privacy of the home. Knowing this, practitioners can avoid the more serious breaches of privacy. For example, the back yard, which is regarded as more private than the front, should be avoided if possible in taking water samples and soil tests.

The anthropological emphasis on context can also be used to help practitioners understand and deal more effectively with local publics. Practitioners need help in understanding that a community with a contamination problem is not a neutral stage on which outside expert actors do their thing, but a part of the drama. Different communities respond differently, depending on several factors in the local context, including community self-image and trust in local government. Thus, practitioners should not expect all communities to respond in the same manner, even to a similar contamination problem. In addition, the technician or official should avoid giving people the impression that he is treating their community as if it were just the same as the last community where he worked. Local uniqueness is a matter of unquestioned belief and considerable pride.

Another context factor affecting people's attitude toward the contamination is their attitude towards its presumed source. People may be more upset by a minute trace of trichloroethylene in their water than they are about a considerably more serious problem of radon in their basements because the latter is perceived as coming from "nature" while the former comes from some factory or "dump." There are also perceived differences among industrial sources. If the factory thought to be responsible for the pollution is symbolically and socially important in the community (not simply as provider of jobs) and is regarded as "part of us," residents and local officials may rally to its defense when the environmental agency's lawyers come to town. Conversely, a pre-existing negative attitude towards a company, especially if it is defined as an outsider, may cause residents to exaggerate the health risks posed by its effluent and to take a more adversarial stance.

Practitioners need help in realizing that they themselves are operating within a local context. An administrator or technical specialist may enter a community with the best intentions of being sensitive to the local public but soon find himself embroiled in controversy and unable to please anybody. In some cases, the water problem acts like a lightening rod, gathering a lot of charged feelings that have been building up in the community. In some cases, earlier schisms and disputes, long dormant, are reawakened by the water problem. Often new anxieties and differing visions of a desired local future (e.g., growth vs. no-growth) become focused and polarized around the water issue. In any case, the outside technical or agency expert needs to be prepared for the fact that she or he is not operating in a vacuum, and is apt to bear the brunt of everyone's discontents.

The anthropological emphasis on process is also relevant and useful here. Contrary to the practitioners' common assumption, resolution of a contamination problem is not a one-way delivery of a product. Rather, it is an interactive process, and the community an active player, even if it is not formally assigned a role. Furthermore, although the world view of agency people leads them to think of process mainly in terms of organizational flow charts and formal lines of communication, our research revealed the importance of indigenous messengers and informal messages. For example, residents' compliance with a health department notice to boil drinking water may be determined less by what the officials say than by what a neighbor or brother-in-law says and does, or the water meter reader, or the man selling water purifiers.

Even people's perception of the problem involves process, for it is fluid and subject to change. Because of this, outside experts should be helped to realize that how they do things matters almost as much as what they do, and also that their actions may speak louder than their words. For example, when engineers come to town dressed in "moon suits" to take soil samples, residents who have previously been calm about the possible health risk from the contamination may suddenly become very upset. This effect could be minimized by showing photos before work begins of cleanup technicians at work in protective gear, and by telling the public ahead of time that the suits are standard operating procedure, required by OSHA, and not indicative of the actual hazardousness of the local problem.

Assumptions and Limitations of Anthropological Explanations

Environmental specialists, like any "natives," are rarely aware of the extent to which they are products of their own enculturation. Therefore, certain assumptions and explanations about culture must be made explicit. Three anthropological assumptions in particular need emphasis.

1. *The existence of American culture.* Engineers, chemists, EPA agents, and environmental lawyers, like most Americans, tend to think that culture is an attribute of the natives of somewhere else; for those others, it is their culture that makes them act as they do. Precisely because the American cultural paradigm emphasizes individual volition and free choice, the applied anthropologist working in the U. S. may have to be painstakingly explicit in convincing technical practitioners that culture does exist in the U. S., and that it shapes the behavior of American publics.

2. *The concept of "cultural rationality."* In the standard American world view, it is assumed that people normally behave with economic rationality, acting in their own best interests to maximize profits, or with an "objective rationality," acting on the basis of knowledge of "the facts." If people do not behave according to either of these rationalities, they can be judged "irrational." But anthropology suggests yet another type of rationality: cultural rationality. Behavior that may be irrational in terms of economic or objective reality could be perfectly rational, understandable, and predictable in terms of the assumptions and values of American culture.

3. *The concept of institutional world view.* To counterbalance the culturally generated notion that the course of events is shaped by people rather than the other way around, applied anthropologists working on U.S. environmental issues may need to emphasize that there are institutional as well as individual explanations for events and actions, that individual actors are shaped by their institutional bases, and that this too lends predictability.

I would also suggest that the applied anthropologist be explicit about the limitations of cultural explanations. I propose three disclaimers or "obligatory caveats" to be made at the outset.

1. *Culture will not explain all of the actions of all of the people.* There are bound to be variations based on region, class, ethnic background, and personal predilection. This point is necessary in part to deflect the argument sometimes made to the anthropologist: "How can you generalize? I'm American, but in my family we don't do it that way." (Individualism strikes again!)

2. *Cultural explanation does not guarantee complete consistency of response.* Because of some conflicting, incompatible values built into American culture, opposing values may coexist, even within the same individual, and will be reflected in different behavior at different times or in different situations.

3. *Culture is not a total or sufficient explanation.* While cultural explanations can help demystify and predict the actions of the American public in responding to environmental problems, applied anthropologists should not oversell the cultural explanation. Reduction to any single explanation, even culture, is totally inadequate in explaining reality.

"There Is a Balm in Gilead": An Interview with Elliot Liebow on His Work with Homeless Women

Margaret S. Boone

In a brief interview with Margaret S. Boone, then a corresponding editor for Practicing Anthropology, *Elliot Liebow, one of the preeminent urban ethnographers of the twentieth century, dazzles with his pithy observations on the persistent but ever-changing problems of the poor, the abused, and the lost of society. Along the way, he offers anthropologists enduring gems of insight on religion, public policy, ethnographic technique, analytical methods, the art of scientific writing, power, fear, humor, computers, and information overload. Together, Boone and Liebow produce an object-lesson on ethnographic interviewing in the anthropology of anthropology. There is, indeed, "a balm in Gilead" in the near-religious inspiration of Liebow's words for novitiate and jaded doubter alike within The Order of Dedicated Anthropologists. Read, enjoy, and take heed!*   J. A. P.

PA: Many people don't know what you did after publishing *Tally's Corner* (*Tally's Corner: A Study of Negro Streetcorner Men* [Boston: Little, Brown, 1967]). What did you do next?

Liebow: I worked for the National Institute of Mental Health forever and ever... I ended up in one or another research unit, then headed up a research funding unit, the Center for the Study of Metropolitan Problems, later the Center for Work and Mental Health.

PA: So you never taught?

Elliot Liebow (1925-1994) was retired from the federal government at the time this article was published, but held a guest worker position with the National Institute of Mental Health and an appointment at the Catholic University of America in Washington, D.C.

Margaret S. Boone is President of Policy Research Methods, Incorporated (2229 Beacon Lane, Falls Church, VA 22043-1709; telephone and fax: (703) 536-4510; <prmi2@aol.com>; http://members.aol.com/prmi2).

Originally published as part of a special section on "The Changing Face of Homelessness in America," guest edited by Margaret S. Boone and Thomas Weaver, in *Practicing Anthropology* 11,1(1989):2,22-23, the interview was conducted on September 23, 1988, in Washington, D.C., recorded in handwritten notes, and edited later by the interviewee. For an update on the work described in this article, see Elliot Liebow, *Tell Them Who I Am: The Lives of Homeless Women* (New York: Penguin Books, 1995).

Liebow: Part time, maybe seven or eight times.

PA: And now you're working with homeless women. How did that start?

Liebow: I retired on disability in 1984 from the federal government. I didn't have much to do with myself. So, I volunteered in a soup kitchen. I started as a "counselor," giving out [bus] tokens, helping people find shelter for the night, that kind of thing… Not one-to-one counseling. But, of course, I got to talk to people; it wasn't very demanding, so I also volunteered to work in a shelter.

PA: So you started as a volunteer?

Liebow: Yes, it was a shelter for homeless women, in a mainline church.

PA: A what…?

Liebow: A mainline church… I thought that was a well-known term. A nice, big granite church in a town just outside D.C.

PA: So, not a storefront church?

Liebow: No… So I started as a volunteer one night a week. I said to myself, "Pick one," and I knew that one, the closest one to where I live. In 1984 it was probably the only emergency shelter for women out there.

PA: Did they take rape victims, too, and battered women?

Liebow: They didn't screen the types of women but there were no children, no men. It was an all-volunteer operation. But then, I kinda got hooked. It was a lot of fun to be with the women. I started going more often. I started taking notes and writing them up at an office I have still at NIMH as a Guest Worker, and at Catholic University's School of Social Work. I never took on my homeless work as *a job!*

PA: So, you took notes while you were with the homeless women?

Liebow: That's not participant observation. Observers take notes, not participants. That's not fun! If you start taking notes when you're with them, you put them off, and you distance yourself from them. I wrote my notes after I got home.

PA: Did you take notes for *Tally's Corner*?

Liebow: Not at the same time I was with the men. Usually I'd just wait. If it was really important to get down what they said right away, verbatim, I'd go to my car or go write it down in a bathroom.

PA: We've all used them for that…

Liebow: But with the homeless women, I asked them for permission to take notes. I made an announcement one night. There were about fifteen women sitting together having dinner in the shelter.

PA: What were their reactions?

Liebow: Well… That was one of the things that was so appealing about them, their sense of humor. This woman, Mabel, leaned over to me and said in a stage whisper so everyone would hear, "You know, Susan has a Ph.D." and Susan said, "No, I don't, but I do have a B.A.—from Duke." And a volunteer at the shelter later recognized her as a graduate teaching assistant… Susan said she'd majored in biology, and said, "All my life I wanted to be an M.D., and now, at the age of 54, I finally made it! I'm a Manic Depressive!"

PA: Was she a manic depressive?

Liebow: She probably was. The women carry all kinds of labels—manic depressive, schizophrenic, bipolar this and unipolar that… Susan, I like her kind of humor. You hear funny stories, and I've come to believe them all, no matter how outrageous; unless, of course, I have evidence to the contrary or they're just too fantastic. For example, one woman told me a story of jumping out of a car because the people she was with were planning to kill her. She said she ran away through the woods and through a creek and lost her shoes and her pocketbook. The police picked her up and she told the police there was $1800 and an airline ticket in her pocketbook! The police brought her to the shelter and asked me, "Should we believe her? Should we look for the money?" I said, "I don't know, but I've learned to accept everything they tell me at face value until I have good reason not to." Two days later, the police called to tell her to come to the station to pick up her $1800!

PA: Well, the guys in *Tally's Corner* had a good sense of humor sometimes, too.

Liebow: You've got to put yourself in some perspective. You've got to step outside yourself so you can laugh.

PA: It sounds like you have a lot of respect for these women.

Liebow: When you see them…when you see how they live, you ask yourself, why don't they just blow their brains out? Why don't they jump off a bridge? How do they do it? How do they keep going?… Part of the answer is religion, but it's a personal kind of religion. Some of the Catholic women go to church, but most of the women are put off by shame, by the way people dress up on Sunday. I guess most of them are "fundamentalists." They believe literally in the Bible but they don't make any fine discriminations [about denominations].

PA: There were types of men in *Tally's Corner*. Do you see types of women at the shelter?

Liebow: One senses that today… I mean, you always see the winos and the ones from skid row, but that's not even the tip of the iceberg! Today, the homeless aren't people who "fall through the cracks." It's something happening all across the board, a lowering of the standard of living of the whole working class. It's the bottom of the working class now, but as time goes on, it goes higher and higher. You have the "working homeless" now, whole families, men, women, and children.

PA: So homelessness is different today.

Liebow: It's partly the *level* of public assistance. Once, it could be that if you were on AFDC [Aid for Families with Dependent Children], you were lifted out of poverty. Today, if you're on public assistance, you're deep in poverty. And, there's a meanness now in our level of support, a meanness in the quality of life for people on SSI [Supplementary Security Insurance], a meanness in

146

the level of public assistance and food stamps, to say nothing of housing! The federal government has completely withdrawn from housing.

PA: None of the men in *Tally's Corner* was completely homeless, right? Did you see the homeless when you did your fieldwork in Washington back in the 1960s?

Liebow: Well, yes, the winos and the skid row guys. But pre-World War II, you don't see references to women in the homeless literature… It's the women's religiosity that is so striking, about knowing God…

PA: There is a word—I'm going to play Devil's Advocate here a little bit—in psychiatry, "hyperreligiosity." Would you use that term?

Liebow: Who's to say what's "hyper" in a belief system!!?? Let them read this book [pointing to Schneider's *The Puritan Mind*, an intellectual history of Puritanism in the 17th and 18th centuries]. So, the Puritans were hyperreligious. "Hyper" suggests "too much." Are the Iranians hyper?… Well, maybe to the Iraqis… Who's to say what are extreme adjustments? You know, if I ever do get around to writing this book, I'm going to call one of the chapters, "There is a balm in Gilead."

PA: There is a…?

Liebow: [singing] There is a balm in Gil-e-ad,
To make the wounded whole,
There is a balm in Gil-e-ad,
To heal the sin-sick soul.

Religion *is* "the opiate of the people"! It *is* "the cry of the oppressed"! If you want to call it "hyper,"… I'm afraid of cliches, especially when people are in such straitened circumstances. It's hard to see how they stay sane! One sees this figure, 30 percent, that 30 percent of the homeless are mentally ill. Well, maybe, but there is the question of whether that's relevant. They're not homeless because they're mentally ill, or because they're unemployed, or disabled, because they "choose a life of freedom." They're homeless because they don't have a place to live! There's no *necessary* connection between mental illness and homelessness. Most of the mentally ill in this country have a place to live. Mental illness doesn't explain homelessness.

PA: You mean that one doesn't necessarily imply the other.

Liebow: It's the same with physical disabilities or unemployment. There's no necessary connection between mental illness and homelessness. People are homeless because they don't have a place to live.

PA: So what would you suggest?… It's a big leap to make between the kinds of observations that anthropologists often make and public programs and policies, which is what this issue is geared to…

Liebow: I'm not convinced that social science makes any difference. Certainly not in the short run. Pete Rossi recently wrote on just that question ("No good applied research goes unpunished," *Society*, Nov./Dec., 1987, pp. 74-79). He says, "Forget it! You do it because it's fun to do!" …You hang out…

I don't think you need to have a defined role, either. You can just be someone that's trusted. You need to have some minimum trust... And, when you get to see people up close, you get an impression... If you stand real close to these women, nose to nose, then they look more different from one another than a random sample of women from the general population. But when you step back and see them as a group, they look more homogeneous. The random sample will have a mix of classes, but the homeless women are almost entirely working class and lower class. Oh, you get an occasional shooting star— a school teacher, a nurse, even a lawyer.

PA: Even a teaching assistant...

Liebow: Even a teaching assistant. But they are mostly working class and lower class, and many of them don't fit in some way. We're a tight-assed society, and we want people to fit. But the homeless women, many of the homeless women, they just don't fit in some way. One woman weighs more than four hundred pounds. Another has a withered hand. Another woman is severely depressed, and here's another with a personality that rubs people the wrong way. They don't conform in many different ways, and there are more ways of being different, of being nonconforming, than of conforming. That's why they are more different from one another than, say, a class of graduate students... The women say, "People don't expect us to behave normally living like this... I don't know whether I'm mentally ill or not. But they expect me to act crazy, so I'll act crazy. I'll please you so long as you give me whatever you give the others." That's what they say. Some women act crazy in order to get off the street and be hospitalized. And, you get involved.

PA: How did they involve you?

Liebow: One wanted me to drive her to the hospital. Another woman had counseled her, "Get a fifth of Johnnie Walker and drink it all at once. They'll take you in." We went to the hospital and I waited for her in the emergency waiting room. Later, I learned she had gone to the ladies' room and overdosed.

PA: Were you sitting there?

Liebow: I waited an hour and a half and finally asked, "Can I go in back and find out what happened to Betty?" They must have had ten people working on her! The doctor said he didn't know whether she was going to make it! She told me later she overdosed to make sure they took her in as mentally ill. And she was a nurse, an LPN. They have ways.

PA: That's frightening...

Liebow: More people are evicted by shelter providers than by landlords. The shelter staff are often tight-assed and rigid. The homeless are fearful of the staff. The staff are fearful of the homeless. The community is fearful of the homeless. The homeless are fearful of the community. The homeless are fearful of the homeless. It's a circle of fear. They're all afraid, and they're right for being afraid.

PA: Why are people right to fear the homeless?

Liebow: Violence. Threats. What is sometimes unpredictable behavior. The very coarseness, rudeness of life on the streets, and the people who live it. The people in the community fear for their children, for the "visual pollution." It's not always fear. It's also aversion to looking at people who look so bad and smell so bad. That's a big thing in the shelters: "I can't stand her! She stinks! I won't stay in the same room with her!"... But the staff does tend to be authoritarian. The volunteers are more likely to be middle class and less authoritarian, but paid staff are more likely to be working class.

PA: Like cops.

Liebow: Yes.

PA: What's the racial composition in the shelter?

Liebow: It's been changing. Originally, in 1984, it was about 10-20 percent black. Last winter we saw a dramatic increase in tough, young, smart black women who are working.

PA: So, these young women see this as a real option?

Liebow: Well, by default. No one wants to be there. More and more you see women whose kids are living with her family or with Social Services. She can't find a place to live, so she uses the shelter as a place "to get her stuff together." It's a jumping off point. She waits out housing assistance, or she stays until she can get the security deposit together for her own place. There are lots of women doing that.

PA: Does she have a more normal social life? Does she visit her family, her children? Does she date? Is it a "normal phase" of a larger process?

Liebow: She's more likely to do those things than the other women, and some shelters take children. The women in such shelters sometimes use paid babysitters. They work and use paid child care. There are more and more doing this kind of stuff—the "new homeless." It used to be that you could always get a room if you worked. But you can't do it now. One woman— a crackerjack typist—got a room in another woman's two bedroom apartment for $325 a month, with very limited kitchen privileges. That's ridiculous! Some women get out by saving. Some women can't work, and shouldn't work. Some get out with the [housing] voucher system—but it's so *few* people. In fact, if the voucher system were to be used for anyone who needs it, it would drive housing costs up and we'd be where we started... I'm generalizing here from three or four urban-suburban shelters that have gone from 10-20 percent black in 1984 to about 50 percent black [in 1988]. Some of the women go back and forth from these shelters to the D.C. shelters.

PA: So, what are your plans now? Are you going to stay there?

Liebow: I haven't been able to start writing. It's been a terrible thing for me. Computers! They seduced me! I took too many notes!

PA: Have you tried ETHNOGRAPH [computer program to sort notes]?

Liebow: No. There's no way I can use a keyword system… The other problem is that I want to be able to encompass it, digest it, the whole thing all at once, and say, "I know this body of material. I know it all." I've collected so much that I can only grab ahold of a small piece of it, a corner, at one time. With other things I've done, I could say, "I have a sense of the whole thing." I only have gross impressions [of the homeless]. The religion thing is very powerful—being able to evoke a different system of logic and a different way to assess life's chances.

PA: You could write about the circle of fear. You could take a program perspective…

Liebow: When I told them I was going to take notes and might eventually publish something, and was that OK with them, one of the women said, "OK, as long as you don't publish before I do!"

PA: You might write about the types of women there.

Liebow: I have an aversion to "types"!… Some of them are just crazy. They joke about it—the craziness. Some are physically disabled… OK, types. There's the young women who come and work full time. They're solid, bright, tough, hard-working. They work in K-Mart, Hecht's, Bradlees, McDonald's. Some have clerical or secretarial skills. Some work in telephone solicitation. So, full-time workers is a new type. Then, there're the battered women, the wives running away from violence and the beatings, the women who can now run away because they finally have somewhere to run. That's a new type. Then, there's another very prominent group—the young women in their twenties and teens. You have to be eighteen years old in this shelter, or technically they can't take you. These women could no longer live at home with their parents. There are awful things that go on in their homes! That's a new type. You know, those people in the community who say that if we build more shelters, there will be more homeless, they're right. We *should* have more places for people to escape to… Most everybody has some income: public assistance, SSI, or they're working, or, less common, from their families.

PA: What about the druggies and the alcoholics as types? People usually talk about the homeless as the mentally ill vs. the non-mentally ill vs. the alcoholic, and the types overlap.

Liebow: That has nothing to do with it! If you gave them an apartment, they wouldn't be homeless. There is an assumption that there are people who *want* to live on the street! That's nonsense. They may choose the street as an alternative to shelters—their only alternative—but that's a far cry from wanting to live on the street.

PA: So, there are the physically disabled, the mentally disabled, and those working full-time. They're there but they're not what you call types.

Liebow: No, I can't deal with them as types. Can't do it… People get to the state of homelessness through *radically* different routes. There are usually three or four kinds of precipitating incidents.

PA: Sounds like you're working on that standard task of all scientists, classification.

Liebow: You could organize by activity, or subject matter. One section could be on "Making It." That would include religion. And humor. One section on jobs, work, money. One on emotions: fear, love. And one on the "round of life." That used to be a standard part of all ethnographies.

PA: You could have a chapter on programs and policies.

Liebow: From the very beginning, I've shied away from that, and that was a mistake. I never dreamt how central the service providers were in their lives! They have life-or-death power over them!…What I wanted was the women's perspective. From their perspective, there's more craziness in the system dealing with the women than in the women themselves.

Cooperation at the Pueblo of Zuni: Common Ground for Archaeology and Tribal Concerns

ROGER ANYON AND JEROME ZUNIE

Since the 1970s native peoples in the United States, Australia, and elsewhere have confronted archaeologists and museum curators on the sensitive issues of excavation of burials, repatriation of sacred objects, and representation of native cultures. In the United States, this issue resulted in the amendment of laws and regulations protecting historical, environmental, and archaeological resources and the passage in 1990 of the Native American Graves Protection and Repatriation Act (NAGPRA). Roger Anyon and Jerome Zunie, writing before the passage of NAGPRA, describe how the Zuni people were already taking their archaeological destiny into their own hands. Many tribes now have their own historic preservation programs, and some have their own Tribal Historic Preservation Officer and are no longer under the oversight of a State Historic Preservation Officer. While archaeologists and Native Americans cooperate in the programs discussed by Anyon and Zunie, applied anthropologists increasingly find themselves serving as cultural brokers between tribes and nontribal archaeologists. J. A. P.

The Pueblo of Zuni is located in west-central New Mexico and east-central Arizona, with a reservation encompassing approximately 655 square miles. Of these, 640 square miles comprise the main reservation in New Mexico, almost one square mile of land surrounds Zuni Salt Lake some 60 miles south of the main reservation, and the remaining 14 square miles of Zuni Heaven (Kolhu/wala:wa), also detached from the main reservation, are located near

Roger Anyon is an archaeologist who was with the Heritage and Historic Preservation Office of Zuni Pueblo at the time this article was written. He is now with Heritage Resources Management Consultants (3227 North Walnut Avenue, Tucson, AZ 85712; (520) 881-4258; <ranyon@worldnet.att.net>).

Jerome Zunie is Supervisory Archaeologist with Zuni Cultural Resources Enterprise, Pueblo of Zuni (Box 1149, Zuni, NM 87327; (505) 782-4814; <zcre@nm.net>).

Originally published in *Practicing Anthropology* 11,3(1989):13-15, this article has been edited and abridged for republication here. For an update on some of the issues discussed in this article, see T. J. Ferguson, Roger Anyon, and Edmund J. Ladd, "Repatriation at the Pueblo of Zuni: Diverse Solutions to Complex Problems," *American Indian Quarterly* 26(1996):251-273.

152

Saint Johns, Arizona. Zuni has a long and unique history and continues to forge its own distinctive path to link its past with its future.

In recent years, relations between American Indians and archaeologists often have been portrayed in a negative light. Issues of reburial, repatriation of artifacts, and who should speak for the past of the American Indian have become polarized. While the extreme views of both sides in these arguments have been widely publicized, very little attention has been given to examples of close cooperation between Indians and archaeologists. At Zuni such collaboration toward mutually defined goals has been practiced successfully for over a decade.

This article describes the goals and roles of the Zuni Cultural Resources Enterprise, a tribally owned small business, and the Zuni Archaeology Program, an arm of the tribal governmental structure. [The latter was renamed Zuni Heritage and Historic Preservation Office in 1993.] Both organizations function under the direction of the Governor and Tribal Council, an executive and an administrative body elected by the Zuni people. Therefore, both the Cultural Resources Enterprise and the Archaeology Program are ultimately responsible to the Zuni people through their elected officials, a situation that promotes cooperation and understanding between archaeologists and tribal members.

Zuni Tribal Archaeology: A Brief History

In the early 1970s, a series of construction projects, such as new housing, flood control dams, and roads on the Zuni Reservation, were preceded by archaeological surveys and excavation. A number of young Zunis, under the direction of experienced archaeologists, worked on these projects and began learning archaeological skills. In previous decades, tribal members had worked on archaeological expeditions including those directed by Frederick Hodge at the ancestral Zuni sites of Hawikku and Kechiba:wa, Frank Robert's work at the Village of the Great Kivas and Kiatuthlanna, and various expeditions in Chaco Canyon. The establishment of tribal archaeological organizations, therefore, was not such an outlandish concept in terms of previous Zuni interest and participation in archaeology. It was, however, a novel concept for archaeologists, in that professional archaeologists would be studying the Zuni past while working for the Zuni tribe.

In 1974, with assistance from the National Park Service, the Pueblo of Zuni established the Zuni Archaeological Enterprise. This was replaced in 1978 by the Zuni Archaeology Program, formally established by Tribal Resolution M70-78-947 to operate under the overall guidance of the tribal government for the best interests of the Zuni Tribe. With changing national economic strategies in the early 1980s, it became increasingly difficult for the program to remain economically viable. In addition, federal budgetary cutbacks of domestic programs and the national recession of the early 1980s had hit hard on the reservation. In fiscal year 1982 half of the Zuni Tribe employees (approximately 200 people) lost their jobs, raising unemployment on the reservation to 77 percent. The need for new economic opportunities at Zuni precipitated creation of several tribal enterprises, one of which was the Cultural Resources Enterprise, a small business dedicated to providing additional employment opportunities for tribal members trained in archaeology. While the Archaeology Program and Cultural Resources Enterprise exist together and share staff and facilities, they have separate and quite distinct roles.

As one of several tribal enterprises created to provide meaningful employment for Zuni people, to protect the resources and culture of Zuni, to generate surplus revenues for the benefit of the pueblo, and to develop financially sound businesses, the Cultural Resources Enterprise is designed to fully utilize the Zuni labor force skilled in archaeology. It is organized as a corporate structure eligible to bid on federal small business set-asides as a minority owned and operated small business. Hence, it brings funds from competitively bid projects both on and off the reservation. The Archaeology Program, which exercises historic preservation responsibilities, is supported through surplus revenues generated by the Cultural Resources Enterprise.

The Zuni Archaeology Program engages in all types of historic preservation on the Zuni Reservation. Its primary responsibility is to manage cultural resources in such a way as to ensure their conservation for the public good. These cultural resources include not only prehistoric and historic archaeological sites, but also historic architecture and other places and objects of traditional and cultural importance. Under its plan of operation the Archaeology Program is charged with the pursuit of five major activities: planning and consultation, research, inventory and curation, public interpretation, and training and development.

On the reservation the Archaeology Program provides professional consultation and technical assistance to tribal leaders and other tribal programs to ensure that cultural resources are fully considered during project planning and protected during the course of a project. The program also helps develop plans for future land use and community development. Under certain federal laws, including the National Historic Preservation Act of 1966, the Archaeological Resources Protection Act of 1979, and the American Indian Religious Freedom Act of 1978, tribes have been provided with the opportunity to become involved in protecting tribal resources of traditional, religious, or cultural importance that are presently off their reservation lands. The Archaeology Program consults with the tribal government and provides recommendations for the protection of Zuni cultural resources located off the reservation.

The Archaeology Program incorporates research into all its projects no matter how small. Of course, it is not possible for all research to be conducted within the framework of cultural resources management. Thus, the Archaeol-

154

ogy Program develops and submits proposals to various agencies for research into the prehistory and history of Zuni. Each of these proposals is reviewed, evaluated, and approved by the Zuni Tribal Council prior to submission. Inventory and curation are also activities of the Archaeology Program. As the historic preservation arm of the tribe, the Archaeology Program is charged with maintaining master files on all cultural resources recorded on the reservation. The Archaeology Program also archives and curates any published and unpublished papers, books, records, photographs, film, and tapes regarding Zuni history and cultural resources. When appropriate, these archived materials are available for use by tribal members and other interested persons.

The Archaeology Program's fourth major activity is public interpretation, involving activities that bring the results of the program's work to Zuni people and also inform the public at large about their rich and unique history. Program members design and install exhibits in the tribal building, visit the Zuni ruins, and publish popular booklets on the results of our research for distribution in the community.

Finally, but by no means least, the Archaeology Program provides employment, training, and development of tribal staff members in all aspects of historic preservation and cultural resources management. This involves providing opportunities for both practical and educational training to interested and motivated staff members so that they can develop and attain professional qualifications. The long-term goal is to enable qualified tribal members to take over the Archaeology Program and effectively manage the cultural resources of the tribe.

Examples of Cooperation

Cooperation between archaeologists and tribal government at the Pueblo of Zuni has been of mutual benefit and has allowed compromise and agreement on issues where cultural differences have surfaced. Perhaps the most obvious example, and certainly the most timely in terms of issues facing tribes and archaeologists today, is that regarding human burials and their associated grave goods. When the problem of what to do with archaeological human remains surfaced almost a decade ago, the Archaeology Program staff, the tribal government, and the religious elders discussed the issue with the goal of solving this problem locally. The issue was settled by establishing a prescribed sequence of events to be followed. First, the burial is removed using standard archaeological techniques with an in-field study of the skeleton by a physical anthropologist after exhumation. A complete documentation of the grave goods is conducted in a laboratory. Reburial of the skeleton along with all its associated grave goods occurs after scientific analysis. The reburial is made as close as possible to its original resting place, but out of harm's way (letter from Chauncey Simplicio to Don Fowler, President of SAA, 1986). On the reservation, the Zuni Tribe will permit human burials to be exhumed only in situations where the burial is threatened with destruction by a proposed development, or where a burial has been disturbed accidentally during activities such as road maintenance, or where a burial is threatened by the destructive forces of natural erosion.

A second example of cooperation between the Archaeology Program and the Zuni community involves historic buildings in the Old Pueblo. The Pueblo of Zuni, a village listed on the National Register of Historic Places, has undergone radical change in the past century, and this change continues at a staggering rate. The Archaeology Program architecturally records structures before they are modified in order to preserve a record of change at Zuni for future generations, while allowing the community to upgrade their houses to modern levels of comfort and efficiency.

A number of years ago there was an attempt by the New Mexico State Historic Preservation Office (SHPO) to rigidly apply standards of house renovations that allowed only the use of original materials. This effort caused misunderstanding and tension between the goals of historic preservation and the modernization goals of tribal members. The Archaeology Program arranged for representatives from SHPO to meet with members of the community. After the SHPO representative had carefully explained the law and the regulations regarding the use of original materials in renovations, an elderly Zuni resident declared that these rules were just fine with her, as long as the SHPO representative was willing come to Zuni each year and replaster her adobe house with a new coat of mud. With the situation instantly clarified by one unambiguous statement, a compromise acceptable to both parties was quickly reached. A commercial plaster substitute of similar texture and color to local mud was deemed acceptable.

Another example of positive interaction between the community and archaeologist involves the Owe:kwe kiva. Members decided to tear down their kiva because it was old and becoming unsafe, and they planned to build a new kiva at the same location. The kiva group invited Archaeology Program staff to completely record the exterior and interior architecture of the old kiva before it was demolished. The kiva group wanted to have a record of the kiva for posterity, but they also specifically requested accurate measurements of interior features and their relationships to one another. The kiva group planned to increase the overall size of the kiva, but wanted to retain the original proportions in the newly constructed interior features. After recording was finished, the Archaeology Program provided the kiva group with a complete copy of all the records generated.

Similarly, the Head Priest of Zuni requested, through the Tribal Council, that the Archaeology Program architecturally record some of his religious retreat rooms to document their structural deterioration. These old rooms have had to be vacated because of their poor condition. This information is, upon the Head Priest's request, being used as documentation to demonstrate the need for moneys to renovate these rooms for their continued religious use. Without an understanding of what the Archaeology Program does, why we do it, and the uses to which community members can put this information, there would have been no record of these important structures. Both the community and archaeologist gain from this collaboration.

In addition, Zuni Archaeology Program staff have worked on a number of legal cases as expert witnesses on behalf of the Zuni Tribe, and they have assisted religious elders in the repatriation of sacred artifacts and objects wrongfully removed from Zuni lands. These efforts have resulted in the collection of data for the Zuni Lands Claims case, the Zuni Lands Damages case and the Zuni Water Rights case. Some sacred items have been returned to Zuni for their proper care and protection. While the Archaeology Program assists in securing the return of these items, "it is the policy of the Program that Zuni religion is something to be lived and experienced by the Zuni people, not something to be analytically studied by anthropologists and historians" (T. J. Ferguson, "Cultural Resource Management at the Pueblo of Zuni: The Zuni Archaeology Program," *Quarterly of the Southwest Association on Indian Arts* 15,4[1980]:6-10).

The Future of the Archaeology Program at Zuni

Despite some ups and downs during the course of the past decade, the Zuni Archaeology Program is now an integral and accepted part of Zuni government. The preservation and development of cultural resources is a priority of the tribe. In the fall of 1988, the creation of the Zuni-Cibola National Historic Park, a joint venture between the Zuni Tribe and the National Park Service, was signed into law. The park is planned to be the first of what should be many national parks that will be joint efforts between the Park Service and tribes on reservations lands. We expect that the Archaeology Program will be a major participant in the development of Zuni-Cibola Park. [Establishment of the park was subsequently defeated by a tribal referendum.]

One goal of the Archaeology Program remains elusive, however. This is the training and development of Zunis as degree-holding professional anthropologists. Few American Indians have ventured into the field of anthropology, and specifically archaeology, at the university level. [An exception is the late Edmund J. Ladd, a Zuni and a professional archeologist educated at the University of New Mexico who worked for many years at the U.S. National Park Service and recently retired from the Museum of New Mexico.] The reasons for this are varied and complex; however, we believe the anthropological and archaeological community is culpable to a large extent for this situation. As a community that spends most of its time studying other cultures and their material remains, anthropologists and archaeologists put too little effort, as a group, into providing higher education opportunities for members of those cultures we study. We see a real need for anthropologists and archaeologists to sink much more effort into actively seeking out and helping American Indians become full professional members of our discipline.

Conclusion

There is no doubt that by living on the reservation and working for the tribe, often for years, archaeologists at the Zuni Archaeology Program develop a much greater respect for and understanding of Zuni values than they would if they only performed fieldwork on the reservation and lived off the reservation. Conversely, there is little doubt that the Archaeology Program, being an integral part of the tribal government, provides tribal members with a much greater understanding of archaeology and the role of archaeologists. This day-to-day, year-after-year interaction of tribal members and archaeologists continues to foster and develop a good working relationship based on mutual understanding and trust rather than the antagonism, fear, and mistrust that we all too often see today. The Zuni Archaeology Program is successful because both the tribe and the archaeologists are dedicated to solving problems and to working together toward mutually defined goals.

158

Agricultural Anthropology: New Disciplinary Blood in an International Research Organization

Robert E. Rhoades

The connection between agriculture and anthropology should be abundantly clear (at least to anthropologists), but Robert Rhoades had to establish the credibility and usefulness of anthropology at the International Potato Center (CIP) in Lima, Peru, where he worked for over ten years. It was only after the successful development of a low-cost storage design for farmers, which was adopted worldwide, that the agronomists and economists working with the CIP paid attention to anthropology and its grassroots approach to research. In addition, Rhoades found that he had to "shed many academic myths" about agricultural development programs. He came to appreciate not only the technical knowledge of his agricultural science colleagues, but also the level of their concern for the common farmer. The CIP ultimately adopted the "farmer-back-to-farmer" model which posits that agricultural research must begin and end with the farmer's perspective and must actively involve farmers throughout the research and extension process. Thus, Rhoades's work, along with that of his teammates and predecessors, resulted in the acceptance of anthropology as part of the working philosophy and official policy of CIP. S. J. F.

When I arrived at the International Potato Center (CIP) in Lima, Peru, in 1979, I became one of three anthropologists working in the Consultative Groups for International Agricultural Research (CGIAR). The CGIAR is made up of thirteen international research centers dedicated to the improvement of agricultural research in developing nations. Their mandates range from improving crop production, seeking alternatives to swidden agriculture, and overcoming animal diseases in Africa to international food policy.

Robert E. Rhoades, who received the 1987 Praxis Award for the project described in this article, is Professor of Anthropology at the University of Georgia (Athens, GA 30602; (706) 542-1024; <rrhoades@arches.uga.edu>).

Originally published in *Practicing Anthropology* 11,4(1989):4-5, this article has been edited and abridged for republication here. For an update on some of the issues discussed here, see Joyce Moock and Robert E. Rhoades, *Diversity, Farmer Knowledge, and Sustainability* (Ithaca: Cornell University Press, 1992).

160

At the time the CIGAR employed some seven hundred researchers, mainly biological scientists, who were directly or indirectly linked to plant breeding programs. While the CGIAR was enjoying tremendous prestige from the successes of the "Green Revolution" (for which one wheat breeder, Dr. Norman Borlaug, was awarded the Nobel Peace Prize), my academic anthropology training had taught me to be skeptical and harshly critical of agricultural scientists. It was, therefore, with some trepidation that I took up at CIP a two-year, post-doctoral post funded by the Rockefeller Foundation. The other anthropologists employed within the CGIAR had come to their respective centers under the same Rockefeller program.

My motivations for wanting to work at the CIP were mixed. On the one hand, the academic anthropology market had virtually closed up shop in the late 1970s and my prospects were dim for a university post. On the other, I was an ecological anthropologist who was born and reared in an Oklahoma farm community and had studied agriculture at a state land grant university before shifting to anthropology. In my mind, agriculture and anthropology seemed to have a connection that had not been fully exploited either by the agricultural research establishment or by anthropology. I soon discovered at CIP, as had my predecessor (Robert Werge), that linking these two fields would be a great challenge as well as a source of professional frustration.

The first major shock I had to overcome when I joined the Potato Center was that anthropology was under trial, and not an accepted discipline with great insights into human behavior as I had come to believe after the intense socialization of a graduate program. "What does anthropology have to offer?" was a common question forced upon me in those early years by both biological scientists and economists. Ethnographic tidbits like "peasant women do not like hybrid maize because it makes lousy tortillas" seemed insignificant compared to the heavy-weight arguments of the agronomists' yields and the economists' increased farm incomes through greater profits. The concept of "culture" did not seem to carry the same clout.

The next five years became for me, therefore, a period of figuring out how to translate anthropological knowledge into a powerful message that agricultural researchers and even policy makers could not ignore. To accomplish this, I had to shed many academic myths that I had earlier absorbed about agricultural development programs. Through increased contacts with biological scientists and agricultural researchers from many countries, I came to realize that a concern for humanity, especially marginal farmers, was not the sole territory of anthropology but was shared by my agricultural science colleagues.

It was clear that my first mark within CIP had to be made in terms of practical payoffs for small farmers in developing countries. I built upon the post-harvest work of CIP's first anthropologist, Robert Werge, who had selected an important technical area—storage and processing—where anthropology offered many new insights.

The story of how CIP's interdisciplinary team of anthropologists and post-harvest technologists set about to build farmers' knowledge and perceptions into the development of a highly successful, low-cost storage design is now well known (R. Rhoades and R. Booth, "Farmer-back-to-Farmer: A Model for Generating Acceptable Agricultural Technology," *Agricultural Administration* 11[1982]:127-137). The resulting storage design had been introduced by 1987 into over forty countries and is being used today by at least four thousand farmers, probably many more. The impact of using the technology, which improves seed quality and gives farmers more planting flexibility, is equivalent to an estimated 12 percent increase in total yield. For some small countries, like Sri Lanka, which depend on European imported seed, this meant an equivalent savings of almost one million dollars per year. The storage project succeeded in great part due to the applied use of such anthropological concepts as farmer adaptation and experimentation, culture of food, social use of space, and indigenous technical knowledge.

The success of the anthropological input into storage research gave credibility to CIP anthropologists and opened the way for greater receptivity to other anthropological ideas. The importance of involving farmers in varietal selection, agroecological zonation for setting priorities, household decision making in technology adoption, and gender issues related to consumption and preparation are but a few examples of new ideas which were proposed by CIP anthropologists, debated and fought for within the center's interdisciplinary setting, and ultimately accepted as part of CIP's research agenda. The result was a gradual incorporation of anthropological thinking into the very values of the research center itself.

Most international agricultural research centers like CIP are only staffed one to two deep in any single discipline, with the exception of potato plant genetics. Research management, therefore, expects each discipline to bring to the center's goals and team research the theories, methods, and special skills which are the comparative advantages of that discipline. All anthropologists who have worked at CIP, including myself, were trained in the ecological school growing from the traditions of Leslie White and Julian Steward. This ecological perspective applied to Third World agriculture is not only a powerful, explanatory tool but is refreshing to biological scientists since it broadens understanding of developing country agriculture.

I decided, as CIP's anthropologist, to focus on those important but neglected themes of Third World agriculture not already covered by other disciplines, including economics. My approach was not to compete with established agricultural scientists, but rather to enrich and broaden through anthropology the scientific understanding of agriculture change. Fortunately, those neglected areas (e.g., ecology, ethnobotany, farmers' perspective, informal research methods) proved to be precisely the topics that had and still have a high payoff for a low investment.

The adoption by the center of the farmer-back-to-farmer model has been the clearest statement of the center's acceptance of anthropology. This model was derived from the interdisciplinary team effort on storage. Farmer-back-to-farmer posits that agricultural research must *begin* and *end* with the farmer's perspective and actively involve the farmer's participation and knowledge through the research process. This approach has also had a strong influence over an emerging development movement now being called Farmer Participatory Research by other agencies. (See John Farrington, "Farmer Participatory Research: Editorial Introduction," *Experimental Agriculture* 14,3[1988]:269-279.)

Use of anthropological knowledge was not limited to primary field research. When CIP called upon me to develop a global understanding of where the potato crop was grown and by whom, I resurrected the Human Relations Area File techniques of George Peter Murdock and applied them to the potato. Following Murdock's style, over three thousand documents from field researchers in Africa, Asia, and Latin America were collected and analyzed. From this material, the first worldwide potato production zone maps were developed just as G. P. Murdock produced similar maps on African subsistence crops thirty years ago (George Peter Murdock, "Staple Subsistence Crops of Africa," *Geographic Review* 2[1960]:523-540). This method is now being used as a model for collecting crop data at other international centers. CIP is also applying it now to its newest mandated crop, the sweet potato.

Another important development at CIP was the legitimization of a new subdiscipline specialization called Agricultural Anthropology. CIP anthropologists gave themselves this name by 1979 as a means to precisely convey the idea that they were anthropologists who focused clearly on agriculture. The name stuck and has continued to gain proponents. In the fall of 1988, for example, Dr. Billie DeWalt of the University of Kentucky taught the first, historic course in this new anthropological subdiscipline.

A decision which was made early on by anthropologists at CIP was to practice what we preach. Therefore, we looked upon our scientific community (CIP) as one with its own internal norms and value system, just as we had been taught as anthropologists to understand small communities. By applying to our own jobs anthropological concepts such as ethnocentrism, cultural relativity, or symbolic interaction, we were able to avoid the polarization that has occurred with many anthropologists in other development or applied research agencies.

The CGIAR itself has gone on to expand its use of anthropology. Every international center, except one, has at least one or two anthropologists on its staff. Anthropology is no longer a strange discipline in the world of agricultural research. The case of CIP and its sister centers illustrates how rapidly new disciplinary blood, such as anthropology, can be incorporated. Above all, however, it requires anthropologists who are willing to translate their knowledge into effective action.

Anthropology and Marine Extension: Can We Make a Difference?

SHIRLEY J. FISKE

Commercial fishermen have been dubbed by some the "last hunter-gatherers," and Shirley Fiske notes that they are often characterized as tradition-bound. Add to that the putative "clannishness" of fishing folks, and it is not surprising that policy makers have been open to using anthropological expertise in managing coastal resources. The potential for anthropology in fishery management got a boost in the 1970s by the high-profile work of a handful of pioneering anthropologists, especially in New England. Thus, marine extension is one of those rare areas of American public life where anthropologists were "in on the ground floor." With the growing crisis in the world's fisheries, Fiske's delineation of the contributions anthropologists can make in marine extension remains timely. Moreover, the themes she develops are applicable well beyond marine extension. In particular, Fiske's observation that "technology is never neutral" has special saliency for the "computer revolution" of the late twentieth century.   J. A. P.

My first exposure to marine extension was a refreshing change from the bureaucratic world of Washington, D.C. In 1984 I was helping the National Oceanic and Atmospheric Administration (NOAA) prepare a management study to monitor outreach services to local communities, businesses, and the general public in Alaska and the Pacific Northwest. I interviewed NOAA officials in the states of Washington and Alaska on the kinds and level of interaction they had with local communities. In the sample were Sea Grant marine extension agents based in Anchorage.

Shirley J. Fiske is Director of Education, Social Sciences and Marine Policy at the National Sea Grant Program (1315 East-West Highway, Silver Spring, MD 20910; (301) 713-2431; <Shirley.Fiske@NOAA.gov>).

Originally published as the introduction to a special section on "Anthropology and Marine Extension," guest edited by Shirley J. Fiske, in *Practicing Anthropology* 12,4 (1990):4-5,8, this article has been edited and abridged for republication here. The author thanks Courtland Smith, Bernard Griswold, and authors of the articles for which this was an introduction (Bonnie J. McCay, Jeffrey C. Johnson, James D. Murray, Madeleine Hall-Arber, John B. Richards, Manuel Valdes-Pizzini, Art Gallaher, and Christopher M. Dewees) for their insights and comments. The views expressed are the author's and do not reflect those of NOAA or the National Sea Grant Program.

When I finished the interviews I realized that this was the closest thing to real outreach that I had seen since I'd been working for a federal agency. The agents spent time on the docks talking to fishermen, were up early in the coffee shops where people congregated, and knew the gear repair shop owners and the fishery management officials. They gave workshops on computer programs for financial management for family-run fishing enterprises, acted as intermediary for fishermen's concerns, and introduced the latest diesel engine developments, cold water survival techniques, or radio frequencies to get superstructure icing information. They knew their constituent group intimately and worked with them on a daily basis on "their turf"—not in a federal office behind stacks of paper.

Not all marine agents concentrate on commercial fishing, as did those in Alaska. Programs in other states work with the marine recreation sector or with individuals interested in aquaculture of clams, shrimp, or fish. Other agents specialize in coastal zone management issues such as beach access, growth management, or estuarine planning and work closely with local government officials, townships, or county supervisors. Expertise of each program reflects the needs of particular states or regions, in part because states provide matching funds, so that priorities tend to reflect geographically important concerns. Most marine extension agents are administratively supported, at least in part, by the National Sea Grant College Program, although they are employed by state universities.

The national network of programs and marine extension agents includes a number of anthropologists who work as agents or directors of extension programs or who are faculty members working closely with marine agents. Most have found a real need for their skills and disciplinary perspective and a challenging role in the community. Anthropology is particularly important because of the social change issues accelerating along the coast of the U.S. With increasing population come gentrification, displacement, and marginality of traditional communities. Along with the dollars and jobs of economic development come problems such as overcrowding, demands for services, transiency, and pollution. These increase the pressures on people who live there and rely on marine resources for their income—watermen, fishing vessel operators, and people who fish for subsistence. Anthropology, with insight and skills in social change and mediation and understanding of community-based resource management systems, is ever more critical to protecting and enhancing the use of our coastal areas.

What Is Marine Extension?

The concept of marine extension is modeled after the idea of the U.S. Department of Agriculture's Agricultural Extension Service. The Morrill Act established the land grant college system in 1862, and the Hatch Act (1887) and

Smith Lever Act (1914) laid the groundwork for agricultural experiment stations and the Agricultural Extension Service. The goal of agricultural extension was to carry the results of university-based research to rural farmers, via a cadre of agents who worked with farmers on their farms, testing and sometimes improving the results of the research, and in turn carrying the reality-tested ideas back to specialists at the universities.

Nearly one hundred years later Congress recognized that marine resources, the Great Lakes, and the coastal environment needed the same kind of attention as the agricultural sector. Congress appreciated the unique features of marine resources: their common property nature, their intensive use, the risk and uncertainty associated with them, and the important roles that local, state, and federal governments play in the management and use of these resources. The National Sea Grant College Program Act was enacted in 1966. The term "Sea Grant" was chosen to emphasize the similarity between the needs of marine resources in the mid-twentieth century and the needs of the U.S. a century earlier with respect to its land resources. Like Land Grant, Sea Grant shares the concept of university research being applied though education and extension advisory service to the public.

Today marine extension is a nationwide network of over three hundred people, organized in state programs. The marine extension leaders at the state level manage program design and delivery, with guidance and coordination from the national office.

The basic tenets of extension are:

- to develop information through applied research;
- to accumulate and transfer information—to educate;
- to stimulate interaction between groups to make something happen;
- to be change agents, providing information that can change values and practice;
- to retain credibility across clientele groups in the community through a non-advocacy stance on partisan issues.

Opportunities for Anthropology and Extension

Marine anthropology has a substantial yet often overlooked record of accomplishment with regard to commercial and artisanal fishing communities and fishery management. [See, for example, the special section of *Practicing Anthropology* 12,4(1990) which this article introduced and J. Anthony Paredes, "Anthropology and Marine Extension," *Practicing Anthropology* 13,4(1991):2,23.] Anthropological contributions have cut across all aspects of the problem-solving cycle, although the predominant focus has been on improving program implementation and service delivery rather than on policy decisions. Much of the activity of marine anthropologists ultimately affects the policy process, however.

More specifically, anthropology has made a difference by encouraging and insuring that local knowledge is used in resource management and by providing tools for better identifying key community leaders and understanding community networks and structures. Anthropology has also contributed critical knowledge of ethnic and other special communities and facilitated better rapport in relating to clientele and improved communication with constituent groups. By providing a better understanding of the paradigms of different groups, anthropology has facilitated both technology transfer and conflict resolution.

I see additional avenues of opportunity for anthropological contributions to fill gaps in current extension practice. These are areas where anthropology and social sciences have the skills, theory, and potential to make a difference, either as part of the system (as extension agents and managers), or as researchers working closely with extension.

Understanding Micro-Macro Linkages and Asking Hard Questions

Increasingly, anthropology is paying attention to the articulation of macro-level forces and micro-level states—that is, seeing technology and information transfer as more than simply the introduction of a new diesel engine, fishing net, or management scheme. Social science fosters ability to see how micro-level introductions articulate with national and international forces such as tax and trade policy, technological advances, increasing foreign investment, internationalization of markets, regional land use changes, and demographic and migration patterns.

The ability to see macro-micro linkages forces the question: "Development for whom?" This is both a blessing and a disadvantage. This is a perspective needed in all approaches that assume that technological development is good in itself. The disadvantage is that it often makes one unpopular.

A major goal of extension is to bring information to people and to assist technology transfer. Yet when one examines this goal closely, it raises the question of who benefits from these activities. Extension agents are information and technology transfer agents for whom or what?

For "progress"? Is a better tomato picker or a more efficient fishing net always better?

For the consumer? To provide us with better seafood?

For small or family businesses? To help improve their efficiency, save fuel, improve safety?

For conservation of fish and shellfish resources?

These goals are sometimes at odds with one another. Will the introduction of better technology (e.g. genetically engineered shellfish) affect family fishing traditions as agricultural technology affected family farming, and result in large, vertically integrated corporations that dominate the fishing industry? While the introduction may be more efficient from an industry standpoint, how will the consumer fare? A related dilemma is to decide which groups should receive extension attention and information. Should an agent concentrate on disadvantaged and low-income groups that require more time and labor, or on mainstream clientele with a greater probability of success?

For the sake of the communities with whom we work, it is important to wrestle with the goals of extension and how technology transfer serves each of those goals. One of the maxims of social science is that technology is *not* neutral.

Changing "Blaming the Victim" Assumptions

Anthropology can play a critical role in helping resource managers, scientists, and extension personnel understand the rationality behind the decisions of user groups, whether they are watermen, shrimpers, small businessmen, recreational boaters, or developers. I often hear the attitude expressed, "The fishermen, they're stubborn. They're set in their ways. They've depleted the oysters and clams and overharvested through greed. They're not reasonable. If they were rational, they'd see that they have to limit their harvests so the stock can recover." This attitude assumes the speaker knows what's best, and that anyone else's way is irrational. It discounts the thinking, knowledge, and perceived constraints of the watermen.

Most of the social science work in innovation, rural development, and farming systems research shows the importance of understanding *and taking seriously* the constraints and perceptions of the producer or family decision maker, whether farmer, fisherman, or small-scale entrepreneur. Greater productivity and receptivity to change are facilitated when those constraints are taken into account. The anthropologist-extension worker is in a good position to understand and demonstrate the reasoning behind apparently irrational behavior with regard to resources.

Empowering Clients

Does extension work make people politically more powerful or engaged? Do users learn how to create useful social knowledge for their own purposes, avoiding the dependent client-expert relationship?

Extension believes that through the provision of information, groups will eventually act on their own behalf; for example, marine extension agents were instrumental in facilitating the formation of fisheries cooperatives in Georgia and the creation of citizen volunteer groups to monitor the water quality of coastal ponds in Rhode Island. Sometimes this philosophy works, as when commercial fishermen negotiated a compromise with environmentalist groups on the sea otter program in California. Through listening to the concerns of groups, extension educates and involves people who otherwise are removed from the political process.

By becoming more knowledgeable and familiar with bureaucratic structure and political process, by informing groups of political channels and helping them get access to resources or receive better services, extension helps groups develop knowledge useful for their own purposes.

Understanding Attitudinal and Structural Bases of Behavior

Medical wastes in our oceans and litter along our coastlines have received national attention in recent years. Problems such as these get knee-jerk responses from federal agencies and environmental groups. The solution usually is a quick education campaign, on the belief that giving people or institutions information will change their behavior. The reflexive response is "Let's educate people about how litter is bad for fish, mammals, and the ocean."

While education is important, in the long run it may be more important to know *why* people litter, to understand regional and subcultural dimensions of littering, and to use what is learned to design educational campaigns that will appeal to specific audiences and tap into particular attitudinal structures. Social sciences provide the knowledge behind the educational campaigns, a kind of social marketing for public goods (i.e., beach clean-ups, anti-littering). The principles of understanding the bases of behavior before designing educational campaigns apply to most environmental and social problems.

Potential Pitfalls: The Nonadvocacy Stance

Since most anthropologists tend to identify with their community, we tend to be advocates for particular groups. The extension goal, on the other hand, is to remain neutral as much as possible—to provide information, to educate, to bring groups together to mediate conflicts. To take the side of one group may alienate other groups, and in the long run may make the agent and process less effective for all concerned.

It is ironic that the "traditional" agricultural extension role in reality encourages agents to be advocates for their commodity groups (e.g., fruit growers, wheat farmers, oyster growers, lobster harvesters) somewhat as anthropologists are advocates for their community groups. In addition, much of the activity of agents, from providing information to policy-making bodies to mediating between user groups, affects policy and political decisions. Nonadvocacy is more of a theory than an actuality.

Extension work with constituent groups in coastal areas is no longer the exclusive realm of those who have degrees in fisheries biology or experience in commercial fishing. The population explosion in coastal areas and increasing multiple uses of the coast have broadened the work of marine extension. This means that there will be greater demand for people who can work with multiple interest groups and who understand marine affairs from a generalist perspective.

The Two Functions of Ethnocentrism in the Process of Modernization: The Tibetan Case

Shengde Zhai

As one of five Chinese ethnographers speaking at the 1989 meeting of the Society for Applied Anthropology in Santa Fe, New Mexico, Zhai Shengde attracted local media and public attention, as well as interest from fellow anthropologists, with his talk on the politically sensitive topic of ethnocentrism and modernization in Tibet. Ethnocentrism, in his view, preserves valuable elements of cultural tradition but at the same time inhibits material and social progress by preventing the adoption of modern elements from other cultures. Zhai would strike a balance between preservation and modernization. People need to maintain their cultural roots as a matter of survival, he argues, but reason must be used to moderate strong ethnic emotion. Like his Western counterparts, he advocates a kind of cultural relativity or universalistic perspective on humanity in which people learn to respect other cultures. While recognizing mistakes made by the Chinese government in the recent past, Zhai does not venture into discussing the merits of Tibetan political independence. With regard to ethnic relations in Tibet, however, he proposes that the Tibetans reduce their cultural exclusiveness and the Han (the dominant Chinese ethnic group) show more respect for Tibetan traditions.   J. A. Y.

A number of scholars have become interested in the intrinsic conflict between emotion and reason that has noticeably shaped recent history. The effects of uncontrolled emotion often are far greater than those of the moderating force of reason, as illustrated by the Sino-Soviet polemics of the 1960s, ten years of chaos during China's Cultural Revolution (which was like a modern God-making movement), and eight years of the Iran-Iraq war. The response to Salman Rushdie's book *Satanic Verses* is a new case in point; it

---

Zhai Shengde is a Tibetologist and was Vice-Director of the Institute for Nationality Studies of the Chinese Academy of Social Sciences when this article was first published.

Originally published as part of a special section on "Applied Anthropology in China," guest edited by John A. Young, in *Practicing Anthropology* 13,1(1991):19-21, this article has been edited and abridged for republication here.

shows that the use of reason, which sprouted from ancient society and was consciously developed in modern Europe, has not really triumphed over emotion. Thus, we must begin now to make better use of reason to examine the relationship between reason itself and emotion. The purpose of this discussion is to promote the development of both reason and emotion to better serve humanity by bringing to light the emotional basis of human reason and the rational basis of human emotion.

Max Weber, in his book *The Protestant Ethic and the Spirit of Capitalism,* remarked that there must be an invisible spiritual force behind any social movement and that the spiritual force must stem from the sociocultural background of the people involved. Shared emotion transforms this spiritual force into physical strength for the achievement of social justice and the advancement of human culture and civilization. Human emotion not only has a psychological dimension but also has social, historical, and cultural dimensions. Consequently, research on emotion has theoretical importance for understanding human behavior, revealing a new perspective on the logic of cultural development, and applying what is learned to solve human problems.

Ethnocentrism as a Human Emotion

One of the most important tasks for the anthropological and ethnological sciences at present is to conduct research on the social and cultural context of emotional expression. A major purpose of such research should be to bring to light the inexorable trend of historic development from ethnocentrism to cultural relativity. This research should also promote mutual understanding between communities of people with different historical and cultural backgrounds living in different natural and social environments.

Human emotion has a complex relationship to social structure when various levels of stratification and different subgroups are taken into account. Emotion is bound up with nationalism, patriotism, ethnic consciousness arising from sharing a common culture and/or membership in a particular group, class consciousness based on economic status and interest, and religious sectarianism based on the common objects of worship and common beliefs. Individual feelings are merely the cellular form of the broader categories of emotion mentioned above.

Among the various kinds of socially expressed emotion, the most conspicuous is that evoked by ethnic consciousness (ethnocentrism). This is because an ethnic group is the carrier of a culture, and the emotional attachment to it is an element of culture that has strong historical continuity, stability, and sense of exclusiveness. *Minzu*, the term for ethnic group in Chinese, refers to a relatively stable community of people whose identity was shaped in the process of history, and who share a common group name, a common origin, a common language, a common historic destiny, a common in-group consciousness and emotional character, and a common psychological predisposition or ethos associated with a common culture.

All cultures have a core, a spiritual or ideological foundation, which includes traditional philosophy, religious beliefs, social norms, and ethical principles. These features associated with the core have a stronger tendency to influence people than do the material and social aspects of culture, but they do not operate fully according to reason; emotion associated with spirituality and ideology is a powerful motivating force behind a variety of behaviors. Thus, it can be said that emotion is the soul of a culture.

Ethnocentrism can be defined as shared attitudes based on common understanding or perception of things regardless of whether they are objectively in the best interest of the group. These attitudes usually have external expressions which the people of other ethnic groups can observe and judge. However, since emotion is also a mental phenomenon, it is very difficult for cultural outsiders to gain an exact understanding of it. We have not yet found a perfectly rigorous method for the study of human emotion.

Anthropologists and ethnologists undertaking research on ethnocentrism must immerse themselves among the people, study their history and language, and closely observe their culture. In the study of ethnocentrism, it is necessary to invite scholars from the ethnic group itself to take part in the research. In addition, we must adopt a relativistic perspective towards other cultures because each cultural characteristic and attitude has its own historical rationality.

I respect the continuity of cultural development. Nonetheless, I also maintain that by no means can historical rationality be used to justify contemporary irrationality. Unquestionably, the development of culture and human emotion should be advanced to a higher stage. In particular, I am delighted to see that the old form of Chinese culture is in the process of undergoing basic change.

At present the world is still composed of a multitude of ethnic groups. Distinctions between ethnic groups play an important role in everyday political and social life and have wide-ranging repercussions. On one hand, our world is enriched by bright and colorful ethnic styles and customs; on the other, it is burdened by complex barriers in the relations between disparate groups.

Nevertheless, because of the development of modern transportation facilities, sophisticated communication technology, and expanded news media, social life is becoming increasingly internationalized. Common values and common ideals based on universal feeling for humanity have begun to transcend cultural differences. Over the past several years dialogue has begun to replace antagonism in the world, and today the peace movement has become part of the mainstream in world affairs. In short, a general trend toward cultural generality is taking shape among various ethnic groups around the world.

We refer to the process or result of adopting traits or patterns of another culture as "acculturation," and when the adoptions are mutual or intracultural, then we use the term "transculturation." In either case ethnocentrism plays an important catalytic role, as it either accelerates or retards the above-mentioned process depending on the particular conditions. Sometimes it can produce positive and negative expressions simultaneously—that is, it can have two opposing functions.

Ethnocentrism in Tibet

For a long time Tibet was shrouded in mystery, and people regarded it as largely unknowable. To uncover the veil from the "roof of the world" Chinese ethnologists, linguists, historians, and specialists on Tibetan Buddhism carried out a large-scale investigation of Tibetan culture, including traditional socioeconomic structure, language, history, and religion. This research began in 1956 and continued through the early 1960s. It culminated in the publication of several large volumes and other monographs, all based on a vast number of field reports. Several films on Tibetan serfdom also were produced before the democratic reforms of 1959. Through my long-term contact with Tibetans and analysis of many of the above investigative reports, I know that the Tibetan people have very strong ethnic pride, which both derives from and continues to reinforce a rich historical tradition, the maintenance of common identity, and a well-defined sense of purpose.

The emotional predispositions of Tibetan people are strongly influenced by the philosophy and ethics of Lamaism. According to the teachings of *karma*, they do not regard happiness and suffering in this life as important. Most Tibetans wholeheartedly seek happiness in the next life. This belief makes the people very tolerant and good-natured while Tibetan society remains short of the initiative needed to develop its poor economy.

Traditional Tibetan society is culturally very conservative and resistant to modern civilization. Even the effort by the Kuomintang officials to build a school in Lhasa during the 1940s could not win the support of the local government. The traditional system of theocracy, based on the belief in reincarnation of living Buddhas, continually reinforces the religious feelings and traditional customs of the Tibetan people.

Today the Tibetans still greatly respect their Lamas and the reincarnated living Buddhas at different levels in the religious hierarchy, especially the Dalai Lama and the Bainqen Erdini. Before 1959, the Dalai Lama was both the highest religious leader and the highest administrative official of Tibet. Now the 14th Dalai Lama, although in exile, is still a personalized god in the minds of Tibetan peasants and herdsmen and a significant ethnic symbol in the minds of the Tibetan intellectuals. It is very important for government policy makers at national and local levels to have a clear understanding of this cultural reality; otherwise their policies may offend the feelings of the Tibetan people.

Tibetans have a strong in-group consciousness and tend to be cautious and reserved toward outsiders. At present, Tibet has a population of 2.07 million, among which 1.98 million are Tibetans; another 1.8 million Tibetans live in Qinghai, Gansu, Sichuan, and Yunnan provinces. Other nationalities in Tibet, such as the Han, Moslems from Qinghai and Gansu, the Monbas, and the Lhobas, have a combined population of only ninety thousand. Nevertheless, some Tibetans have expressed worry about the prospect of assimilation. This fear reflects both the strong sentiment that Tibetans feel towards their own culture and their suspicion of outsiders. To dispel the distrust it is necessary for the government to respect and support the efforts of the Tibetan people to preserve their own language and writing system, their traditional customs, their religious system, their literature, art and folkways, and their autonomous political rights.

The ethnocentrism of Tibetans reinforced internal solidarity and engendered pride within the Tibetan community throughout history, and these factors have played a very important role in maintaining the stability of Tibetan society. During the past eleven centuries no large-scale class war ever took place in Tibet. Such stability was beneficial for cultural accumulation. For this reason the cultural heritage of the Tibetan people, which includes their architecture, literature, art, and medicine, is an important component of the cultural treasure-house of humankind.

Of course, internal solidarity and pride also reinforced the exclusiveness of Tibetan society. It was very difficult for any modern scientific achievement or advanced technology to enter and find acceptance, and so it seems that the advance of modern civilization has had nothing to do with "the roof of the world." From this point of view, exclusiveness was obviously not beneficial for either the development of Tibet or the welfare of the Tibetan people.

Today Tibet is open to the outside world, and an increasing number of Tibetans have been affected by this change. A modern educational system has grown out of nothing. Some Tibetans who have bachelor's, master's, and doctor's degrees now are able to educate and to choose between the old and the new. It is important, beyond doubt, to preserve the valuable tradition created in the past and to pass on this tradition to the next generation—to preserve the Tibetan heritage and cultural identity. If the Tibetans neglect their cultural tradition and concentrate only on pursuing economic interests, then like stunted grass they will lack strong roots for full growth. If, however, Tibetan society is completely preoccupied with tradition, it will stagnate and cannot expect to advance or develop to keep pace with changes in the modern world.

Thus, Tibetan intellectuals face the challenge of how to combine emotion and reason. Today the globe seems to be growing smaller because of the progress of modern science and technology. All ethnic groups must be linked to the rest of the world, and they must justify their existence and evaluate their societal objectives by assessing their contribution to the development of humankind.

The Future of Tibet

As far as the future is concerned, the traditional religious system of Tibet restricts the capability of the people to advance. Their traditional philosophy and associated ethnic emotion make it very difficult to acquire beneficial elements from other cultures. This is one reason why the living standard and educational system in Tibet still lag behind.

I define nationalism as the ideology associated with ethnic consciousness that mobilizes people to promote the unity, independence, freedom, and development of their own ethnic group. Some Tibetans living abroad now are appealing to nationalism to arouse hope and high-spirited emotion by advocating the "independence" of Tibet. Here, I do not intend to discuss how reasonable or realistic this possibility might be, but I would like to express my views on nationalism which is an outgrowth of ethnocentrism.

It is not a fault, but a virtue, to love one's own ethnic group. However, once this love goes beyond a certain limit, it becomes blind and gives rise to illusory perceptions, idolatry, and an exclusive ethnic chauvinism. Without being tempered by thought and reason, nationalism will certainly deviate from the right path and become a harmful tool of a self-indulgent group. I believe that nationalism today should become a well-reasoned ideology seeking the development of the whole of humanity.

Today, Tibet faces two major tasks. First, the region must speed up economic development with special attention to religious believers. If this can be accomplished, an improved living standard will have a calming effect. Second, the Chinese government must carefully examine its policies regarding Tibet and evaluate both positive and negative experiences. After the democratic reforms were carried out in 1959, China embarked on a wrong political path, unavoidably causing a series of grave mistakes that offended the feelings and pride of the Tibetan people. Since the end of the Cultural Revolution, the government has corrected some mistakes, but some losses are irreparable. During recent years the economy of Tibet has developed fairly rapidly, and consequently, the living standard of the people has improved. I believe the future of Tibet is bright, although more time is needed to solve some difficult problems.

Anthropology of Development vs. Development Anthropology: Mediating the Forester-Farmer Relationship in Pakistan

Michael R. Dove

Social forestry and development anthropology are areas of research and extension critical to sustaining the world's growing population. Anthropology has much to contribute to these efforts. Working on a team contract to USAID in Pakistan, Michael Dove provided research insights and used persuasion and managerial skill to influence the nature and interpretation of national forestry policy. His research provided credibility for the shift of policy focus from state lands and large landowners growing trees for profit to small farmers cultivating trees for household needs. When he discovered that state foresters' incorrect assumptions and long-standing patron-client relationships made them part of the "problem" in implementing the new national forest policy, he used innovative means to bring local farmers' knowledge to the foresters and to change the ways foresters relate to farmers. To be effective, Dove argues, anthropologists need not only to involve themselves in development but also to study the process, offices, individuals, and policies that implement development.   S. J. F.

The Forest Service of Pakistan has concerned itself since colonial times largely with the production, protection, and extraction of trees in the nation's state forests. The only contact that its officers had with most farmers (except large landowners, with whom they had traditional patron-client relations) was to levy punishments for violations of forest laws or gather fees for the use of forest resources. In recent years, the state forests have declined in area and

Michael R Dove, who received the 1989 Praxis Award for the project described in this article, is Professor of Social Ecology in the School of Forestry and Environmental Studies at Yale University (205 Prospect Street, New Haven, CT 06511-2189).

Originally published in *Practicing Anthropology* 13,2(1991):21-25, this article has been edited and abridged for republication here. The analysis was written during the course of fellowships at the East-West Center and benefited from the comments of Carol Carpenter. For an update on some of the issues disucssed in this article, see M. Dove, "The Existential Status of the Pakistani Farmer: A Study of Institutional Factors in Development," *Ethnology* 13,4(1994):331-351.

importance, and the need to increase on-farm supplies of tree products and halt resource degradation has increased. As a result, the Government of Pakistan, with the assistance of the U.S. Agency for International Development (USAID), decided to change the basic direction of the Forest Service—away from state lands to private lands, away from commercial to subsistence or mixed subsistence/commercial production, and thus away from the rural elite to the small farmer. The vehicle chosen to accomplish this was the bilaterally funded Forestry Planning and Development Project, Pakistan's first major social forestry project.

The mission assigned me as project anthropologist was to assist the Forest Service to make this transition to a public service agency by helping it to identify and communicate with its intended clientele, the small farmers of Pakistan. It was initially assumed that my work would focus on ways of "motivating" the farmers, based on the then-widespread belief within the Forest Service and USAID that small farmers were inherently ill-disposed towards trees and tree cultivation. My field research soon revealed that this was largely a myth, and that the real constraint to the development of farm forestry was that many foresters were ill-disposed towards working with small farmers. A large part of my mission shifted, therefore, from motivating farmers to plant trees to motivating foresters to help farmers plant trees, and from communicating forestry technology to farmers to communicating farmers' attitudes and needs to foresters.

The Role of the Project Anthropologist

As the project anthropologist I was one of four long-term, expatriate experts on a technical assistance team assembled by the Windrock International Institute for Agricultural Development under contract to USAID. The other expatriate experts were a farm forester, a research forester, and a training expert. On the Government of Pakistan's side, a special project cell was established in the federal office of the Inspector General of Forests to provide overall supervision and guidance, and individual project offices were established in each of the country's four provinces to carry out field operations. My direct counterpart in all activities was a Deputy Inspector General of Forests in the federal project cell. I was assisted in my work by one full-time and eight part-time Pakistani sociologists and by thirteen farmers hired to assist in village-level data gathering.

The specific goals of the project anthropologist were (1) to carry out a national program of research to establish a baseline for farm forestry in Pakistan, monitor farmer response to the project, and promote research relevant to farmers' needs within the Forest Service; (2) to assist in developing practical extension strategies based on this research, with special attention to the involvement of women and the landless; and (3) to assist in the development of socially-relevant curricula at the Pakistan Forest Institute and to develop in the forest service generally an appreciation of the utility of a social science perspective. A project-wide goal, to which I also devoted a good deal of my time, was to develop a national policy to better manage the forest and tree resources of Pakistan.

My approach to the first goal, involving a national program of research, was to carry out a series of surveys in the three project provinces of Baluchistan, the Northwest Frontier Province, and the Punjab. There were five stages to this research, each more focused than—and to some extent based on—the results of the previous stages: (1) group interviews on basic village characteristics (in 118 villages); (2) interviews on basic household characteristics in 1132 households; (3) in-depth interviews on farm ecology and economics in 589 households; (4) in-depth interviews on village ecology with 40 village groups and village religious leaders; and, finally, (5) daily monitoring of farm dynamics for 18 months in 13 households.

I adapted anthropological techniques for analyzing and reporting on these data to the time constraints, pragmatic interests, and expository style of government forest officers. Ten timely, succinct reports were issued, focusing on identifying the proper clientele for project services, describing their needs, and predicting their responses. Highlights of these reports were the presentation of complex data in easily-understood, computer-generated graphs. One graph, for example, showed that interest in planting trees for use as fuel is uniform among Pakistani farmers, regardless of farm size. This finding refuted the widely-held belief in social forestry that farmers (especially better-off farmers) were not interested in planting trees for use as fuel. Another highlight of the reports (for me, if not my intended audience) was the use of the prose of the biological sciences (for the benefit of the Pakistani foresters) and the U.S. government (for the benefit of USAID). This expository style differs from that of anthropology in its emphasis on brevity, use of numbers rather than prose, and implication of authoritativeness.

I used these reports as the basis for developing extension strategies, which was another goal of the project anthropologist. This included preparation with my Forest Service counterpart of a manual on social forestry extension, emphasizing simple techniques for contacting and communicating with common farmers. The social and political structure of Pakistani society normally rules out any contact between visiting government officers and common villagers. Many foresters initially regarded meetings with local officials as the beginning and end of their "extension" activities, with the focus of these meetings being on what the Forest Service could do for the officials. In our manual we emphasized that meetings with local officials are just the beginning and that their focus should be on what the officials can do for the project. In addition, we strongly encouraged the foresters to contact local farmers themselves, rather than relying on local officials to set up meetings. Meetings arranged by local officials are invariably limited to a tiny minority of economically and politically influential farmers, those who have the least need of extension services.

With the same counterpart, I established an Urdu-language quarterly, *Farm Forestry Newsletter*, focusing not only on communication to farmers of simple, useful information, but also on communication to foresters of the farmers' own skills and knowledge. Foresters tended to be slow to appreciate this knowledge because of a cognitive block against the perception of tree cultivation in nonconventional patterns, locations, and strategies. For example, the most common farm forestry system in Pakistan, the thorn fence—incorporating a wide variety of trees, bushes, and grasses (some wild, some managed, and some planted) variously used for fuel, fencing, fodder and timber—is invisible to most foresters. In each issue of the newsletter we highlighted traditional practices of tree cultivation and implicitly made the point that the farmers knew how to cultivate trees before the Forest Service came along, that some of this knowledge is unknown to the Service, and that there are things that the forest officers could learn from—as well as teach to—the farmers.

A notable example of farmer knowledge is the traditional system of lopping and pruning, which is part of a sophisticated management system for maximizing desired impacts and products of trees and minimizing undesired impacts and products. One widespread custom is lopping trees just before the winter wheat planting in order to reduce shading of the wheat seedlings and energize the soil and at the same time ameliorate a seasonal shortage of fuel and fodder. I discovered that this management system is based on an indigenous system of humoral classification of trees and tree shade, the understanding of which should offer promising new perspectives on research and extension concerning the critical tree-crop interface. (See M. Dove, "Perceptions of Tree Shade among Farmers in Pakistan," in M. Dove and C. Carpenter, eds., *Sociology of Natural Resources in Pakistan and Adjoining Countries* [Lahore: Vanguard Press, 1992] pp. 98-107.)

These efforts to stimulate a flow of knowledge from farmer to forester reflected my concern for institutional development, the third goal assigned to the project anthropologist. My efforts in this regard included co-sponsoring an international seminar (with the Office of the Inspector General of Forests) on the need for a more people-oriented forestry policy in Pakistan. I also co-authored with this same office a review of past national forest policies and a draft of the new policy. I used anthropological techniques of textual analysis to reveal the implicit structure of past policies, which produced some novel and useful perspectives for policy revision. For example, I showed that past forestry policies in Pakistan have relied most heavily on planning or organizational changes to attain policy goals and least heavily on study or research.

For the Pakistan Forest Institute, I developed a syllabus for a course (in the M.Sc. curriculum) in "Rural Sociology/Anthropology" based on South Asian case studies of the use of anthropology and rural sociology to solve extension problems in natural resource use. I subsequently co-edited a textbook, *Sociology of Natural Resources in Pakistan and Adjoining Countries* (cited above). [In the eight years since this article was published, Pakistan's Forestry Planning and Development Project and its infrastructure have dissolved—with the end of foreign funding—and internal literature on the project has become inaccessible, leaving only this and other academic publications as a legacy of this applied project—a condition of institutional amnesia. Anthropologists are starting to pay more attention to questions of writing and audience: who benefits from our writing for one audience versus another; who, indeed, is served by institutional amnesia versus institutional memory? These are the sorts of questions that will lead the next generation of practicing anthropologists toward better practice and better memory. M. R. D.]

Use and Impact of Anthropology in the Project

I drew on ecological anthropology and ethnoscience to analyze Pakistan's farming systems, recommend directions for forestry extension, and prepare extension tools like the farmer newsletter. I looked at what tree species the farmers were already cultivating; how, where, and why they were cultivating them; and what the principal perceived constraints were. One finding, for example, was that farmers decide when to plant trees based not only on climatic conditions, but also on the availability of labor, a constraint that the foresters had not previously had to consider (when planting trees with hired labor in state forests).

I drew on the traditional tools of social and economic anthropology to correlate variables of interest to the Forest Service, such as willingness to plant seedlings, with important differentiating variables in rural Pakistani society, like land tenure or access to irrigation. I then identified for the Forest Service the household types likely to be most receptive to extension efforts, as well as those where the net impact of these efforts would likely be greatest. I established that landless tenants possess some traditional rights to trees, and that rural women play a major role in the production and consumption of tree products, and I accordingly recommended an increased extension focus on both groups.

I attempted to meld the anthropological focus on local-level dynamics and perceptions—which I believe is essential to revealing farmer needs—with the short time-frame and broad scope of a national development project. I did this through use of open-ended questionnaires emphasizing local perceptions and knowledge and strategic mixing of sample size and interview focus. I also utilized the novel method of having farmers keep records of their own activities to provide the in-depth and long-term data normally used by anthropologists but typically missing from development projects. The application of

180

anthropological methods was not limited to farmers alone: I utilized techniques of unstructured interviewing, with senior officials as my expert informants, to produce the first draft of the new national forestry policy. This proved to be a very successful exercise and suggests a new avenue for contributions by anthropologists—drawing on our special skills in eliciting and structuring informants' beliefs—to development and policy formation.

Of most importance perhaps, I drew on anthropological tools for institutional analysis to help mediate a conflict over the basic philosophy of the project. The explicit design of the project—to assist small farmers to cultivate trees to meet household needs—initially met with resistance from some forest officers who contended that there were no small farmers in Pakistan, and if there were, they would not be interested in planting trees. These officers pressured for a redirection of the project to the cultivation by large farmers of block tree plantations for the market. My documentation of the interest of small farmers in tree cultivation, and hence of the practicality of the project design, contributed to a subsequent decision by the Forest Service to discourage efforts to redirect the project towards a market-oriented project for large farmers and refocus attention on improving implementation of the existing project.

After three and one-half years there was abundant evidence that the value of these anthropological inputs was appreciated within the Pakistan Forest Service. The sample and methodology of the base-line study was adopted for use in two major Forest Service research projects; reports on the results of this study were accepted for publication in the *Pakistan Journal of Forestry* (the foremost publication of forestry research in Pakistan), the first ever by an anthropologist; in the revision of the national forestry policy in which I participated, social forestry was elevated to a position equal to traditional commercial or protection forestry; and the federal government unilaterally requested USAID to extend the position of project anthropologist beyond the original commitment. This represented an about-face from the start of my appointment, which one provincial forestry office had attempted to block and which the USAID project officer had called an "experiment." (This starting position—not at "go," but at some point considerably behind it—is, unfortunately, still the norm rather than the exception for anthropologists working in international development.)

Anthropology of Development vs. Development Anthropology

The most stimulating work that I did in Pakistan, and the work that drew most heavily on my anthropological training, involved the analysis not of peasant behavior and beliefs, but of the behavior and beliefs of government officials. It was not small farmers, but government officials that posed the principal development challenge in my project. This is often the case in rural development, yet the belief systems of government officials in developing countries are rarely studied by anthropologists (or, indeed, by any other discipline). Why is this?

I suggest that anthropologists do not study government officials (at least not in developmental contexts), do not treat them as the anthropological "other," because to do so is to call into question the conventional perceptions of development. To treat the *object* of development, the farmer, as "other" is fine; but to treat the administering official as "other," to study (and hence implicitly question the basis for) their perceptions, is to acknowledge that there is a subjective element in the management of development programs. Institutional and personal aversion to making this acknowledgment has contributed to a tradition of study in which the anthropological "other" is firmly located outside of government, development, and aid offices.

This positioning of the "other" in nongovernmental contexts is part of a more general effort in post-World War II anthropology to draw a boundary between research and application, selecting nonapplied topics for basic research, and then attempting to apply the insights gained to development problems. The result is a theoretical anthropological literature that has little to say about development, and a (gray) development literature that has little to say about anthropological theory.

The conclusion to be drawn from this unfortunate schism is that relevance and theory are mutually developed not by the application of research findings to relevant topics, but by the selection, in the first instance, of relevant topics for research. An "applied anthropology" is good for neither application nor theory (recognition of which is reflected in the use of "practicing" instead of "applied" in this journal's title). Many of the most relevant topics involve the development process itself; the use of anthropology within development must not, therefore, preclude the study *of* development by anthropology.

In fact, the development process should be one of the foremost topics of anthropological study. This is one of three lessons that any anthropologist with an interest in "praxis" should bear in mind. The second is that a sincere commitment to the first lesson will inevitably, as in any such self-reflective exercise, create conflict with some colleagues and counterparts. The third lesson is that the practicing anthropologist must be willing to assist in any activity, whether strictly anthropological in nature or not; this will provide the data needed to honor lesson number one, and it will provide the political capital needed to survive lesson two.

The study of the development process (as opposed to the study of the objects of this process) implies that the anthropologist has an agenda of his or her own, over and above the particular tasks assigned within the context of the development project. The existence of a personal agenda raises a number of problematic ethical issues, but so does the absence of a personal agenda. To bring one's own agenda to a development project is to bring one's own moral conscience. There is nothing in recent development history to suggest that this is not needed, and much to suggest that it is.

Applying Anthropology to American Indian Correctional Concerns

Elizabeth S. Grobsmith

*Though anthropology might have had its beginnings among con-
quered peoples, seldom have anthropologists worked among truly captive people (work in World War II Japanese American relocation centers
being an important exception). In this essay on her work with American
Indian prisoners, Elizabeth Grobsmith lays bare the special advantages
and problems of anthropological intimacy in such a setting. Grobsmith's
utter openness about so much—gender relations, the stigma of being an
anthropologist, the value of being an "expert," trust and mistrust, ignorance and knowledge—is refreshing yet profound. She shows how the
many roles of anthropologists—old-fashioned collector of ethnological
esoterica, small-group ethnographer, teacher, counselor, cultural broker, and expert witness—converge in successful practice of anthropology among American Indian prisoners. The practitioner must understand not only historical and contemporary American Indian cultures
but also the institutional and occupational cultures of prisons, courts,
lawyers, and various kinds of "service providers."* J. A. P.

Opportunities abound for the application of anthropological methods, techniques, and data in addressing issues relative to incarceration. Over the last
sixteen years, I have worked in a variety of capacities with and on behalf of
Native American inmates incarcerated in the Nebraska Department of Correctional Services. My roles as teacher, consultant, trainer, and expert witness
have evolved over the years, in response to the changing concerns of the Indian prisoners.

In Nebraska, Indian inmates represent about 4 percent of the prison population, which is disproportionately high compared to the 1 percent of Nebraska
population that is Indian. As their understanding of their rights to religious
freedom has increased, so has their demand for anthropological consultation.
I receive letters from Indian prisoners throughout the United States who are

Elizabeth S. Grobsmith is Dean of the College of Letters, Arts and Sciences at the University of
Colorado at Colorado Springs (1420 Austin Bluffs Parkway, Colorado Springs, CO 80933-7150;
(719) 262-4550; fax: (719) 262-4200; <egrobsmi@mail.uccs.edu>).

Originally published as part of a special section on "Addressing Issues in Criminal Justice," guest
edited by Irene Glasser and Livingston D. Sutro, in *Practicing Anthropology* 14,3(1992):5-8.

184

seeking similar professional expertise. Becoming such a resource person can easily turn into a full-time job. Furthermore, Native Americans are only one of a number of ethnically diverse groups within the prison population that could benefit from the work of anthropologists.

Teaching

My work with Indian prisoners began in 1975 when Native American inmates were awarded a Consent Decree by the U.S. District Court in Nebraska which enabled them to practice their religion and culture behind the walls. One of the first provisions of the decree that Indian prisoners wished to implement was access to education, so the prison, in negotiation with the State of Nebraska Indian Commission, provided academic programs in American Indian Studies.

Teaching in such a program is a rather different experience from teaching large groups of undergraduates at a typical college campus. The educational preparation of Indian prisoner students is quite variable; offering a college course may be unrealistic when members of the class are from nonliterate societies and have dropped out of school by the third grade. Indian prisoners are also rather different constituents from ordinary college students in that they may wish to hear more about their own tribal heritage rather than about other traditions, and they are not afraid to say so. This can be an even greater problem when the number of different tribes represented in a single class may be ten or more.

Being a non-Indian anthropologist carries with it some genuine hazards, including being accused of exploitation and having to deal with sensitive, volatile issues such as religious beliefs being presented from the perspective of a non-native outsider. Another challenge was being a female in a maximum security prison. While there were some disrupters, the majority of inmates behaved in a most gentlemanly manner. This included one occasion when all the electricity in the prison went out and I stood in front of fifty maximum-custody male inmates in complete darkness for twenty minutes. While this might appear to be a very threatening situation, in actuality, the inmates were so desperate for educational services that any outsider offering such a service would have been greatly protected.

Teaching under these circumstances does leave something to be desired, as we are not accustomed to constant criticism, class disruption, and challenges, if not outright disagreement with what we are teaching. After two semesters, I decided that it was time to give someone else the learning experience of teaching Indian prisoners about their history and culture in prison. Though difficult, the role of teacher is extremely important, for prisoners are acutely in need of education, and they stand to profit both from an academic perspective and from the increased self-respect which education affords. Their culture gains credibility by being the subject of a prison college class.

Consulting for Prison Authorities

The Consent Decree led to increased tension between inmates and correctional officers. Indian inmates now had opportunities to conduct religious ceremonies in prison, and guards encountered unusual and therefore suspicious religious paraphernalia and procedures. Sage, cedar, and sweetgrass burned at ceremonies and during private prayer can easily be mistaken for the smell of marijuana by the untrained. The Sacred Pipe, wrapped carefully with special religious articles, requires special protocol in being unwrapped and used and poses a challenge to normal inspection procedures. Healing ceremonies conducted by medicine men and women from outside the prison, sometimes in a totally blackened room as required in Lakota Sioux ceremonies, and the taking of skin sacrifices with scalpels or exacto blades understandably makes guards nervous.

The contribution of the anthropologist can be great here, serving as consultant to correctional authorities and guiding them as to the legitimacy and meaning of these religious practices. Absence of regular training programs and turnover of employees result in ignorance and insensitivity on the part of correctional officers and continual mistakes which prisoners deeply resent. Guards may be unaware of how "count" in prison can be conducted at a sweat lodge and at what points in the ceremony the "doors" (flaps, tarps) to the lodge may—or may not—be opened. Inmates are offended by accusations of drug use at their sacred sweat lodge grounds and would rather refuse a urinalysis and suffer an automatic conviction of "guilty" than humiliate themselves by consenting.

Anthropological expertise is of benefit not because the inmates are incapable themselves of explaining their traditions. Rather, the use of an "outside expert" or consultant affords legitimacy to the entire process. The consultant attests to the fact that these traditions are real—that they exist outside the prison walls and have not just been invented to inconvenience the prison system. Greater dependence on such consultation could only improve prisoner-guard relations, and it could potentially reduce the involvement of prisons in continual litigation.

Another area in which anthropological consultation can be beneficial is in dealing with alcoholism among the inmate population. Intake procedures normally ask very limited questions about personal histories, and an inmate's criminal record may be but a skeletal overview of involvement in a criminal career. Nebraska prison data estimate that 40 percent of Indian inmates have a chemical dependency problem. On the other hand, my 1986-87 interviews with forty-five inmates in the Nebraska Department of Corrections (a 56 percent sample) revealed that 100 percent of Indian prisoners claimed to be chemically dependent. The actual involvement of alcohol or drugs in offense commission was unknown by correctional authorities for nearly 74 percent of Indian inmates; in my research, I discovered that between 91 and 100 percent

186

of offenses were alcohol or drug-related. (See Elizabeth S. Grobsmith, "The Relationship between Substance Abuse and Crime among Native American Inmates in the Nebraska Department of Correctional Service," *Human Organization* 48,4[1989]:285-298.)

These data should have a tremendous impact on the estimate of services required by and for this population. Anthropological consultation on data gathering procedures used during the intake process can upgrade the quality of inmate intake profile data, which in turn can reinforce the prison's request for resources to develop treatment programs.

Anthropological consultation can also improve the design of treatment programs. Underuse of prison programs concerns prison mental health staff who do not understand why their programs are not popular among Native American inmates. Anthropologists have worked extensively with Indian populations, and they recognize the need to accommodate Indian religious and cultural practices in the design of alcohol and drug treatment programs. Native Americans share—or perceive that they share—certain cultural bases for alcoholism; consequently, addressing the causes and cure must reflect an understanding of Indian values and culture. Indian clients in prisons express hesitation to self-disclose unless they are assured the safety of relating exclusively to other Indians. Usually this means separate Indian therapy groups, which prisons hesitate to employ. In addition, incorporation of traditional spiritual elements such as the sweat lodge and use of the pipe can have a significant impact on the degree of commitment to rehabilitation Indian inmates are willing to make.

The consequence of ignoring Native America prisoners' needs is the ultimate return of most Indian inmates to incarceration. A follow-up of the forty-five inmates in my original study showed that within three years of their release from prison, two-thirds either had returned to prison or were confined in a city or county jail following an alcohol-related offense. (See Elizabeth S. Grobsmith and Jennifer Dam, "The Revolving Door: Substance Abuse Treatment and Criminal Sanctions for Native American Offenders," *Journal of Substance Abuse* 2,4[1990]:405-425.)

Consulting for the Parole Board

Anthropological consulting can be even more effective as inmates prepare to seek release from prison. They typically face a parole board which, like the correctional system, has little knowledge of or sensitivity to Indian cultural approaches to rehabilitation. For example, the Nebraska Board of Parole commonly requires that an offender who has a history of substance abuse attend Alcoholics Anonymous (AA), but the general rejection of AA by the Indian prison population makes such a requirement meaningless. While attendance may result, sincere involvement in addressing one's alcoholism cannot take place in an environment which is distrusted.

Native Americans are, once again, far more willing to involve themselves in the therapeutic environment when clients are exclusively Native American, an option which is often available at urban Indian centers. Outpatient therapy available at specific Native American treatment centers is also a far superior option to attending AA in a "generic" group with which Indians fail to identify. Most cities with even small Indian populations have some Indian treatment programs or centers, or at least an Indian counselor. In some cities, Indian AA meetings are available which incorporate principles of AA but in a less Judeo-Christian way. Anthropologists' understanding of native perspectives on alcohol treatment can be invaluable in helping to implement systems which inmates *will* use and which are more likely to be effective.

One step is to educate the parole board about Native American perspectives. Some members of the Nebraska Board of Parole have been very receptive to such ideas and have even attended Native American prison club functions to discuss the parole process with Indian inmates. I served as liaison in this process, bringing the two parties into the first dialogue they have ever had and giving inmates the opportunity to express their preferences for referrals in the alcohol rehabilitation process.

I have also served as cultural interpreter or broker and have used ethnographic documentation to support Native American requests. For example, an Indian inmate wanted to attend the funeral of his grandfather, but prison and parole regulations prohibit inmates from attending funerals of anyone but an "immediate" family member. Anthropologists can provide cross-cultural perspective on the extended family and the frequency with which Native Americans are raised in extended family networks or by grandparents alone. As another example, Indian prisoners sometimes request to attend rituals such as the Vision Quest or Sun Dance. In Nebraska inmates with minimum custody are eligible to attend ceremonies away from the prison, but permission to attend these activities is normally denied Native Americans. If parole authorities understood that for most American Indians in prison, attending a Vision Quest or Sun Dance is a principal avenue for alcohol rehabilitation, it would hardly seem reasonable that they would deny such access. The provision of ethnographic information to a parole board serves to educate, and also to lend credibility and thus support to inmate requests.

Serving as Expert Witness

When prison authorities continue to refuse Indian inmates access to the religious practices which inmates believe are within their Constitutionally guaranteed rights, they file grievances and lawsuits. In these instances, there are many ways anthropologists can be and are involved. First, and basic to all positive settlements, is the education of attorneys with reference to Indian prison religious practices. All suits filed by Nebraska Indian inmates are reviewed by the Chief Judge of the U.S. District Court for the District of Nebraska and a law firm appointed by the judge. If the judge deems the grievance relevant to the original Consent Decree and worthy of being litigated, the case is assigned to an attorney. The attorneys have rarely had any experience with Native American inmates, however, and generally know nothing of Indian culture. On the other hand, the Nebraska Attorney General's Office, which always conducts the correctional system's defense, has excellent knowledge of Indian prison practices.

Attorneys who find themselves in this position are desperate for assistance, and they are extremely grateful for anthropological involvement, both to educate them and ultimately to serve as expert witness in the legal proceedings. They gladly petition the court for expert witness fees to help the scholar prepare material in support of the case.

But getting to court is further complicated by the fact that the Indian plaintiff and his or her attorney may not "speak the same language," both figuratively and literally. Not only must attorneys achieve a greater understanding of Indian culture, Indian inmates must also come to understand the legal negotiation process. They must realize that they cannot always win on every point and that settlement and compromise with correctional officials may be the best avenue to making some gains. On one memorable occasion in my work as liaison between plaintiffs and attorneys, an attorney and I were invited to come to prison and smoke an inmate's Sacred Pipe to bless the negotiation and cement our ties.

I have served as expert witness in suits brought by Indian inmates against the prison in seven instances. The role of the anthropologist here is to inform the court of the content and validity of cultural and religious practices. In this vein, I have testified, as have other anthropologists, about the Native American Church and its use of peyote, the Sun Dance, sweat lodges, pow-wows, hand games, and religious principles in general. This is probably the most significant role the anthropologist can play, for in this environment we submit our credentials for the court's review and, when permitted, offer testimony that explains the historical and cultural bases for Indian religious practices. In one lawsuit success in alcohol therapy was at issue, and my own research data—rather than the ethnographic literature—were presented as testimony in support of the claim that prison data seriously underestimate the extent of alcohol and drug addiction and that the prison is unable to provide suitable therapy for its Indian population.

Ethical Issues

A statement about the role of anthropologists in corrections would not be complete without a comment on ethical dilemmas. Numerous issues surface, not the least of which are reciprocity and safety. Inmates who participate in research also get released from prison and, in the Indian tradition, they expect reciprocal kindness. These are delicate issues for the anthropologist, for one does not want to convey that one is happy to "use" informants *in* prison, and then refuse to associate with them once they have been released. But neither can one allow the expectation that the anthropologist is willing to go to dinner or to park for a quiet, private visit with an ex-offender.

Teaching and/or consulting in prison may carry with it some obligation of continued involvement with Indian prisoners, but the issue is most pronounced for researchers. Ethnographic and interview research brings the investigator and the subject into much closer personal contact. The prisoner who opens up and shares his criminal as well as alcohol or drug history with a researcher is revealing an intimate part of his or her past, and that self-disclosure requires a very high level of trust. The bond which results can easily be misinterpreted by prisoners as personal affection or willingness to do favors; at a minimum such prisoners are likely to feel that since they shared an important and deeply personal reflection of their lives, the researcher has an obligation in turn to be sympathetic. While teaching and consulting also bring prisoners and the service-provider into contact, the depth of one-on-one contact is greatly increased in research with personal interviews, particularly where sensitive information is revealed.

Other ethical concerns revolve around discovery of sensitive information in prison and the protection of confidentiality and anonymity for one's informants. Discovery of intended crimes, illicit drug or alcohol use in prison, or information about unsolved crimes all bring the anthropologist's moral decision making into play. From my perspective, anthropologists can make only one choice—that is, to maintain the strictest confidentiality under all circumstances—for without that, informants will withdraw their trust and ultimately refuse to participate in research of any kind. Protection of the confidentiality of data is particularly difficult for researchers whose data are requested in court testimony. Divulgence of one's sources for verification may be requested, but revealing the identity of our research subjects is forbidden according to the ethics of our discipline, and the anthropologist must be prepared to defend the privacy of the research data.

Conclusion

There is a tremendous need for anthropologists in correctional affairs. With the largest number of inmates representing minorities, and correctional staff seldom representative of those same groups, anthropologists are frequently sought as liaisons, cultural resource persons, and simply savvy outsiders who can help minority individuals interact with the complex, legal world in which they live. Correctional authorities benefit from this interaction as well, through improved inmate-staff relations, decreased litigation, and prison accreditation standards which reward institutions that permit and cooperate with research.

For the anthropologist the rewards of this type of involvement are numerous, but they are not primarily financial. While there may be enough work to keep an anthropologist busy full-time, the court is not accustomed to paying for expert witnesses, and the clients are nearly always indigent. Attorneys are appointed to cases by the court and normally receive no compensation for their services. However, in the cases in which I have been involved, attorneys have attempted—sometimes successfully—to obtain a small expert witness fee for the consultant. Anthropologists may, then, receive a fee for the preparation and delivery of their testimony or service, but it can in no way compensate them for the amount of time that must be expended in preparing for court. Also, the irregularity of litigation would preclude providing such a service on any but a periodic consultation basis.

The rewards of this type of advocacy lie, rather, in a sense of accomplishment from the activities conducted and services rendered. Few activities are more satisfying than helping to mend an intercultural communication network that has broken down. The satisfaction of such a role is primarily in the process, for the actual gains often seem few and far between. Those that do occur are extremely gratifying professionally, and they may put the anthropologist in a situation of great demand and generate numerous additional opportunities for applied work.

Between Practicing and Engaged Anthropology in Israel

Jeff Halper

A purely academic anthropology, focused on intellectual issues irrespective of their social import, is commonly contrasted with applied or practicing anthropology, in which the results of research and analysis are used to address practical problems. A third form of anthropology is identified here by Jeff Halper—a form that he calls "engaged" anthropology. Like applied or practicing anthropologists, engaged anthropologists use their professional training to address practical problems, but the problems are those associated with furthering a social or political cause to which the anthropologist is personally committed. Engaged anthropology is almost by definition outside the system; hence, it is even more often lost to the discipline than is the work of applied or practicing anthropologists. Halper cites Zora Neale Hurston and Kathleen Gough as engaged anthropologists of earlier eras, but his primary examples come from his own work in Israel—a setting which in many ways demands engagement of its residents. Halper describes how he has used anthropological insight and methods to foster his position that Israel is and should be a secular, democratic state. While not all will agree with the distinctions drawn here between academic, applied, and engaged anthropology, Halper's conceptualization and examples can expand our thinking about the utility of anthropology. P. J. H.

Whether or not Israeli anthropologists choose to respond, the overbearing political and social situation of the country certainly places pressures on them to become "engaged" in one way or another in issues and events beyond the purely professional. The Anthropological Association of Israel, which numbers around one hundred in all its various subdisciplines, has passed and publicized resolutions on a variety of political concerns, from supporting Bedouin claims to land, to calling for more culturally sensitive policies of immigrant "absorption," to assailing the government's actions during the Palestinian Intifada.

Jeff Halper is Coordinator of the Israeli Committee Against House Demolitions and directs the applied anthropology program at Ben-Gurion University of the Negev (<halper@iol.co.il>).

This article was originally published as part of a special section on "The Practice of Anthropology in Israel," guest edited by Jeff Halper and Anita Nudelman, in *Practicing Anthropology* 15,2(1993):27-30.

192

Anthropologists have been prominent among the leaders and activists of the Israeli peace movement. Until Here, a group of Tel Aviv University professors organized to protest the Israeli occupation; Women in Black, who hold a weekly vigil against the occupation; Peace Now and different organizations "to the left of Peace Now" (as that part of the political spectrum is called) all boast prominent members who are anthropologists. Similarly, anthropologists stand out as advocates for the Middle Eastern Jewish underclass, for immigrant groups, and for Arabs, both Bedouin and Palestinian, supporting the latters' claims to land and civil rights. Nor are anthropologists missing from the ranks of the religious right wing supporting the Jewish settlers' claims to Judea and Samaria (the West Bank), although they tend to be few in number.

As in other countries, in Israel the involvement of anthropologists in pressing political affairs tends to be personal—something added to, but not displacing, normal academic, applied, or professional activities. The small size of Israel, coupled with the pressing and often intimate issues that constantly confront its citizens—the unyielding pressures of immigration, economic hardships, and the myriad effects of its conflicts with the Arab world, to name but a few—foster a degree of involvement in which professional and personal spheres are intertwined. Yet while anthropologists may adopt activist positions in certain political contexts, they normally maintain a separation between their personal, political, and professional lives.

A few Israeli anthropologists, myself included, do not maintain these divisions. We practice a form of anthropological involvement that goes beyond both the university and usual forms of applied or practicing anthropology, a kind of professional involvement in the world that I call "engaged anthropology." This form of anthropology is not really new, although many of those who have practiced it have been "lost" to the formal discipline called anthropology. Zora Neale Hurston is a well-known engaged anthropologist that comes immediately to mind. Indeed, engaged anthropology has many expressions, from following a political career or engaging in business to writing novels, helping to organize disempowered communities, or teaching in public schools.

I am concerned here with an engaged anthropology of a political kind, linked to what Paulo Freire calls "transformative intellectuals," those who use their professional knowledge to advance critical analysis and emancipatory social action. Engaged anthropology had a bright if brief moment during the sixties when colleagues such as Kathleen Gough urged us to oppose American imperialism, Anthropologists for Radical Political Action (ARPA) published incendiary newsletters, and books like Dell Hymes's *Reinventing Anthropology* (New York: Random House, 1969) asked us to "study up" and to lead anthropology into socially responsible activities. Since then, however, a tight academic job market and the ubiquitous Reagan era have all but eliminated the transformative side of anthropology. "Contract anthropology," conservative by nature, as well as other forms of applied and practicing anthropology have developed subsequently along primarily practical and task-oriented lines.

Following the hallowed French conception of intellectuals who are *engagé*, I would define engaged anthropology according to the following characteristics, fully aware that they shade into those of practicing and applied anthropology as well.

- Engaged anthropology is characterized by commitment to a cause or concern that transcends the discipline. Like many practicing anthropologists, engaged anthropologists operate in situations that may have only tangential connection to their chosen field. They act as anthropologists, nonetheless, because anthropological concepts, views, and tools suffuse their activities and because they consider themselves anthropologists-in-action.
- Engaged anthropologists usually do not enjoy formal, paid, and well-defined positions in their area of activity. On the contrary, their activities tend to be in opposition to the formal structures of their society.
- Often forced to find employment in nonanthropological settings; having to apply their anthropology in nonconventional, nonacademic ways; lacking resources or time to attend professional meetings; and lacking access to professional networks and publications, engaged anthropologists are often lost to the discipline—or so it seems. Professional recognition and support certainly are lacking.

In a word, engaged anthropologists are wholly engaged people-in-action in the wider society. They bring to both their personal and professional activities (which are largely indistinguishable) anthropological skills and concepts acquired through training as anthropologists; but their anthropological expression is directed towards the issues in question rather than towards a task for which they have been hired or towards publication or other common forms of professional activity.

Let me illustrate what I mean by engaged anthropology through my own experiences in Israel.

I am an American-Israeli who has lived in Israel for the past twenty years. Having come to maturity in the United States during the sixties, I adopted an approach to life typical of many other activists: I would follow my commitments rather than some career path. Indeed, part of the attraction of anthropology was the possibility to engage in social change side by side with the people themselves.

Beyond the tragic conflicts between Israel and her Arab neighbors, I found myself involved in an internal Kulturkampf in which two radically different views of what Israel is and should be are pitted against one another. On one side is the Israel envisioned by the Zionists of the once-dominant Labor movement, a secular democratic state which, while constituting a national home for

194

the Jews, nevertheless grants equal rights of citizenship to all its inhabitants, Jewish and Arab alike. This definition of Israel, which belongs to what I call the *"State* of Israel" forces, held sway in the country from the early years of the century until the mid-1970s. At that point, when the nationalist Likud party came to power, a coalition which I call the *"Land* of Israel" forces arose to challenge the Labor paradigm. Rather than emphasizing self-determination within for Jews the framework of a secular democratic state, the Land of Israel forces, composed of orthodox Jews, followers of Menachem Begin, and Jews from Muslim countries, placed ultimate importance on settling the entire historic Land of Israel, West Bank and Gaza included, as part of an exclusively Jewish patrimony. The division between the two groups involves fundamentally different conceptions of what Israel should become: one (which I support), a society defined by its citizens; the other, an exclusively Jewish entity based on a kind of tribalism.

The contest between these two paradigms is waged on many levels, from political battles at the voting booths to the content of the educational system, including competition over national and religious symbols. The State of Israel paradigm has weakened over the years, especially as the children of the socialist pioneers leave off the collective struggle for an ideal society in favor of more individualistic ends. The Land of Israel forces, led by anti-socialist parties who control many of the society's most emotive symbols, especially those of religion, portray themselves as the "true" embodiment of roots. Such a movement possesses the double attraction of offering a collective, even tribalistic, mission of redemption to disaffected young people without challenging their individual materialistic goals. In this context, the ongoing conflict between Jews and Palestinians, so close to everyone's lives, only strengthens the tribal character of Israeli Judaism.

The question of cultural and class paradigms is crucial here. Information is not lacking, for example, as to the price Israel is paying for its conflict with the Arabs; how religious and ethnic tribalism creates intolerance and oppression; and how the Jewish African-Asian working classes of Israel work against their own interests by supporting a political right wing that diverts financial resources from their needs into settlements on the West Bank and Gaza. Nor does the European-dominated middle class lack information as to the concerns and values of the working classes. Israel possesses a highly critical press, television, and radio, and in-depth discussions among opponents on a wide variety of issues is much more common than in the United States. Yet few seem to be persuaded by the other side (notwithstanding the recent election results) and polarization continues to grow.

As an engaged anthropologist, I have two preeminent concerns here. The first is to facilitate communication so that the issues—including their underlying implications—be understood by all sides and a true national dialogue may occur. Second, as a partisan (and it must be assumed that engaged anthropologists use their anthropology in favor of some position), I seek to advance the positions of the State of Israel peace forces among the general population. The means I have chosen is to establish a Center for Contemporary Israeli Culture, supervised by a board representing grassroots organizations in the fields of peace, Jewish-Arab dialogue, women's issues, the disadvantaged, and human rights. Funding comes from grants, various local fund-raising activities, and contributions of the participating organizations themselves. The center's primary goals and areas of action are three:

1. to promote public awareness of Israeli culture—including those elements which unite Israeli Jews and Arabs—through exhibits, multimedia presentations, seminars, research on popular culture, publications, and outreach programs;
2. to generate educational materials dealing with dialogue, conflict resolution, and intercultural communication, for use both in the schools and in other spheres of public discourse; and
3. to serve as a meeting place for activist groups seeking to advance a State of Israel agenda, creating conditions for intergroup cooperation and lobbying.

The anthropological base underlying the center's activities is its concern to articulate conflicting paradigms so that dialogue, as well as persuasion, may take place. The focus on grassroots activist groups also reflects an anthropological approach; just as practicing anthropologists tend to work closely with local groups, so too, in the political sphere, an anthropologically oriented group might be expected to work more closely with grassroots organizations than with formal centers of power (although the latter, of course, cannot be ignored). Let us look briefly at a recent center activity to illustrate.

The center sponsored a day-long symposium at a kibbutz near Tel Aviv which was attended by representatives of more than twenty grassroots groups active in the areas described above. The central question of the symposium was, "How Can We Get Our Messages Across to the Wider Israeli Public?" The very question—decidedly "anthropological"—proved novel to groups used more to protest, confrontation, and debate than to attempts to understand why their positions are often rejected by the wider public. Almost all previous gatherings had revolved around ideological debates and plans of action, with little attention as to how effective such actions were in influencing public opinion.

It quickly became apparent in the planning process that simply presenting an "anthropological" question to these groups was not sufficient; although the participants were highly informed and articulate, they lacked tools to communicate beyond their own circles. The idea of "engagement" suggested a practical way of dealing with the issue. The separation of professional from personal life, so natural in industrial societies, had led to a situation in which activists or their supporters would participate in political events solely as *personal* activities. It never occurred to anyone to inquire about the professional skills of the person holding the sign at the peace rally; he or she was simply another supporter.

Upon inquiry at several rallies and meetings, I discovered that a number of participants were active in the Tel Aviv advertising world. Drawing on the practical eclecticism for which anthropologists are famous, I crossed the line between activists' personal and professional lives and dipped into a professional community which few would have suspected held anything of use to the peace movement. Here were people, after all, whose professional core consisted of deciphering paradigms and finding "openings" for communication. Without trivializing the importance of the issues involved, is there not a connection between selling beer and "selling" peace? One result of the symposium, therefore, was the creation of a group of people in advertising, supplemented by others in such fields as communications and anthropology, who advise grassroots organizations as to the effectiveness of their messages and materials and help them understand where resistance to their messages might arise among different groups and how such resistance might be overcome.

Focusing on aspects of the conflict that involve clashing paradigms and not simply clashing personalities or groups, the internal logic and interests of the competing parties can be brought out, examined, and dealt with, rather than simply being dismissed. This led some to explore paradigms they had previously rejected outright, perhaps even to incorporate some of their elements. Several participants in center activities began what became known as the "Context Group." They met regularly with individuals from groups which had radically different paradigms: West Bank settlers; inner-city African-Asian Jews; members of different orthodox sects, both Jewish and Muslim; advertising executives; politicians across the spectrum; and others. A fundamental principle of anthropological thought, that every group develops a worldview that is internally consistent and "makes sense"—if only one is able to penetrate it—became a basis for dialogue among vastly different Israelis.

One very brief example might illustrate this breakthrough. Israelis from the Labor Party and groups farther left reject out of hand the West Bank settlers' claims to the greater Land of Israel. From their perspective—the State of Israel as it has emerged since 1948—the West Bank is tangential to the country and Jewish attempts to settle it are merely provocative. The "Context" discussions revealed a much different perception among the settlers themselves. Mainly religious, they conceived of Israel in biblical terms. That meant, among other things, that the ridge of mountains between Nablus, Jerusalem, and Hebron where the Hebrew tribes settled represented, in their eyes, the "true" core of the country. Tel Aviv, the center of modern Israel for most secular Israelis, was for the settlers tangential—all the more so because it remained in Philistine hands through much of the biblical period. This perspective was one that Israelis among the State of Israel forces had not previously appreciated. It "made sense" of the settlers' actions and was an issue that had to be addressed in any dialogue that was to take place. Certainly strategies of communication and opinion change across paradigm lines that rely solely on confrontation or argumentation are doomed to fail.

Dialogue groups have long been a staple of Israeli educators. Arab and Jewish school children are often brought together for such dialogues, as are Jewish school children of different ethnic and class backgrounds. Based upon the common-sensical "contact hypothesis"—that people from different backgrounds will discover their common humanity if they only meet—such "dialogues" often descend into shouting matches and end up reinforcing negative stereotypes. Left-wing political groups often hold dialogues of their own, but they tend to be among the already persuaded: Jews and Arabs sharing similar political views; middle-class European Jews finding "progressive" African-Asian Jews with whom to talk, or selected (but nonrepresentative) segments of the Jewish religious community.

One of the main activities of the center has been to initiate dialogues among groups with truly different views and interests, preceded, however, by carefully formulated "paradigm studies" of the parties. These have not only stimulated fruitful discussions, they have also stimulated questioning within the various groups over certain aspects of their own paradigms. We cannot boast any major breakthroughs in the Middle East peace process, but "pre-dialogue" models that have emerged from our dialogue activities are being used by an increasing number of schools and other organizations.

The interminable political, economic, and social pressures permeating every aspect of life in Israel will continue to push Israeli anthropologists into involvement in wider issues of social change. Whether these forces will produce more engaged anthropologists or merely thrust anthropologists into sporadic and personalized activism remains an open question. I have attempted here to sensitize us to that borderland of engaged anthropology which exists between the applied and practicing forms on the one hand and the simple involvement of individuals who happen to be anthropologists on the other. In the meantime, recognized or not, engaged anthropologists will continue to be occupied with what may be described as the anthropology of what-has-to-be-done.

Ethics and Contract Archaeology

Patrick H. Garrow

Archaeologists have led the way in the nonacademic professionalization of anthropology. Perhaps they could be regarded as the "miner's canary" for the rest of applied anthropology. Here Patrick Garrow, a respected leader in contract archaeology, describes bluntly and precisely some of the pitfalls of anthropology as a business. As Garrow notes, changes in government policies in the 1960s and 1970s did much to drive the demand for what one American Indian anthropologist wag calls "mercenary archaeology." Academic archaeology— despite a tradition of salvage work on highway and large-scale construction projects—was largely unprepared for the kind of ethical questions that archaeological entrepreneurship raises. Garrow's gripping descriptions of employee abuses, client demands, and competitive pressures serve as an object lesson for all would-be anthropological practitioners. Garrow shows how economic forces drive questionable practices in contract archaeology, chides government regulators for accepting shoddy work, and offers valuable advice for breaking the vicious circle of cheap archaeology. Here is a classic precautionary tale for all applied anthropologists.   J. A. P.

Contract archaeology as practiced today is a product of the environmental movement that began in the 1960s. The National Environmental Policy Act (NEPA) of 1969 required that a number of environmental factors, including archaeology, be taken into account prior to initiation of federal projects or actions. Additional legislation since 1969 has further strengthened requirements, and federal undertakings have been broadly defined to include not only federally funded projects, but also all projects that require federal permitting. The current application of cultural resources laws and regulations means that thousands of archaeological projects are conducted each year in this country. This translates into hundreds of millions of dollars spent annually on compliance-based archaeological research in the United States.

Contract archaeology did exist prior to NEPA, but in a much different form. Often called "salvage" or "rescue" archaeology, most centered on reservoirs

Patrick H. Garrow is Vice President of TRC Garrow Associates, Inc. (32772 Pleasantdale Road, Suite 200, Atlanta, GA 30340; (770) 270-1192; fax: (770) 270-1392; <garrow@mindspring.com>), a contract archaeology firm with branch offices in Tennessee, North Carolina, and Pennsylvania.

Originally published in *Practicing Anthropology* 15,3(1993):10-13.

200

or highways and was conducted by universities or museums. The vast majority of projects were severely underfunded and depended on free, or nearly free, student and volunteer labor. It was common practice on pre-NEPA projects to use all available funding for field investigations, saving nothing for analysis and reporting. This meant that a number of the pre-NEPA projects were never reported or were reported only in preliminary form, and that the reports that were done often fell short of modern standards for archaeological reporting. The full impact of NEPA did not hit the field until the mid-1970s. Initially the same universities and museums that had conducted salvage archaeology attempted to meet the rapidly expanding needs for contract archaeology. It soon became evident, however, that most universities and museums were poorly suited to meet this demand for services, and most had withdrawn from contracting or drastically reduced their contracting programs by the early 1980s. University-based contract archaeology programs were replaced by private sector programs which have dominated the field since then.

Most early private sector programs were situated in architectural and engineering (A&E) firms, which simply added archaeology as a service area as demand increased. The trend over the past decade has been toward the development of specialized contract archaeology firms, which can generally offer lower overhead costs than A&E firms and are thus more competitive.

Contract archeology created thousands of jobs in a profession where few jobs had existed previously, and a number of new programs were established to train contract archaeologists. The rapid increase in demand for archaeological services and the changing political and professional environments in which those services have been offered were not matched, however, by development of a strong, explicit, and pertinent code of ethics for practitioners.

Existing Codes of Ethics

Most archaeological societies or organizations address ethical issues in one sense or another. Codes of ethics formulated by the Society for American Archaeology (SAA) and by the Society of Professional Archaeologists (SOPA) have been chosen for discussion in this article because they are the codes most widely recognized by practicing anthropologists.

The SAA Four Statements for Archaeology (*American Antiquity* 27,2[1961]:137-138) includes one entitled "Ethics for Archaeology." Five primary principles briefly discussed under this statement are: (1) collections and associated data have to be kept available for study by "competent" archaeologists; (2) archaeologists are obligated to prepare reports of findings for all investigations; (3) buying and selling artifacts is "censured"; (4) archaeologists are not to engage in excavations on sites under investigation by others without proper coordination; and (5) "…willful destruction, distortion, or concealment of the data of archaeology…" constitutes grounds for censure or expulsion from the SAA. When this code of ethics was framed almost all archaeological research was conducted by universities or museums. Unfortunately, the Four Statements for Archaeology are not specific enough to provide the type of ethical guidance that is currently needed, especially with respect to contract archaeology.

The SOPA Code of Ethics and Standards of Research Performance (*1993 Directory of Certified Professional Archaeologists*, pp. 5-9) provides more detailed guidance for the practice of archaeology. The Code of Ethics is organized into three broad sections which define the responsibilities of professional archaeologists to the public, to colleagues, and to employers and clients. Each section is further subdivided into obligations archaeologists should meet and behavior archaeologists should avoid.

Professional archaeologists are obligated, according to the SOPA Code of Ethics, "...to represent archeology and its research results to the public in a responsible manner," while being "...sensitive to, and respect[ing] the legitimate concerns of, groups whose culture histories are the subject of archaeological investigation...." Professional archaeologists are also instructed to support the preservation of archaeological sites and to discourage illegal or unethical trafficking in artifacts. The Code further states that it is unethical to undertake research that the individual is not qualified to conduct or to "... engage in conduct involving dishonesty, fraud, deceit or misrepresentation about archaeological matters."

Concerning colleagues, the SOPA Code of Ethics is fairly straightforward. It requires that due credit be given to others for research contributions and that the professional archaeologist keep up with the literature and developments in the field. It also requires that research be reported promptly, that the archaeologist communicate and cooperate with colleagues with similar research interests, that the mutual interests of colleagues in particular sites or lines of research be recognized and respected, and that all pertinent laws and ethical codes be complied with during research. The archaeologist is obligated to report violations of the Code of Ethics by colleagues, but is admonished not to make false accusations or maliciously attempt to harm the reputations of others. Plagiarism in verbal or written form is defined as a violation of the Code, as is misrepresentation of qualifications on a SOPA certification application.

The third section of the SOPA Code of Ethics addresses the member's "...responsibility to employers and clients." It reiterates that an archaeologist must not attempt research that is beyond his or her level of expertise. It also states that the archaeologist must respect the client's confidential information, but restricts this to "non-archaeological" information, and that the archaeologist cannot use the client's confidential information for personal gain, or personally gain from recommending the "...employment of another archaeologist or other person..." without full disclosure. In addition, the archaeologist must refuse any "request on demand" made by a client or employer that "…conflicts with the Code or Standards."

SOPA's Code of Ethics is supplemented by their Standards of Research Performance, which establish broad technical parameters for the proper conduct of archaeology, and their Institutional Standards, which define the minimal facilities and services that must be maintained by an institution that conducts research.

Current Ethical Issues

Most of the precepts of the SAA and SOPA codes of ethics deal with the ethical considerations of archaeologists as scientists, and here they generally do a good job. There are still many undefined or ill-defined areas in relation to contract archaeology, however.

One area that needs further discussion concerns the ethical considerations faced when the archaeological findings themselves are considered confidential by the client. For example, when a client asks the archaeologist to do background research on a series of properties from which a final site will be chosen, premature release of the archaeological findings can compromise the client's interests. It probably is unethical to sign a contract that forever forbids release of project information to the scientific community, but it may not be unethical to agree to withhold information for a period of time.

Another area not adequately covered is the obligation each archaeologist has to attempt to find viable preservation alternatives for significant sites identified within areas to be developed. Archaeological excavation is a destructive activity, and techniques of excavation and analysis are rapidly improving. It can be assumed that a site excavated fifty years from now will yield much more information than the same site explored in 1992. Data recovery should be conducted only after it is determined that preservation is not feasible or is unlikely to be feasible over the long term. Application of this principle might still result in very few sites being set aside, but preservation should be considered and ruled out before moving on to excavation.

The existing codes of ethics are less helpful for archaeologists as business persons. The development of specialized archaeological firms, without the buffer of a trained business management or university superstructure, has put many archaeologists in the position of making decisions for which they were not trained. Unfortunately, as in all fields, some archaeologists have found ways to cut corners with personnel and administration that make their businesses more price-competitive in the short run, but that are questionable from an ethical standpoint.

Some of the most blatant ethical abuses can be seen in the treatment of employees. Salaries are abysmal in many contract archaeology programs; technicians are often paid wages barely above the legal minimum. Some firms (and academic programs) do not pay *per diem* until they are in turn paid by their clients. This means that the employees, including people who are barely earning a livable wage to begin with, actually front the cash needs of the firm. Paid vacations, paid company holidays, health insurance, and sick leave are benefits that are taken for granted in most professional fields, yet are not available to most archaeological employees.

One of the most insidious abuses involves hiring project staff as private contractors. Under that approach an employer pays no benefits, takes out no payroll deductions for taxes, and evades paying employers FICA, which is about half of the amount paid into an individual's annual Social Security account. As James Hester has pointed out ("Stop Selling Yourself Short!!" *SOPA Newsletter* 13,2[1989]:3), if a person was paid $8 per hour as a private contractor, that person's effective wage was actually $6.20 per hour after taxes and Social Security were accounted for. As Hester also points out, according to IRS rules, specialists such as floral and faunal experts, geomorphologists, and the like who can perform discrete elements of a project with no real supervision can easily qualify as private contractors. It is virtually impossible, however, to have a technician or crew chief legally work for a firm as a private contractor, and crew members working in the field or lab workers who are working under supervision generally do not qualify under the IRS rules.

Maintaining a safe work environment is another issue that has not received enough attention in contract archaeology. Some archaeologists still send staff members into unsafe trenches, and all too often we excavate sites without attention to possible toxic substances in the soil. It may surprise some archaeologists to learn that we are not exempt from the Occupational Safety and Health Administration provisions and that we have a legally defined responsibility for insuring a safe work place.

Recognizing that serious problems exist in the treatment of employees in many contracting programs, SOPA appointed a committee to investigate. Their recommended additions to the SOPA Code of Ethics (*SOPA Newsletter* 5,1[1990]) dealt only superficially with the problems, however, and said little more than that employers should obey the law.

Employees, in turn, have reciprocal ethical and legal obligations to their employers. These obligations vary with the level of defined responsibility, but employers have the right to expect honesty from everyone who works for them. Employees are obligated to be productive and attentive to detail, to show reasonable care for the equipment and vehicles provided as a part of their employment, and to endeavor to keep up with the latest developments in the field. Employees are also obligated to maintain those confidences reasonably designated as privileged information by the employer. They should be aware that the program they work for will be judged by the client's representatives and local residents at least in part by their actions.

As business people, contract archaeologists must also deal with clients. Most client problems arise from the client's lack of understanding of archaeology, although some clients occasionally try to get away with something that even they perceive as unethical. We have not done a particularly good job of defining archaeology to the public, and our education system has failed to instill the type of respect for the past and for knowledge that is needed to fully appreciate a field like archaeology. We must educate clients and inform them of our own ethical framework so that they can understand our rules and why we must follow them.

It is important to know how and when to tell a client "no." For example, one major client tried to have data recovery recommendations systematically reduced before a series of testing reports were submitted to state and federal regulators for review. An agreement to reduce the effort on our part clearly would have been unethical, as the recommendations would no longer have been made on archaeological criteria. The answer to that request had to be "no," even though some work was lost as a result. It is also important to know when to stop providing services to a particular client.

The results of contract archaeology are sent to other professionals employed by state or federal agencies who must approve our work before a client's project can proceed. Those individuals represent ultimate quality control for contract reports. They decide whether project recommendations are reasonable and well supported, and they can literally hound substandard contractors out of the field if they choose to exercise their legal prerogatives.

In practice, most state and federal regulators are overworked, and they are also subjected to constant and severe political pressure that can influence their judgment on particular projects. A remarkable number have retained their love for archaeology and are truly trying to do a good job. At the same time, too many of those archaeologists who are in a position to demand ethical and competent project performance have been so battered by the system that they lack the energy or resolve to do more than perfunctory reviews.

Toward Better Business Practices

A successful archaeological contracting program is a partnership between employers and employees, based on competence and mutual trust. Both employers and employees must be dedicated to performing technically excellent projects within budgetary and scheduling constraints. No client will simply hand a program a blank check and be unconcerned about performance or schedule.

Eventually more archaeologists who manage contract programs will learn that their product consists of the time and professional efforts of their staff. Low salaries, lack of benefits, and unsafe working conditions will ultimately result in employers cutting themselves off from the best and fastest workers who could make them more competitive. Hence, not only are many of the practices referred to above unethical, in the long run they are inefficient as well.

The practice of bidding professional archaeological services has probably led to more abuse than any other single factor. Many clients (including an unfortunate number of state and federal agencies) demand that archaeological contracts be done at the lowest possible price. The lowest bid often equates to the least effort expended by the most poorly trained and inexperienced staff. Cut-rate firms tend not to last, but there never appears to be a shortage of them. We must find a way to insure that those who work in this field receive at least minimal benefits, a livable wage, and a safe working environment.

Perhaps the greatest responsibility for the perpetuation of low-bid archaeology and all of the ills it implies rests with the regulators. The basement of the contract market is determined by what state and federal regulators are willing to accept as compliance reports. The minimum amount needed to insure report acceptance sets the "lowest possible price." Perhaps what we really need is a strong and published code of ethics for state and federal regulators; we need to let them know that we desire the type of strong regulation that will benefit both the field and the resources in the long run.

Substantive changes are needed in contract archaeology, and at present we do not have a code of ethics adequate to support those changes. It is certain that the employees of at least some contract firms will not put up with the way they are being treated for much longer. It is equally certain that the needs of archaeology will not be adequately met if we allow the current system of low-bid archaeology to be perpetuated. Contract archaeologists must address the need for more explicit ethical guidance.

At the Edge...: Visual Anthropology and HIV Prevention

Nancy E. Tongue, Jay Wheeler, and Laurie J. Price

Nancy Tongue, Jay Wheeler, and Laurie Price describe how they used anthropological concepts and methods in the design and filming of a nineteen-minute video for use in HIV prevention counseling. General evidence of the power of video plus research among drug users in northern Arizona convinced the authors and their colleagues in the Flagstaff Multicultural AIDS Prevention Project that a video anchored in the local community and highlighting participant stories would be an effective tool. While the impact of the video on behavior cannot be precisely measured, viewer response testified to the value of using local context, insider viewpoints, and culturally relevant narrative and imagery to convey health messages. As the authors point out, visual anthropology— although traditionally focused on documenting cultural patterns and communicating anthropological messages—has tremendous potential for promoting cultural and behavioral change. P. J. H.

The representation of video imagery in a printed medium is frustrating when the images speak so eloquently for themselves. Our video, *At the Edge... Arizona at Risk*, was created for the Flagstaff Multicultural AIDS Prevention Project (FMAPP) to be used as an integral part of its HIV prevention counseling. Funded by the National Institute on Drug Abuse, FMAPP educates drug-using adults about HIV risk factors such as needle sharing and unprotected sex. In addition, the project addresses concerns of sexual partners of drug injectors and of cocaine/crack users.

Nancy E. Tongue works as a visual and medical anthropologist through her company, Four Directions Cultural Advocacy (160 East Astro Lane, Flagstaff, AZ 86001; (520) 774-6856; <fourdirect@aol.com>).

Jay Wheeler is completing his master's thesis in applied anthropology. He can be contacted at 90 Chinle Place, Durango, CO 81301; (970) 375-2324.

Laurie J. Price is Associate Professor of Anthropology at Northern Arizona University (Flagstaff, AZ 86011; (520) 523-6565; <laurie.price@nau.edu>).

Originally published as part of a special section on "AIDS Outreach, Education, and Prevention: Anthropological Contributions," guest edited by Kathleen A. O'Connor and William L. Leap, in *Practicing Anthropology* 15,4(1993):9-12, this article has been abridged for republication here.

Media studies attest to the strength of visual messages in promoting beneficial behavior changes; printed messages do not have the same impact. American culture revolves around visual messages, and this kind of communication can reach the general population, regardless of educational level. A similar video, *Shooting Smart* (Fen Rhodes, director; 1992), was found to have significant impact in promoting a sense of personal vulnerability to HIV among drug users. Yet our project participants could not relate to the California boat-yard scenes, the ocean, or the community depicted. With *Shooting Smart* as a springboard, we decided to tailor a new production for FMAPP clients that would address concerns specific to our location.

Identifying the Need

Flagstaff is a multi-ethnic community of 48,300 in northern Arizona. Major cultural groups in the town and surrounding service area include Anglos, Native Americans, Hispanics, and African Americans. Citizens think of their community as insulated from such urban problems as drugs and HIV. In fact, people are not confronted with HIV/AIDS to the extent that they are in major cities because HIV infection is still relatively rare and people with AIDS tend to migrate out of the area. Yet, the common assumption of isolation is misguided given that two interstate freeways and a railroad run through the area and that high-volume tourism is generated by the nearby Grand Canyon and other national parks. This false sense of isolation exists within the drug-using as well as the general population and has perpetuated unsafe needle use and an unrealistic perception of personal sexual invulnerability.

Thus, acknowledgment of risk and susceptibility is pivotal in FMAPP's intervention process. As many of the FMAPP staff come from anthropological backgrounds, the intervention design used methods, principles, and concepts from applied anthropology from its inception. (See James M. Potter, Jr., V. Davis, George S. Gotto IV, Anthea V. Hajjar, and Robert T. Trotter II, "A Small Town Model for HIV/AIDS Prevention," *Practicing Anthropology* 15,4[1993]:5-8.) One such principle is that motivational aspects of counseling may best be addressed by a "personal narratives" format which highlights local and/or ethnically specific knowledge, symbols, and stories.

FMAPP's quantitative research data (e.g., Risk Behavior Assessments) were instrumental in understanding where *Shooting Smart* failed to serve project participants. For instance, about half of our project's clients are not injectors, but use other modes of drug self-administration. Since the Long Beach video focuses almost entirely on injection drug use, it does not address many of the needs/risks encountered by noninjection drug users and the sexual partners of drug users.

In addition, we carried out open-ended interviews with twelve clients who viewed *Shooting Smart* as part of the intervention process. They were asked to tell us how they liked the video overall, and they were also queried as to which specific parts of the video had the most and the least impact on them and why. Their comments confirmed the power of video images but also pointed to the cultural incongruence of the Long Beach production.

Thus, we had five major goals in designing the video. We wanted to visually and substantively anchor the production in northern Arizona. We wanted to address sexual risks and sexual negotiation processes which were not emphasized in *Shooting Smart*. We wanted to highlight participant stories by allocating as much "air time" to video participants as possible. We worked to include drug culture "insider" information regarding when and where drugs are used in this region. Finally, we sought a background narrator with a warmer, less authoritarian, less Anglo and paternalistic voice than the narrator of *Shooting Smart*.

Making the Video

We began by making initial contacts to locate participants and constructing the overall video treatment (plan for scenes and themes). FMAPP's outreach personnel, most of whom are recovering drug users, introduced us to community members who were currently injecting drugs and/or partners of users. With staff help, we were able to conduct field interviews both with and without the video camera, and we learned the locations and contexts in which northern Arizonans would most likely use drugs.

It was clear that the video should focus on Arizona residents of diverse ethnic and gender groups who had contracted HIV through drug use or sexual activity with drug users. As mentioned, AIDS cases are not highly visible or prevalent in northern Arizona. Thus, we needed to go elsewhere to tape people willing to talk frankly about their HIV status and/or showing actual symptoms of AIDS. Shanti, a day care, support service, and in-patient hospice unit serving people with HIV/AIDS, has a number of clients from northern Arizona at their Phoenix center. A day-long visit built rapport with key personnel and selected clients and clarified the purposes of FMAPP and the video we were proposing. One Shanti counselor was especially supportive of our educational aims and helped locate clients to take part in the video.

In all, we video taped twelve individuals in various stages of HIV infection, including two who died shortly after completion of the video; each added something unique. We also video taped seven health professionals who provide HIV/AIDS care, two at Shanti in Phoenix and the remainder in Flagstaff.

The interviewer had certain themes, derived from ethnographic interviews and project data, to cover with each participant. The first theme was that of the personal narrative. HIV-positive participants introduced themselves with their name and a short statement about their personal HIV situation (e.g., how and when they contracted the virus). Another important theme was the false sense

210

of security many drug users feel about not contracting HIV. When asked to comment, participants responded with powerful statements, e.g., "I was sure that I wouldn't get it, but I did"; "I didn't think I was big-time enough, but I caught it."

The gravity of AIDS, the disease, was also a theme. The Long Beach footage of people with visible symptoms of AIDS had enormous impact on FMAPP clients; the same was true of graphic description of opportunistic AIDS-related illnesses. Consequently, we made special efforts to locate video participants who were very compromised. We had to convince staff members at Shanti, an institution which maintains an upbeat ambiance and de-emphasizes sickness and death, of the importance of this kind of footage for HIV prevention. For counseling HIV-positive people, such footage might be inappropriate, but prevention was our main program objective. The final video devotes almost one minute to Philip, a very sick gentleman, as he explains his experience with AIDS, including blindness and virtual immobility. He finishes with the cautionary statement, "to sum it up, just be careful."

Another theme is the invisibility of HIV status. The video challenges common misconceptions that HIV-positive people look sick and that a few questions about lifestyle reliably indicate HIV infection. Video participants provided shocking admissions about transmitting the virus to others by continuing to share syringes and having unprotected sex even knowing they were infected. This theme is accompanied by participant and narrator reminders to bleach needles and use condoms.

In a final theme we asked participants to comment on why they agreed to do the video. Responses show the personal investment they had in self-expression through video and also in protecting other people from HIV.

One strategy for contextualizing the video locally was to open with shots of northern Arizona and to repeat these scenes periodically throughout the production, e.g., the freeways through Flagstaff, the hospital, the train station, local bars, the San Francisco Peaks. Flagstaff drug culture experts helped further situate the video by suggesting drug use simulations in a gas station, a home, and outdoors at a phone booth. We video taped the sexual partner of a local injection drug user talking about her fears of HIV infection. We also video taped a recovering drug user describing risky activities she had observed in the area.

Technical Issues

Our technical format in making *At the Edge* was Hi-8, edited on a desktop editing system. This "in-house" approach allowed us to control every aspect of the video's production (e.g., participant choice, interviewing, filming, editing, narration, music, credits) and to keep costs to a bare minimum. It also allowed us to maintain an interactive approach, consulting with project staff members, video participants, outreach personnel, and local health educators throughout the process.

The video makes use of most of the documentary styles from the 1930s to the present. (See Bill Nichol, *Representing Reality* [Bloomington: Indiana University Press, 1991].) The expository style is used in two and a half minutes of the nineteen minute production. The narrator introduces key themes and underscores constructive behavioral changes such as "bleach your works." The observational documentary approach is incorporated in cut-away shots of an HIV-positive family playing in the park, a participant doing his laundry, a hospital patient brushing her hair. This technique allows viewers to "know" the video participants and to feel more empathy with them.

By using persuasive techniques, we echoed the reflexive documentary style. The video shows a man staggering in the street "high," a wild party scene, and people leaving a local bar in couples. This footage builds image-based scenarios to encourage viewers to entertain the idea that people they know, including themselves, are at risk for HIV through their sexual behavior. Finally, the interactive documentary style of film making (from the 1960s and 1970s) is used in our interviews. This style acknowledges the active role of the film maker as catalyst and participant in the filming.

An interactive approach validates informants' views and supports the importance of their contributions. As a natural extension of the interactive emphasis, we have stayed in touch with video participants; we grieve when they are sick and rejoice when they rebound.

Responses to At the Edge

Qualitative evaluation of *At the Edge* (in use since January, 1993) supports the proposition that local context is important in communicating health messages. For example, Burton, a Hualapai Indian, agreed to be in the video to spread the word about HIV, particularly among Native Americans whom he perceives as very naive about AIDS. Surprised by the video's straightforward approach and honesty in portraying his experience, he was pleased, nevertheless, with the video and enthusiastic about showing the production to his small tribe in northern Arizona. Diane, who continues to attend substance abuse counseling workshops at Shanti, has found that the video has a strong positive impact when shown to substance abuse clients. She feels proud to be a part of a video that she perceives to have a direct affect upon those around her.

FMAPP clients have affirmed the impact *At the Edge* has had on increasing their personal awareness of AIDS and risks; counselors, too, report great success with the video as a stimulus for identifying personal risks and solutions. When asked which part of the video had the greatest impact on them, most clients referred to seeing people sick, with comments such as "didn't realize how it deteriorates the body" and "the dying guy in bed, makes me want to

212

quit using drugs and use a condom all the time." In discussing their overall impressions of the video, clients commented, "fear for everyone I know," "didn't know it (AIDS) was so severe," and "it's good because it tells you how not to get AIDS." The descriptive terms clients used have a hard edge: fear, hard, reality, depressing. The video and the counselors work to address these negative emotions by providing reinforcement for the client's belief in his/her ability to reduce risks. Thus, these hard-edged reactions may well initiate personal contemplation and, ultimately, behavior change.

FMAPP is in the process of measuring HIV risk behavior changes six months after clients view the video. Because it is embedded in a larger, multifaceted intervention, the video's impact cannot be precisely measured as a separate variable. Future research may address the question of the impact of the video, in particular, on behavior change.

At the Edge as Applied Visual Anthropology

Visual anthropology began as a means of documenting cultural forms, especially in disappearing tribal societies. Such documentation has continued, expanding to include distinctive subcultures in complex societies. In addition, visual anthropology has been concerned with communicating anthropological material and theories to the general public. Visual anthropologists also strive to understand the collaboration process as it shapes film and video and to make effective use of collaboration, both with other experts involved in production and with those who are chronicled in film and video. *Applied* visual anthropology engages in all these activities, but it gives priority to using anthropology to design and implement effective change programs for target audiences.

Because the authors and film makers of *At the Edge* are anthropologists, anthropological methods and perspectives were used in every phase of video production, including conception, planning, scripting, interviewing, narration, editing, educational application, and follow-up evaluation. This proved beneficial in three ways. We were able to emphasize the insiders' view consistently and to represent the language and outlook of our drug user and HIV-positive video participants authentically. In addition, we were able to employ anthropologically informed educational strategies, which are more effective because they are based on powerful cultural and community images. Finally, we were able to engage in an on-going reflexive process by repeatedly exploring values and commitments with video participants during the production. This promoted a sense of ownership among video participants as well as increasing the cultural accuracy of our production.

If visual anthropology is to succeed in applied aims, particularly in helping to stem the HIV pandemic, we must break away from the "us" vs. "them" frame of mind in media production. We must instead concentrate on risk behaviors that potentially affect us all. This entails acknowledgment of HIV threats in one's own locale and increasing recognition of personal vulnerability. The urgency of the AIDS epidemic underscores the need for applied anthropologists to understand and utilize the power of video productions to convey culturally relevant and potentially life-saving messages.

Archaeology and Community: A Village Cultural Center and Museum in Ecuador

COLIN MCEWAN, CHRIS HUDSON, AND MARIA-ISABEL SILVA

In a dramatic story of successful collaboration and community involvement, Colin McEwan, Chris Hudson, and Maria-Isabel Silva trace the development of the Agua Blanca Archaeological Project in Ecuador. The authors provide an absorbing case study of how archaeology can enable local people to engage actively with their own past, which highlights the connections among culture, ecology, and community development. Through dialogue, consultation, and public display of their work, the archaeological team harnessed the energies of a rural Latin American community in mapping, excavating, and conserving an archaeological site. Eventually, as funding was secured, they worked together to build a village cultural center and museum. The project resulted in the village affirming its cultural identity and demonstrated a "viable alternative to 'top down' development strategies" that so often exclude local populations from planning and implementing projects that address their problems. The Agua Blanca site is now recognized as "one of the major pre-Columbian centers in the northern Andes...visited by over ten thousand people each year." This case study shows that archaeology can play a vital practical role in asserting community identity and catalyzing local initiative. R. O. S.

In mid-1979 the Pacific coast of Ecuador lay in the grip of a fierce and prolonged drought. The seasonal winter rains had failed to materialize for

Colin McEwan is Curator of the Central and South American collection in the Department of Ethnography, The British Museum (Burlington Gardens, London W1X 2EX, United Kingdom; 44-[0]171-323-8070; fax: 44-[0]171-323-8013; <cmcewan@british-museum.ac.uk>).
Chris Hudson is a free-lance designer and museum consultant (Chris Hudson Designs, 21 Grafton Rd., London NW5 3DX, United Kingdom).
Maria-Isabel Silva is an anthropologist and founder and president of Fundacion Tercer Milenio which supports projects related to culture, ecology and community in Ecuador. She can be contacted at 904 S. Race, Urbana, IL 61801 or P.O. Box 17-21-1055, Quito-Ecuador.

Originally published in *Practicing Anthropology* 16,1(1994):3-7, this article has been edited and abridged for republication here.

several years, and, unable to make ends meet, many *campesinos* fled rural farms and villages to seek a change of fortune in the sprawling shanty towns of Guayaquil, Manta, and Libertad.

In the *comuna* of Agua Blanca, a typical village in the province of Manabí, one in every three families had been forced to leave. With no moisture to nourish their crops, people intensified the felling of timber from the surrounding forest. The best of the lumber was hauled out by horse or donkey, destined for house and boat construction. Much of the rest was converted into charcoal for a meager cash income, while a small portion met domestic cooking needs in the *comuna* itself. Slowly but surely the forest was being consumed, aggravated by the ravages of goats and foraging cattle.

The forest harbored other resources too. Amid the dense underbrush villagers often stumbled upon the foundations of the houses and temples of what had once been a thriving indigenous town. Carved stone seats were found grouped together in some of the more imposing public buildings. The ruins yielded delicately worked figurines, and the occasional exotic object such as a copper ax. Some of these were kept as curiosities, but many were sold to itinerant dealers for much needed cash, eventually finding their way into museum collections or onto the illegal market in prehistoric antiquities.

That same year, the Machalilla National Park was created—a 35,000 acre reserve designed to protect and preserve the extraordinarily diverse coastal fauna and flora as well as marine life on the nearby islands of Salango and La Plata. Want it or not, the *comuna* of Agua Blanca in the Buena Vista Valley found itself at the heart of the park and dependent for its very survival on the resources that the park was intended to protect.

The year 1979 also marked the beginning of the first archaeological survey of the Buena Vista Valley. Archaeologist Colin McEwan reconnoitered on foot from the river mouth at Puerto López, past Agua Blanca some eight kilometers inland and up the farther reaches of the narrow gorge cutting deep into the northern Colonche hills. The survey revealed a series of pre-Columbian settlements which once comprised a powerful alliance of coastal trading towns described by the Spanish chroniclers as the Señorío of Salangome, belonging to the Manteño culture (800-1530 AD). Agua Blanca is located on top of a sector of the largest of these pre-Hispanic towns and thus gave its name to the archaeological site.

The story that unfolded in the course of the 1980s revolves around the active role that this small rural community has played in collaboration with archaeologists and other professionals to investigate, conserve, and protect its cultural heritage. Through participation in the mapping, excavation, and conservation of the nearby archaeological site, the *comuna* has recaptured a sense of cultural identity. The process has also aided in the community's struggle to maintain itself as an independent, legally constituted *comuna* and to achieve a sustainable economy in the face of vagaries of climate and the park's policy of environmental protection.

Ironically, at the time the Machalilla National Park was created, park authorities were quite unaware of the existence of the archaeological remains at Agua Blanca. Despite Ecuador's rich pre-Columbian heritage, the National Park Service had never faced the challenge of managing cultural resources. As a result of several seasons of fieldwork by the Agua Blanca Archaeological Project, the site is now recognized as one of the major pre-Columbian centers in the northern Andes, and it is visited by over ten thousand people each year.

Campesino and Comuna: The Right to Exist

The arrival of the Spanish *conquistadores* on the South American mainland in 1528 brought devastating epidemics against which indigenous people had few defenses. The ensuing population collapse and social disintegration resulted in the abandonment of most of the major pre-Columbian towns. Within fifty years, only one family is recorded as still living at the port of Salango, out of a population in the Señorio of Salangome that once numbered many thousands.

Early colonial maps record a scattering of isolated fishing villages until the late nineteenth century, when European colonists and merchants began to exploit local products such as the *tagua* nut—highly valued in Europe for making coat buttons. By the early 1920s the *hacienda* Agua Blanca had attracted a few migrant *campesino* families as seasonal work hands. Some stayed on to become year round residents, and in 1967 Agua Blanca achieved legal status as a *comuna*. A few years later the *hacienda* went bankrupt—a blessing in disguise, as the 1971 Agrarian Reform Law empowered the *comuna* to appropriate cultivable land left unattended.

During the 1970s the village's struggle to assert its identity and to secure right of access to the surrounding land was sharpened by the encroachment of herds of cattle driven in from far afield during the dry season to forage in the moist vegetation of the upper slopes and hills. Owners ordered their cattle hands to fire the forest to convert it into pasture. Not only did the villagers see the vegetation going up in smoke, their maize fields were often trampled and the crops eaten as well.

The creation of the Machalilla National Park was perceived as a further threat to the villagers' land and livelihood, with good reason. The Ministry of Agriculture which manages the Ecuadorian national park system did not include any provision for addressing the needs of a human population already resident in the designated protected area. During all the preliminary planning, pilot studies, and surveys, no explanation was offered to local people to allay their fears. Despite good intentions, a deep mutual distrust developed between

218

park officials and *campesinos,* who found their apprehensions confirmed by the harassment they began to suffer. Each week witnessed one *compañero* or another complaining bitterly of hard-earned sacks of charcoal being impounded and weekly earnings lost. From the park's perspective the *campesinos* were the willing agents of the forest's destruction. To the *campesinos* the very word "park" was synonymous with arrogance and unknown officials in a remote government bureaucracy taking decisions that would affect their lives. Worst of all, word got out that a plan was being considered to eject the villagers forcibly from the park and "resettle" them elsewhere.

When a topographical survey of the archaeological ruins began in 1981, members of the *comuna* plied the archaeologist with requests to explain what he was doing and why. This time the request met with a response. A meeting was arranged and collaboration between professionals and community was born.

Conscious of the Past, Building for the Future

In 1985 the third phase of the archaeological project began. Two field assistants were hired from the *comuna* for the clearing of brush and undergrowth from the ruins. The director took up residence in a corner of the *casa comunal* (a village hall, built by the community with assistance from a German volunteer organization in 1980) and used this space to assemble and sort the finds coming in from surface collections. This material was accessible for all to see, and questions could be asked and answered.

It soon became apparent that the archaeologist was interested in all the debris of prehistoric occupation that people were accustomed to finding in and around the ruins: bits and pieces of broken pottery, fragments of stone tools, scatters of marine shells. An impromptu class was held in a nearby gully to examine the layers of rubbish accumulating there. Laughter erupted as the "archaeological" remains of modern Agua Blanca culture were recognized: tin cans, a discarded shoe, bottle tops. Thoughtful glances probed several layers beneath.

"There are clay floors and hearths with identifiable Manteño pottery!" "So that's what stratigraphy is—one layer on top of another—and that layer down there must be older than the one on top!" "Who were the Manteños anyway?" "How big were their houses?" "Did they have a *casa comunal* too?" With their curiosity aroused and myriad questions to ask, villagers and archaeologist joined together in the search for answers.

In 1986 support from the Anthropological Museum of the Central Bank of Ecuador enabled the scope of the project to grow. Gradually members of the *comuna* were incorporated into the archaeological team and trained by Maria-Isabel Silva in the various tasks of drawing and excavating on site as well as washing, labeling, and classifying excavation finds in the field labora-tory. At each midday recess a different find was chosen for discussion and animated debates developed. Where was the material for a certain stone tool found? Why was lime encrusted on the inside of a vessel? How did the Manteños smelt the copper used to fashion delicately spiraled ear-rings? Why were the dead buried in funerary urns? Did the Manteños suffer droughts too?

The practiced eye of the *compañeros* in the archaeological team detected subtle differences of soil color and texture during excavation which would have eluded others unfamiliar with the local terrain. Machetes in hand, the mapping team cut sight lines. Then instructed by topographers, they mastered the intricacies of plumb bob, tape measure, and stadia rod to lay out the site grids. Reference collections of shells were gathered during expeditions to lo-cal beaches. A small storeroom and guest room were constructed adjoining the *casa comunal*.

Interest was further galvanized by the accidental discovery of an intact stone seat. This resulted in the opportunity to build a community archaeologi-cal exhibit designed by Chris Hudson in the *casa comunal*. (See "Focusing Pride in the Past," *Museum* 154[1987].) This exhibit, located in the center of the village, was a tangible expression of the community's links with its past. It also showed that the community was prepared to assume responsibility for caretaking that past. Its inauguration drew a crowd from all over the province: *campesinos* from neighboring hamlets and villages, school teachers from nearby towns, family and friends. As they guided visitors through the site, villagers belonging to the archaeological team explained in their own words their experience of discovering the past. This has now grown into the annual *encuentro cultural* (cultural festival) in which villagers celebrate their experi-ence with people from all parts of the country.

As the excavation progressed, the *casa comunal* became the venue for evening classes for the archaeological team dealing with all aspects of Manteño culture. Visiting specialists contributed with lectures and field excursions to explain their work. In addition, the project director took members of the ar-chaeological team with him on visits to other projects and archaeological sites all over the country. This allowed them to learn about the scope and variety of archaeological investigation and to see how other sites were being managed, mismanaged, or even neglected altogether. Team members could appreciate that the participatory approach to archaeology in Agua Blanca was something new.

In addition to setting up the field laboratory, Maria-Isabel Silva arranged meetings with national institutions in Quito, the capital. Slowly, backing was found for the task of building up site infrastructure. The British Council re-sponded to a request for funds to install two relief models and rest shelters, to better accommodate and inform visitors. The National Forestry Service released funds to build a boundary fence around the site, consolidate footpaths, and construct stairways. In due course, the Central Bank Museum in Guayaquil recognized the need for year round maintenance of the site and provided a budget to make this possible.

Casa Cultural: A Village Museum

One idea that arose from discussions between the project directors and village leaders was to create a permanent cultural center—a building that would display finds from the excavation and that would extend facilities available to both the archaeological project and visitors. By using local materials, it would be possible to create a structure that would fit into the village and landscape and that would also be inexpensive to build. In 1988 funding was obtained from the Ecuadorian Oil Corporation, and a British Council travel grant enabled Chris Hudson to return to the village to supervise construction.

Labor for the project was entirely drawn from the village itself, and in addition three *mingas* (an Andean tradition entailing communal labor on public projects) were organized to get things going. At the suggestion of the village president, one of these was made up of school children who enthusiastically collected stones for the foundations; even the children would be able to say that they helped to build the *casa cultural*.

The building is of timber, split bamboo, palm thatch, and *quincha*—a render made of manure, earth, straw, and water. It comprises a generous porch with a shop, plus an exhibition hall on the first level. An office, storeroom, and living accommodations for the archaeological project are upstairs. The entrance porch and balcony afford a magnificent panorama of the valley and welcome shade in which to sit and rest.

Nearly every one of thirty-five foundation holes yielded pre-Spanish remains—floor levels, potsherds, hearths, and animal bones. In two places stone walls were uncovered, which were excavated, mapped, and photographed by the archaeological team. One was later cleaned up and roped off to become an exhibit right at the entrance to the museum.

The display in the eight-by-eight meter exhibition hall is modest, but bright and informative. Its purpose is to orient visitors concerning the extent and significance of the prehistoric town before they tour the archaeological site on foot. Simple glass modules on plywood bases protect the exhibits, and larger pieces, such as stone seats, are on open display, which also includes a "please touch" table. Information is provided by text, photos, maps, and a simple time-chart incorporating real potsherds. The display will be upgraded to include new finds as resources become available, and funds are currently being sought to produce a ten-minute audiovisual introduction.

Living, Learning, and Celebrating

The overwhelming reality facing the *comuna* has been limited material and financial resources. This has also had its positive side, however. Nearly everything that has been attempted by the *comuna* and archaeologists working together has had to be based on careful deliberation and discussion. Much thought has gone into determining the *comuna's* real needs and, equally important, what is feasible. This community-based approach poses an alternative to "top down" development strategies which risk excluding or deliberately overriding the creative contribution that a local population can make toward solving problems of environmental and cultural resource management.

In the Agua Blanca Archaeological Project, respect for, and willingness to work with, the existing *comuna* organization went hand in hand with recognition of the pressing economic realities of a community whose natural environment is in jeopardy. The close involvement of the archaeological project with the village opened new possibilities in the cultural life of the community which have proved to be a tool for education in the broadest sense. A conscious attempt has been made to involve a wide range of institutions and individuals.

The process has met with many obstacles—some stemming from ignorance, some from indifference, and some from outright hostility to new ways of working. On the other hand, vital interest and support has sometimes come from unexpected quarters. While more challenges lie ahead, we are optimistic; these first steps have shown how a knowledge of the past, and an identification with it, can be catalysts for change in rural Latin America.

Human Rights and the Environment

BARBARA R. JOHNSTON

Human rights advocacy has a checkered history in anthropology. Some anthropologists have resisted the role of advocate. Others see the notion of universal inalienable rights as contradicting observed cultural diversity and violating the principle of cultural relativism. The 1980s, however, drew many anthropologists into the struggle for basic human rights of the peoples with whom they work. Barbara Johnston reports here on an effort to link environmental protection with human rights and to use anthropological knowledge and perspectives to influence policy on an international scale. A United Nations inquiry led Johnston to mobilize a Society for Applied Anthropology-sponsored study project which argued that the right to a healthy environment is a basic human right and which showed that exposure to environmental degradation is selective on the basis of cultural, class, or racial identity. The project's results were re-ported to the United Nations and distributed to a variety of influential policy institutions. An expanded version of the project report, Who Pays the Price? Examining the Sociocultural Context of Environmental Deg-radation, *was published first by the Society for Applied Anthropology and then in 1994 by Island Press.* E. B. L.

1989. The pre-Earth Day 20 media blitz had reached its fevered pitch. Chico Mendez was murdered, and the images of rain forests burning and rubber tappers nervously awaiting the bullets were seen on TV screens across the world. Birds dropped from the trees in Mexico City, their lungs and intestines lined and even their feathers coated with cadmium, lead, and other heavy metals. Ships circled the globe searching for a port to land their stores of garbage. With "glasnost" discourse encouraged, information flowed in new directions, and overnight Poland was recognized as the most polluted spot on the planet.

Ecoactivism was suddenly politically correct. Burger King joined the boy-cott on Amazonian beef. McDonalds switched to paper packing. Melitta in-troduced unbleached coffee filters. In this time of idealistic

Barbara R. Johnston is Director of the SfAA/EPA Environmental Anthropology Project (http://www.sfaa.net/eap/abouteap.html) and Senior Research Fellow at the Center for Political Ecology (P.O. Box 8467, Santa Cruz, CA 95061; <bjohnston@igc.org>).

Originally published in *Practicing Anthropology* 16,1(1994):8-12, this article has been edited and abridged for republication here.

224

neoenvironmentalism, the media brought loud voices into our homes. They also brought images of strident voices being silenced.

It was in this context that the Sierra Club Legal Defense Fund, with the help of Friends of the Earth International, presented the United Nations Sub-Commission on Prevention of Discrimination and Protection of Minorities a position paper on environmental rights. They urged the Sub-Commission to examine the relationship between human rights and environmental problems. They argued that people who experience torture, imprisonment, or death as a result of their access to, effort to acquire, and/or attempts to disseminate sensitive environmental information suffer an abuse of human rights. They also noted increasing global awareness of links between government-sanctioned action, environmental degradation, and the deteriorating health and welfare of communities. In essence, they challenged the Sub-Commission to consider broadening the scope of international human rights conventions to include consideration of environment-related abuses, and to provide an international forum to hear individual cases of human environmental rights abuse.

Much to the surprise of the Sierra Club Legal Defense Fund, the Sub-Commission accepted their challenge. They appointed one of their members, Mdme. Fatma Zohra Ksentini, a lawyer from Algeria, to make a preliminary investigation of the linkage between human rights and environmental concerns and to report back to the Sub-Commission in 1990 on the feasibility of a comprehensive study of the topic.

In August 1990, Mdme. Ksentini reported to the Sub-Commission that a study of human rights and the environment was warranted. Mdme. Ksentini noted that few international human rights instruments include specific environmental provisions. She argued that a study was needed to determine whether one or more new instruments should be adopted to apply existing human rights principles in an environmental context, or whether an entirely new statement of human environmental rights is needed. Other issues include whether substantive standards should be established for rights to clean air, drinkable water, or self-sustaining forests; whether new procedures should be made available, such as rights to participation in decision making and rights to information from governments, intergovernmental organizations, and corporations; and whether new mechanisms need to be structured to allow international and national tribunals on the violations of these rights. Mdme. Ksentini recommended examining human rights as they apply to four broad areas of potential environmental harm: natural habitats, natural resources, human settlements, and human health.

The Sub-Commission accepted Mdme. Ksentini's preliminary note, voted to undertake a comprehensive three-year study of human rights and their application to environmental problems (extended in 1992 to a four-year period), and designated Mdme. Ksentini as special rapporteur in charge of the project.

The Study Process

Within the United Nations system, it is the Sub-Commission on Prevention of Discrimination and Protection of Minorities which generates and develops international law in the field of human rights and makes recommendations for the adoption of standards by other bodies, including the Commission on Human Rights, the Economic and Social Council, and the General Assembly. By designating a special rapporteur, the Sub-Commission initiated a formal process of study and consideration of recommendations. This action was taken with full awareness that this study and its recommendations might go well beyond existing human rights norms. The decision to undertake this study was subsequently endorsed by the full Commission on Human Rights and by the United Nations Economic and Social Council at their meetings in Spring 1991. (The United States was the only country to vote against authorization of the study, as the Bush administration opposed any moves to encompass environmental concerns within the framework of human rights; Japan abstained.)

To undertake a study, the Sub-Commission relies upon the resources of the Centre for Human Rights and on the voluntary contributions of nongovernmental organizations and individuals. In this case, the Sierra Club Legal Defense Fund, acting at the request of Mdme. Ksentini, has served as the coordinating agency for voluntary contributions—disseminating information about the study, organizing efforts to contribute to the study, and directing contributions to Mdme. Ksentini and the Centre for Human Rights.

I first encountered a reference to this study process in *Earth Island Journal* (Fall 1991). I was compiling material for a textbook, and I contacted the Sierra Club Legal Defense Fund in hopes of establishing a collaborative information exchange. Most responses to their call for contributions had been from human rights lawyers and interest-specific environmental organizations. At that time, materials for the Sub-Commission study consisted of reviews of national constitutions, legislation, and international human rights conventions; a few case studies of ecoactivists experiencing human rights abuse; and descriptions of various environmental problems. My offer to provide anthropological documentation of community-based experiences of human environmental rights abuse represented the sole offer of social science input.

Realizing the huge need and my limited capabilities, I asked Society for Applied Anthropology (SfAA) President Carole Hill for help publicizing the study and organizing broader anthropological involvement. Eventually the SfAA Executive Committee approved the formation of a Committee on Human Rights and the Environment. Meetings with the Sierra Club Legal Defense Fund, the SfAA Executive Committee and SfAA officers, representatives of Cultural Survival, and other fellow anthropologists led to a plan. Our contribution could be most effective, we decided, in broadening the definition of victims of environmental rights abuse and in illustrating the processes and

226

mechanisms which initiate, structure, legitimize, and reproduce victimization. As anthropologists, we could provide the descriptive rationale for human environmental rights.

A research and action plan was prepared by the SfAA Committee outlining a three-phase effort that would rely on contributions by committee members and colleagues and that would result in a preliminary report, a final report, and a summary overview. The goal was to present well-documented examples of the relationship between government action (or government-sanctioned action), environmental degradation, and subsequent human misery. Regional overviews would be followed by a series of cases describing situations of human environmental rights abuse and identifying the contexts which predispose certain groups to victimization. The final report would be prepared in time for consideration and inclusion in the 1993 Sub-Commission report to the United Nations Commission on Human Rights. A booklet providing a summary of the study with representative examples of human environmental rights abuse would be distributed to national and international policy and advocacy groups in support of the U.N. Sub-Commission's effort to articulate human environmental rights.

In March 1992 the SfAA Executive Board approved and endorsed the draft preliminary report of the committee and authorized limited financial support for its duplication and dissemination. Last minute case studies were added to the draft, and the preliminary report was formally released in May 1992. After a year of review and revision and of expansion of case materials, the final report, entitled "Who Pays the Price? Examining the Sociocultural Context of Environmental Degradation," was completed in May 1993.

In July 1993 a summary of the study was published in booklet form. This booklet was prepared with the assistance of the Nathan Cummings Foundation, Human Environmental Rights Fund. The booklet represented an abbreviated version of the final report.

Conceptualizing Human Environmental Rights Abuse

In my role as Chair of the SfAA Committee on Human Rights and the Environment, I was responsible for organizing the study, coordinating research efforts, editing contributions, and preparing introductory materials for the report. My biggest difficulty was finding a conceptual strategy to link individual cases in a cohesive fashion. For this purpose, I developed the concept of "selective victimization" as an expansion of the environmental racism thesis.

The environmental racism thesis is based on the observation that people of color bear the brunt of the United States' pollution problems. Various studies demonstrate the role of racial discrimination in environmental policy making, in the enforcement of regulations and laws, in the siting of toxic waste disposal facilities, in the siting of polluting industries, and in the legal sanctioning of minority community exposure to poisons and pollutants. (See, for example, Bunyan Bryant and Paul Mohai, eds., *Race and the Incidence of Environmental Hazards* [Boulder, Co.: Westview Press, 1992] and Robert Bullard, ed., *Confronting Environmental Racism* [Boston: South End Press, 1993].)

The notion of environmental racism encourages analysis of linkages between histories, cultures, political and economic conditions, and environmental concerns. We found, however, that the focus on race loses its usefulness in contexts where other cultural variables structure the differential environmental health experience. In searching for a term broad enough to include diverse variables (race, class, caste, gender, age, ethnicity, religion), we developed the notion of "selective victimization."

Selective victimization, like environmental racism, is a product of cultural differences as well as political and economic relationships and particular histories (of colonialism, imperialism, ethnocide, and ecocide). Cultural values and ideals inform and structure the goals and development agendas of governments, of national and multinational corporations, and of the local elite. These values combined with preexisting social conditions result in and legitimize the exposure of certain groups to hazardous environmental conditions while others are free to live, recreate, procreate, and die in a healthy setting.

Study Findings

The final report of the SfAA Committee on Human Rights and the Environment incorporates this concept of selective victimization and includes, as planned, regional overviews with case-specific examples of human environmental rights abuse (Latin America and North America), country-specific overviews (China, Botswana, and Russia), and issue-specific studies (nuclear testing and mining). Also included are two position papers, one assessing the role of natural resources in nation and state conflicts in the twentieth century and the other providing a summary discussion of the concept of "indigenous peoples." While our focus is the general relationship between environmental degradation and human rights abuse, many of the examples we use involve indigenous people and the state. Given their typically isolated homelands and the presence, in many cases, of previously unexploited and/or recently discovered resources (mineral, energy, timber, etc.), indigenous peoples are a significant group of victims.

Taken together, these cases argue that the right to a healthy environment is a basic human right; that some people have been more vulnerable than others in experiencing the human consequences of environmental degradation; that their collective experiences represent a form of selective victimization where some people (and their rights to land, resources, health, and environmental protection) are expendable in the name of national security, national energy, national debt, and natural resource conservation; and that significant biases

228

exist in the present system of identifying victims, forms of abuse, and adequate compensation for loss. Our study concluded that selective victimization is a significant problem in structuring resource management, environmental preservation, and sustainable development policy. Our findings suggest:

- that human rights violations occur as both a preceding factor and as a result of environmental degradation;
- that processes, as well as individuals and organizations, can deny human rights;
- that it is important to consider group as well as individual rights;
- that the category of "victim" is shaped by preexisting contexts of power and powerlessness: gender, race, and ethnic-based inequities, as well as occupation, generation, and poverty and class, are all significant categories of concern;
- that resource rights (e.g., to land, timber, water), the ability to organize to protect land and resource bases, and the ability to transform traditional resource management systems to meet modern needs are crucial factors in ensuring sustainable life-styles;
- that there is a need to document the immediate as well as long-term implications of change; and finally,
- that the process of protecting a "healthy environment" may, in some cases, result in human rights abuse.

Applying Anthropology in the Policy Arena

The findings of our committee are not startling or new if your perspective is anthropology, but we believe they can have a significant impact in the policy arena. Originally we expected to submit our report to one person: the special rapporteur assigned to study the relationship between human rights and the environment and to prepare preliminary recommendations for the United Nations Commission on Human Rights. As the SfAA study progressed, awareness of our study and interest in receiving our findings increased. We submitted copies of our preliminary report to Special Rapporteur Ksentini, the Sierra Club Legal Defense Fund, the Centre for Human Rights in Geneva, the SfAA Executive Committee, and study contributors and interested colleagues.

This initial circulation prompted requests from numerous quarters. The preliminary report was distributed by the Sierra Club Legal Defense Fund to environmental nongovernmental organizations (NGOs) attending the Earth Summit/United Nations Conference on Environment and Development meetings in Rio de Janeiro. Our study was written up in the Fall 1992 issue of *Race and Poverty* (a newsletter for environmental equity/social justice NGOs), prompting requests from grass-roots activist organizations throughout the

United States. The study was also described in the Culture and Agriculture unit news column of the *Anthropology Newsletter* (October 1992) which resulted in requests for material from colleagues and students as well as additional contributions for the final report.

After the November 1992 elections, a summary briefing and our preliminary report were submitted to the Clinton transition team with copies delivered to Al Gore, Bruce Babbitt, and Timothy Wirth. Portions of the report were also distributed with the summary briefing to the in-coming Congress, thanks to study contributor Greg Button, who is the American Anthropological Association Congressional Fellow for 1993.

Informal reproduction and circulation of the report resulted in its use as a supplementary text in the classroom and as background material for the human environmental rights media. Alan Durning, of World Watch, used the report extensively in his 1993 paper, "Guardians of the Land: Indigenous Peoples and the Health of the Earth" (World Watch paper no. 112; also Chapter 5 "Supporting Indigenous Peoples" in *State of the World 1993*, by Lester Brown et al. [New York: W. W. Norton]). We also received a call from a producer from the Public Broadcasting System series "Rights and Wrongs" who requested a copy for background material and to develop possible program themes.

Our final report was distributed to a limited group of contributors, politicians, environmental and human rights organizations, and United Nations Human Rights and the Environment Special Rapporteur Ksentini. This report was twice the length of the preliminary report (197 pages) and included case studies and essays from 17 contributors. The limited nature of our distribution strategy reflected our minimal funds, as well as the nature of our primary target audience (politicians, environmental and human rights advocates, and other members of the international policy community). Recognizing that constraints to applying anthropology in the public arena include issues of "readability" (the language used, the length of the report, the varied nature of cases and essays), we placed greater emphasis on preparing and distributing our booklet.

With the July 1993 release of our booklet, "Human Rights and the Environment: Examining the Sociocultural Context of Environmental Crisis," we entered the final stages of this study process. Some 300 copies were printed and distributed. Over 150 copies of the booklet were mailed to international NGOs, to colleagues in the academic community, and to various politicians. Another 150 copies were distributed at international conferences and United Nations meetings, including the August 1993 International Hunter-Gatherer meetings in Moscow, the July 1993 International Union of Anthropological and Ethnological Sciences Congress in Mexico City, and the October 1993 Third World Studies Association meetings in Tacoma. Our booklet was distributed in Geneva and presented to the Sub-Commission by the Sierra Club

Legal Defense Fund. As an NGO officially recognized by the U.N. Commission on Human Rights, the Sierra Club Legal Defense Fund can formally present information to the Commission and have it enter the United Nations record. Thus, our study findings and selected cases were formally received by all members of the Sub-Commission and the Human Rights Commission, as well as entered into U.N. records. The booklet was also distributed to members of the Working Group on Indigenous Populations.

Assessing the Efficacy of our Efforts

Our efforts to broadly distribute our booklet continue to generate interest. I have received letters of support and requests for additional copies from all levels of the political arena: state legislators, members of the U.S. Senate, representatives of various arms of the United Nations, and others. Such requests have also come from social science researchers as well as activists working in various nongovernmental organizations (everything from Amnesty International to the National Resources Defense Council). I have also had requests to present our ideas and study findings to other disciplines at their professional meetings. Thus, I was a featured speaker at the October 1993 meetings of the Third World Studies Association and will be a featured speaker at the Association of American Geographers meetings in San Francisco in April 1994.

In regards to our initial objective of influencing a specific United Nations study process, we have had limited direct effects. Our material is not quoted or cited in the 1992 or 1993 report from Special Rapporteur Ksentini to the Sub-Commission, or in the Sub-Commission's report to the Commission on Human Rights. At an indirect level, we have played a role in broadening the scope of the U.N. study from its initial focus on individual instances of human rights abuse to its present acknowledgment of the abuse of group rights. The degree to which the distribution of our findings affects public policy at international as well as national levels remains to be seen.

Where we have clearly had the greatest success is in influencing public awareness of the problems and processes of selective victimization; the *State of the World* series, for example, is published in twenty-three languages and distributed across the world. Perhaps even more significant in the long run is the way this study has stimulated numerous colleagues around the world and across applied social science disciplines to reorient their research and writing efforts. Many more are now exploring links between government action or government-sanctioned action, environmental degradation, and subsequent human misery, and directing their writing efforts to the public and policy arenas.

Redefining Relationships:
American Indians and National Parks

DAVID RUPPERT

Often an instrument of colonial domination in the late nineteenth and early twentieth centuries, applied anthropology in the late twentieth century aspired to facilitate a collaborative approach to problems of conflict and change. In this essay, National Park Service ethnographer David Ruppert describes how, partly through the force of federal law and policy, a government agency has begun to take seriously the wishes of American Indian tribal governments in the treatment of buried human remains, geological features, and wild game. Though a huge power differential remains, it is now advantageous for federal agencies to treat official representatives of Indian tribes with the kind of equanimity not shown them since the days when their ancestors sometimes held the balance of power between competing colonial military forces. Like the administrators of treaty parlays in olden days, Ruppert served, as he describes it, as a "cultural broker." His account makes clear that, if viable agreements are to be reached and lasting changes made, understanding the corporate culture of the government agency is at least as important as understanding the culture of what used to be called "the target group."

J. A. P.

What are now federal lands and resources have been for centuries part of the cultural heritage of American Indian tribal communities. Management of these lands and resources, as well as relationships between agencies and tribes, should reflect this fact. In the past, these relationships have been characterized by one-way communication, dominant-subordinate relations, and the imposition of non-Indian methods of interaction. Today, a growing tribal political awareness and resulting legislation dealing with American Indian links to natural resources are forcing federal agencies to redefine their relationships with American Indian peoples.

David Ruppert is a cultural anthropologist with the Intermountain Region Support Office of the National Park Service in Denver, Colorado (12795 West Alameda, Denver, CO 80225).

Originally published as part of a special section on "Federal Law, Native Americans, and Cultural Resources," guest edited by Inga E. Treitler and Richard W. Stoffle, in *Practicing Anthropology* 16,3(1994):10-13, this article has been edited for republication here.

This article summarizes a few of the efforts made by the National Park Service (NPS) in the Rocky Mountain Region to establish new ways of doing business with American Indian communities. The region includes [in 1994] forty-one national parks in the six states of Colorado, Wyoming, Utah, Montana, North Dakota, and South Dakota. Well over fifty federally recognized Indian tribes have historic and culture ties to these parks.

New ways of conducting business for the NPS means establishing a new set of rules for fielding and responding to tribal concerns. These concerns have revolved around the management of American Indian items in storage or collection facilities, the treatment of Indian burials and burial sites, and the protection of natural resources considered culturally important by tribal communities. For American Indian peoples these concerns are not new, but they have been repeatedly ignored by government agencies for decades, if not centuries. For federal agencies, these concerns *are* new, in the sense that federal agencies have only recently been forced to acknowledge them and have only just begun to craft ways to respond.

The following examples of consultation with Indian groups illustrate recent efforts by one agency to bring American Indian concerns to the table on an equal footing with other factors normally considered by federal agency management in environmental assessments.

Human Remains at Mesa Verde National Park

During a construction project at Mesa Verde National Park in 1992, a water pipeline trenching crew inadvertently uncovered human remains from an Indian burial site estimated to be six hundred years old. In the past, such a discovery would have forced a halt of construction activities until professional archaeologists had a chance to excavate and evaluate the site for its importance to the archaeological record. The primary concern would have been for the loss of a cultural resource as defined by non-Indian people, and remedial action would have aimed at preserving information relevant to the archaeological record.

Today, the Native American Graves Protection and Repatriation Act requires consultation with Indian groups affiliated with any human remains found on federal lands. The site at Mesa Verde was back-filled to protect the remains. No effort was made to study them outside of a cursory determination by the monitoring archaeologist that the remains were most likely of Anazasi origin. Since there was no way to determine specific contemporary tribal affiliation of the remains, the park superintendent notified all the Pueblo Indian communities, the Hopi Tribe, and the Navajo Nation, as well as the Ute Mountain Ute and the Southern Ute tribes whose reservations border the park.

A series of meetings with representatives of these tribes resulted in a formal agreement regarding an acceptable means to treat the remains. Close collaboration with tribal traditionalists provided guidance on what constitutes culturally appropriate management and how specific elements of the agreement were to be implemented (e.g., proper storage of remains already disturbed, preparation of the site for complete exhumation, location of the reburial site, proper positioning of the body for reburial, respectful handling of the remains). The agreement was extended to address any future discoveries made during the pipeline replacement project.

My role in this process was to serve as a cultural broker between the groups involved. There were disagreements between representatives of the various Indian tribes, but these were worked out in executive sessions or in private without my participation. The greatest need for cultural brokerage was between the tribes and park staff. Some park staff viewed reburying the remains as a loss of scientific data and a loss for park interpretive programs that could teach visitors about Mesa Verde. For the tribes, the burial remains were part of their past and present identity as Indian people. The unearthed remains constituted a disturbance of an important set of relationships between the living, the dead, and the earth; reburial was seen as means of restoring these disturbed relationships.

Successful collaboration on reburial has led to increased participation by tribal communities in the management of Mesa Verde's resources. Mesa Verde was established precisely for the purpose of preserving and interpreting the unique remains of large American Indian village sites, including houses, grain storage buildings, religiously important structures (kivas), and burial sites. Thus, the park holds a special interest for many American Indian communities. Meetings with tribal representatives, funded by the NPS, will now be held on a regular basis to cover a wide range of management issues at the park.

Climbing Devil's Tower National Monument

Devil's Tower National Monument was established by Congress in 1906 to preserve and protect, for scientific purposes, a spectacular outcropping of igneous rock in the Black Hills in eastern Wyoming. The enabling legislation did not recognize that this same rock tower was (and still is) considered a sacred site by a number of American Indian tribal communities. Management of the Tower has recently become entangled in a web of conflicting cultural values involving the national and international rock climbing community and a number of American Indian tribes.

Devil's Tower has posed a challenge to rock climbers for years. Early in the century few attempted to climb the tower, but recently climbing has increased at a remarkable rate. From 1937 (first year of an official count) to 1947 a total of nineteen people attempted the climb. In 1973, 312 climbed; in 1984, 3,136 climbed; and in each of the past 6 years over 6,000 have climbed the Tower. Since climbing is normally concentrated in the warmer months of

May to August, the rock face of the Tower has become a busy place with an average of fifty people per day attempting the climb. The areas around the Tower and the Tower itself are used for vision quests and traditional prayer activities by members of many American Indian tribal communities. As climbing activities increased, the American Indian community became more vocal about the intrusion at a site they consider religiously important. For these tribal communities, recreational climbing of the Tower is viewed as "sacrilegious," as would be recreational climbing of the dome of St. Peter's Cathedral in Rome for members of the Roman Catholic Church.

In 1992 the park began preparation of a "Climbing Management Plan" which includes assessing the impacts of climbing on the Monument. In the past, such a plan would have focused almost exclusively on the effects of climbers on natural resources, such as raptor nesting sites or the viability of fledglings, or on damage to the rock itself through the placement of bolts along climbing routes. Due to recent legislation, and to increased expression of American Indian concerns, several American Indian groups were consulted for the impact assessment.

A confrontational climate involving both cultural and legal values was set. Climbers operate from a set of values deeply rooted in Euro-American traditions of self-reliance and individualism. American Indian values associated with the Tower focus on the earth as the source of group origins and spiritual identity. American Indians insisted that climbing be stopped altogether in order to end what is, in their view, damage to a traditional religious site; climbers insisted that the Tower was an important international site for climbers and that restricting their access was an infringement on their legal rights.

I was asked to organize and facilitate the planning process in a way that recognized the multicultural elements of impact assessment. A work group was formed which consisted of representatives from the county government, national climbing organizations, national environmental groups, and American Indian organizations. Tribal affiliation and interest was determined through research that documented the historic and cultural affiliation of various tribes with the Tower. The group met over a period of eighteen months to help formulate a plan to address the needs of all. As a result, the proposed management plan offers restrictions on climbing (but not a total ban) as well as a means for the NPS to explain to the general public the traditional Indian religious values associated with the Tower.

Compromise was reached through a process of cross-cultural education. American Indian representatives initially felt that if they understood the reasons non-Indians climbed Devil's Tower, the conflict between the groups would be easier to address. For their part, the climbers listened to Indian accounts, often allegorical, of the religious importance of the Tower.

Much of my time was spent facilitating dialogue. At later meetings discourse between work group members became less strident. The style of presentation and the choice of vocabulary changed almost imperceptibly as mutual understanding grew and as the need for comprise became apparent. I took these changes into account in the planning and presentation of issues at subsequent meetings.

The dialogue established through the work group has brought out points of conflict, but it has also brought opportunities for greater understanding and mutual respect. In addition, all work group members have come to a better understanding of the government planning process. To a large extent, positions remain polarized, and the work group's compromise solution remains to be judged by the public. Nevertheless, the work group has provided a forum within which all interested cultural groups can ensure that their perspective is represented in at least one, if not more, alternative management solutions. [In 1999 the U.S. Court of Appeals upheld the National Park Service's 1995 accommodation that asks rock climbers to refrain voluntarily from scaling the tower during June, when Indians perform sacred ceremonies there.]

Hunting at Badlands National Park

Located in the southwestern corner of South Dakota, Badlands National Park is divided into northern and southern units. The northern unit of the park is under federal ownership and control. The southern unit (133,300 acres), added to the park by an act of Congress in 1968, rests within the boundaries of tribal trust lands of the Pine Ridge Indian Reservation. Although Congress instructed the NPS to manage this southern unit as a park, it also instructed the NPS to come to an agreement with the Pine Ridge tribal government to ensure retention of certain tribal rights.

Among the reserved rights was the tribal right to hunt in the southern unit. In 1993, the tribe decided that the time had come to exercise this right and announced plans to issue hunting permits for tribal members beginning in the fall of 1994. Wary of impacts to the game population and concerned that a hunt would set an unwanted precedent for parks, the park agreed to work with the tribe to prepare a game management plan. (Grand Teton National Park is the only unit with the designation "park," outside of Alaska, which allows a controlled hunt. Controlled hunting is allowed in other units with other designations, such as Glen Canyon which is a National Recreation Area.)

The unique feature of this cooperative arrangement is that the Oglala Sioux Park and Recreation Authority (OSPRA), the tribal office charged with managing the hunt, asked that the NPS incorporate traditional Oglala cultural elements into the game management plan. As a result, the Park Service has provided funding for a cultural anthropologist/ecologist to work with OSPRA, game biologists, and tribal members to document salient Oglala cultural features to be used in the game management plan. The resulting plan, not yet completed, will be a joint tribal/NPS document emphasizing the maintenance of sustainable game populations by combining western and traditional Oglala methods of game and habitat management.

The task of documenting contemporary Oglala methods of game and habitat management has just begun. It is unknown to what extent the specifics of Indian and non-Indian management practices can complement one another or be combined in a coherent, workable plan of operations. The greatest challenge may be in finding ways to incorporate or combine Oglala traditional knowledge about the environment with non-Indian, western views. Nevertheless, the incorporation of tribal values and cultural practices in a plan of this type will, it is hoped, provide improvements in game management. It will also signal a significant change in the relationship between the park and the tribal community—from one of federal government domination to one of joint management or partnership in resource stewardship.

New Directions for Agencies

Since the turn of the century Euro-American perspectives have dominated judgments regarding cultural meanings and values associated with National Parks. Today it is necessary to redefine these relationships as "partnerships" with an emphasis on two-way communication, a commitment to egalitarian tenets, and greater attention to potential cross-cultural barriers to communication. These partnerships should be aimed at joint tribal-federal management of historic, cultural, and natural resources in parks that are linked to the cultural identity of Indian communities. The form and content of these partnerships will take time to develop. It will also take a willingness on the part of both tribes and agencies to work out a new way of doing business which is responsive to the cross-cultural environment in which they both must operate.

It is easy to talk or write about new procedures or relationships, but quite another matter to design, fund, and implement them such that they become part of the internal structure of a bureaucracy. The present processes of interaction (or lack of them) between federal agencies and American Indian tribes have had centuries to develop, and they have become solidly institutionalized within the structure and organization of the agencies themselves. The challenge is to make the new procedures and relationships become the conventions or "customs" of the federal agency. Once they are part of the normal operating procedures of an agency, it will be easier to find funding and staff to work on long-term relationships that meet the needs of the agency and of distinct tribal groups.

Cases such as those described here offer insights into how these new relationships can be initiated. The Mesa Verde case shows how agencies and tribes can tailor agreements to accommodate the needs of specific cross-cultural situations. The Devil's Tower experience illustrates a planning process in which representatives of different cultural groups can negotiate settlements while maintaining the integrity of their unique value systems. The Badlands hunting issue presents an important opportunity to develop a model for cooperative cross-cultural comanagement of natural resources. In each case individual formal agreements with different tribes set in motion a defined process of interaction as well as a set of mutual obligations. They also set a period of time after which agreements can, and should, be modified to reflect changing agency and tribal needs.

Anthropologists can identify problems in current interactions and make recommendations for the creation of a more cooperative environment supportive of conflict resolution between agencies and tribes. Bureaucracies are conservative by nature, however, and recommendations for changes are often difficult to implement. Through research and intercultural facilitation, the National Park Service's ethnography program at the Rocky Mountain Region has helped redefine relationships not only between the NPS and American Indian communities, but also between American Indians and non-Indian groups. The goal now is to institutionalize these relationships.

238

Translating Research into Policy: What More Does It Take?

MERRILL EISENBERG

*Based on her work as a consultant in program planning and evalua-
tion, Merrill Eisenberg argues that to have an impact on programs and
policies anthropologists must not only do well-grounded, scientifically
solid research and present the results in ways comprehensible to policy
makers and the public. They must also be thoroughly acquainted with
the political context and policy culture surrounding each project, and
they must act on that knowledge. To highlight some revelant contextual
features and the actions anthropologists can take, she compares two
projects—one a well-executed study of sexually transmitted diseases,
commissioned by the Connecticut Department of Health, which had no
impact on policy or programs; the other a study of disability services
commissioned by the Department of Human Services which resulted in
changes in policy, programs, and administrative organization. Eisenberg
stresses that it is every bit as necessary and as legitimate for
anthropolgists to use their skills and knowledge to change the behavior
of policy makers as it is for them to attempt to change the behavior of
the intended beneficiaries of policies and programs.*   P. J. H.

Public assistance, health, and social service programs are under increasing
pressure to address what are viewed by the press, the general public, and politicians as critical problems in the communities they serve. At the same time,
programs are increasingly required to account for the way in which public
funds are spent and to prove that they are having an impact. This climate has
led to a variety of opportunities for anthropologists and other social scientists
to participate in program planning and evaluation. I have worked in this capacity as a consultant for almost a decade.

A common thread in the applied anthropology literature is that planning
and evaluation activities that are informed by anthropological perspectives,
concepts, and methods are more responsive to community needs and will

Merrill Eisenberg conducts contractual research for various state agencies, municipalities, and
private nonprofit groups. She can be contacted at 3001 E. Drachman Street, Tucson, AZ 85716-
3544; <merrill@azstarnet.com>.

Originally published as part of a special section on "Welfare Policy and Practice," guest edited by
Irene Glasser, in *Practicing Anthropology* 16,4(1994):35-38.

240

therefore result in policy and programs that are more sensitive and effective in ameliorating community problems. The role of anthropology is often formulated around the contribution of objective information to the policy makers. The research process is removed from the policy-making process. Understanding the culture of the policy process is addressed primarily to alert anthropologists to the need to present information in a format that policy makers recognize and understand. (See, for example, *Applied Anthropology in America*, Second Edition, Elizabeth M. Eddy and William L. Partridge, eds. [New York: Columbia, 1991] and *Anthropology and Public Policy: A Dialogue*, Walter Goldsmidt, ed. [Washington: American Anthropological Association, 1986].)

My work has demonstrated, however, that it takes much more than good anthropology well presented to change public programs and policy. Factors that anthropologists must consider and act on if they want to have an impact on public health, social service, and assistance systems include (1) the sponsors' commitment and capacity to effect policy change, (2) the temporality of the problem being addressed, (3) the policy process and culture to be affected, and (4) resources available for involvement in the policy debate.

I will demonstrate these points by comparing two projects on which I have worked. The cases were chosen as best and worst scenarios in order to highlight my points. We'll start with the bad news.

The Bad News: Great Study, No Change

Connecticut, like every state, tracks the incidence of sexually transmitted diseases (STDs). Statewide rates for syphilis and gonorrhea are reported nationally, and states are ranked against each other. From 1988-1989 the syphilis rate increased 57 percent in Connecticut. This was cause for alarm at the Department of Health Services (DOHS). After examining the data, the DOHS determined that the city of Bridgeport, where the rate had increased 120 percent, was contributing heavily to the statewide increase.

DOHS and the faculty of the Department of Community Medicine at the University of Connecticut School of Medicine entered into an agreement whereby two anthropologists would conduct a study in cooperation with the Bridgeport Health Department to determine how best to address this critical "problem." The DOHS wanted an in-depth analysis that would lead to the development of an innovative approach to addressing STD prevention at the community level. The DOHS stated that its intention was to fund an experimental intervention based on the findings. This was an ideal opportunity for anthropologists to inform public policy and programs.

The research effort was placed within the STD unit of the Bridgeport Health Department. This unit receives all reports of positive STD tests, operates an STD clinic, and is responsible for contacting all individuals who have a reportable STD and identifying and tracing their sexual contacts. AIDS and STD programs are bureaucratically separate at both the state and local levels. Although many of the issues we were researching had direct implications for AIDS prevention, the project operated solely in the realm of the STD program.

The study included mapping all reported cases of sexually transmitted diseases (excluding AIDS, which is not a reportable disease) by census tract and analyzing formal and informal community resources in two focal neighborhoods. Then, using a "grounded theory" approach, more than fifty open-ended interviews were conducted with neighborhood residents to identify language, meaningful behavioral categories, and attitudes about sex, sex partners, and safe sex. Four research assistants from the neighborhoods were trained to conduct interviews; they also acted as key informants in interpreting findings. The interviews were followed by a multistage sample survey also implemented by the research assistants. Survey data were computer analyzed at the medical school and interpreted by the research assistants and the two anthropologists.

Midway through the project there was a gubernatorial election, and when the governorship changed, so did the commissioner of DOHS. The new commissioner had different priorities with regard to departmental interests and expenditures, and she replaced key DOHS staff, including the person who had shepherded the STD project. The new staff were preoccupied with defining and learning their roles and did not have the interest in this project that the previous staff had. In addition, the STD rate in Bridgeport and in Connecticut had moderated.

Although focus was lost at the state level, the research continued. Policy and program development recommendations were formulated by the research team and shared with the Bridgeport Health Department and its community advisory structure. These recommendations were then presented to the state health department in the form of a proposal for funding of a community-based prevention program.

Scholarly papers about the study were presented at the annual meetings of the American Anthropological Association, the American Public Health Association, and the Northeast Public Health Association. The utility of using this approach for community health planning was also documented in an article in the *Journal of the American Public Health Association* (Stephen L. Schensul et al., "Translating State Data into Local Programs: Targeted Research for Intervention Planning (TRIP)," April 1994).

The intervention that was designed, however, was never implemented. While the research was commissioned by the state health department with the full cooperation of the local health department, was "good" grounded research that focused heavily on the problem from the viewpoint of the affected persons, and was specifically designed to develop an intervention that would be tested and evaluated, the project ended when the final report was submitted.

242

The Good News: State Bureaucracy Can Be Changed!

In Connecticut, in 1987, if you were a person with a disability but did not have mental retardation or a mental illness and were not visually or hearing impaired, or if you had some combination of these disabilities, there was no state agency you could call your own. Services to assist you with housing, employment, transportation, income maintenance, rehabilitation, or independent living (to name a few) were scattered among several different state agencies. There was no focal point for services, and no "point of entry" into the system. In fact, there was no "system of services" at all. Every state agency had different policies, and services delivered by different agencies were not coordinated.

The disability rights community, which was well organized and vocal and had strong self-advocacy skills, wanted the situation changed. There was no consensus, however, as to how the change should be accomplished. Some factions wanted a new agency that would collect all of the programs under one bureaucracy, while others thought it better to leave programs in their "generic" agencies, but increase coordination and planning.

The disability rights advocates had the ear of the then new commissioner at the state Department of Human Resources (DHR). The advocates and the commissioner made their concerns known to the chairmen of the legislative committee that oversees DHR. As a result, the legislature approved an appropriation for DHR to study the delivery of services in Connecticut and to report back with recommendations in one year. I was chosen to conduct the study.

Much of the research involved tracking programs from agency to agency—work that was based on review of state documents and interviews with state workers. I also conducted interviews with clients of the services being described. While the project did not call for a complicated or elaborate research design, anthropological concepts and methods did form the basis of the study. I sought to understand the programs from both the client and providers' points of view, and I used participant observation and open-ended interviewing techniques. I worked closely with representatives of the disability rights community to formulate recommendations based on my findings. I was careful to facilitate input from all factions and to develop a consensus within the disability community on how best to organize state services.

When the draft document was given to the commissioner, he objected strongly to the recommendations in one section. He was able to produce additional data that persuaded me to suggest to the disability community the changes he wanted. The disability community agreed to the changes, the report was finalized, and the contract was fulfilled one week before the beginning of the next legislative session.

The commissioner then offered me additional funding to "represent the report" at the legislature, and I accepted. I worked with the disability advocates to mount a strong lobbying effort to have the report's recommendations implemented. This included translating the findings into everyday language, free of professional jargon, so that the people who would be affected by the recommended changes would be able to understand and comment, and into even simpler, more concise language that the legislators could understand. I was part of the "team" of disability advocates who organized the disability community, identified "fires" that had to be put out, disseminated information, coordinated direct contacts between people with disabilities and legislators, and "counted heads" as key votes in committee, House, and Senate came up. I also kept the DHR apprised of our progress, identified "trouble spots" for the department to address, and coordinated with the department's lobbyist.

In the end the legislation was passed. All disability programs stayed in their generic agencies, but DHR was made the "lead agency." DHR was required to organize a statewide consumer advisory board to plan services for people with disabilities and to set broad disability policy. DHR was also required to head an interagency management committee to coordinate efforts across agency lines and ensure consistency in agency policies. The legislation also provided new funds to staff a disability unit to support these efforts.

Discussion

Comparison of these two projects highlights factors—apart from the quality of the research effort—that inhibit or allow our research to affect public policy.

Commitment of the Sponsor

Planning and evaluation studies are conducted for many reasons aside from wanting to develop better programs or change public policy. For example, "study bills" are often passed by legislatures in order to postpone or avoid addressing an unpopular or politically dangerous issue. At the agency level, I have been asked to do planning studies solely because "planning money" had to be spent before a certain date, or because "it's required in the grant." These types of studies are unlikely to have an impact on programs or policy.

Commitment to program or policy change may be strong initially, as it was in the Bridgeport STD project, but weaken later. By comparison, commitment at DHR for the disability services project was consistently strong, and it came from the highest level. Whether the commissioner was motivated primarily by concern for people with disabilities or by a desire to carve out a larger mandate for his agency is not relevant. Newly appointed, the commissioner was likely to stay in office through the research and policy-making process, allowing for sustained commitment to the issue.

Temporality of the Issue

Commitment of the sponsor is often influenced by the temporality of the issue. The Bridgeport STD project was stimulated by an especially large increase in the STD rate; when the STD rate moderated, as would be expected from an epidemiological point of view, commitment waned. By contrast, the disability services issue was a long-standing one related to the structure of state government. It was unlikely to improve on its own.

The Policy Process

In order for the Bridgeport project to have had an effect on the way STD prevention services are delivered, funding for the second step—development, implementation, and evaluation of the intervention—had to be secured. We researchers had no idea how an item like this would get into the budget of the DOHS, let alone when that would take place, who the players would be, or in what context our item would be considered. Nor did we attempt to build a constituency for the project. We conducted our research diligently, with little worry about the next step, assuming that the DOHS would take care of it.

Ultimately, the DOHS told the Bridgeport Health Department to take funds for the proposed intervention "out of your (state) AIDS money." Even though the issues and intervention developed would also address risk factors for AIDS, the local AIDS unit had no ownership of the project nor interest in providing funds for the intervention. In retrospect, it would have been logical to integrate the project from the start with AIDS efforts, which were well organized, crossed program lines, and were visible in the community.

For the DHR project, the policy process was well understood by the commissioner, his lobbyist, the advocates, and me. We knew a policy change would require a legislative decision. We knew which committee hurdles would have to be passed, who the key players were, and what their interests and biases were. Even as the research model was being constructed, the data were being collected, and the report was being written, we had the ultimate policy process in mind. We concentrated heavily on building consensus among the interested parties, and we analyzed our opponents and developed retorts to their arguments.

Resources for the Policy Debate

All other things being equal, a study that is supported by an outpouring of public sentiment on an issue is more likely to produce policy change. In Bridgeport, although we had considerable community input into our plan, we had no community support. The issue had originated at the state agency level and had never been raised to the level of public attention in the community.

On the other hand, the issue of scattered, disjointed services for people with disabilities originated from within the disability community and was championed by a network of politically active individuals with long-standing ties with both DHR and the legislature. This group had linkages with individuals with disabilities across the state and with private, nonprofit agencies that could contribute staff time and materials to getting the word out. In addition, the commissioner financed my continued involvement, which not only enhanced what the disability groups could accomplish, but also kept me, and therefore the issue, visible among the policy makers.

Conclusion

If applied anthropologists want their work to have an impact on public policy they must do more than carry out good research and present the results to policy makers in an understandable format. They must also:

1. understand the context and motivation for the study and the sponsor's commitment and ability to effect change;
2. assess the probability and impact of staff turnover on support for the study and implementation of its findings;
3. evaluate whether the problem situation is likely to change, compromising the salience of the study or making it obsolete;
4. determine how the issue is viewed in the community and whether the community will be interested in and able to advocate for change;
5. design the research to link the study to other issues, populations, or organizations in order to build broad consensus and expand the resources available in the policy arena;
6. understand the culture of the relevant policy arena and know the players, the process, the context, and the world view of allies and opponents;
7. identify and work closely with community groups to bring the research findings to the attention of policy makers; and
8. design the project to include the time necessary to present and interpret results in the policy arena.

Anthropologists are often uncomfortable setting out to change the way policy makers think and behave. I have been told that it is not our role to get involved in "politics" and that this type of involvement will "compromise the credibility of our research." Such protestations are based on a lack of understanding of policy culture. If efforts are not made to translate and communicate our findings to policy makers, and to convince them to adopt our recommendations, policy will simply be made without our input. Influencing policy makers to change public programs is no different than designing programs to change sexual behaviors to reduce the risk of disease or devising ways to change child feeding practices to improve child survival; applied anthropologists do these things all the time.

Anthropological research can inform public policy, influence the way social welfare programs are administered, and improve the way those programs are experienced by clients. To do so, however, good research must be combined with strong linkages to the community being affected and an understanding of and credibility within the policy culture.

The Funds of Knowledge for Teaching Project

Norma E. González

No question has concerned educational anthropologists more than how to bridge the gap between the culture transmitted by the schools and that of minority students. Diversifying the curricula through multicultural education has been one response embraced by many educators. Here, Norma González deftly skewers the shallowness of the "foods and folklore" approach to multicultural curricula. Drawing from Eric Wolf's "household fund" paradigm, the "funds of knowledge" approach shows how a more dynamic conceptualization of culture can enrich education in multicultural classrooms. González provides a crisp case history of a teacher-training project based upon reshaping the time-honored (but seldom-practiced) custom of the teacher home visit into a vehicle for greater multicultural sophistication. With proper guidance and follow-up discussion, home visits were transformed into ethnographic experiences for teachers that brought them to a far less static understanding of the cultural contexts of their students. These experiences also generated concrete and novel ideas for incorporating "household knowledge" into lessons "designed to enhance traditional curricula, not to replace them." And, the teachers' ethnographic interviews generated mutual trust between home and school and produced greater parent involvement in the schools as well. J. A. P.

Although multicultural education has been bandied about in policy arenas for decades, substantive contributions by anthropologists have been limited. Yet anthropologists, above all other social researchers, have insights to offer on cultural phenomena, the processes of social change, and the educational implications of ethnic diversity.

It is axiomatic in multicultural education that teachers must come to "know the culture" from which their students emerge. This approach is laudatory in

Norma E. González, Co-Project Director with Luis Moll of the Funds of Knowledge for Teaching Project, is Associate Research Anthropologist at the Bureau of Applied Research in Anthropology, University of Arizona (Anth Bldg, Room 316, P.O. Box 210030, University of Arizona, Tucson, AZ 85721-0030; (502) 621-6282; <neg@u.arizona.edu>).

Originally published as part of a special section on "Educational Innovation: Learning from Households," guest edited by Norma E. González, in *Practicing Anthropology* 17,3(1995):3-6, this article has been edited for republication here.

its conceptualization, but its application has run aground on two key issues: the manner in which teachers come to "know" their students' culture and the way in which teachers understand the concept of culture.

With respect to the first issue, teachers' awareness of cultural diversity is too often prepackaged and predigested for ease of consumption. Typically, in-service training programs or after-school meetings are held in which experts transmit to practitioners certain traits of "Culture X" or "Culture Y." Rather than grappling with the complexities of cultural processes, exposing teachers to cultural practices firsthand, and developing a historical consciousness of how different groups came to exist in their present circumstances, in-services tend to offer a homogenized and standardized prescription for dealing with children of the "other." This type of cultural awareness program may simply succeed in replacing previous sets of stereotypes with new ones, albeit more positive or benign.

The second issue that proves problematic is dealing with the concept of culture. As evinced by multicultural curricula, prevailing notions of culture in the schools center around observable and tangible markers: dances, food, folklore, ethnic heritage festivals, and international potlucks. While including a diversity of such cultural features may foster tolerance, this practice often obscures more fundamental issues of minority status. Furthermore, there is in this practice an unspoken assumption of a normative and clearly defined culture "out there" which may not take into account the students' everyday lived experiences. Anthropological understanding of culture has moved away from univocal, harmonious, and integrated visions, but current ethnographic theory has not been transferred into educational arenas.

An innovative approach to addressing these two issues is the Funds of Knowledge for Teaching Project, a collaboration among teacher-researchers from elementary schools and university-based researchers from the disciplines of anthropology and education. The basic premise of the project is that classroom learning can be greatly enhanced when teachers learn more not just about their students' culture in an abstract sense but about *their particular* students and their students' households. In our version of how this can be accomplished, teachers engage in ethnographic research involving participant observation, interviewing, elicitation of narratives, and reflection on field notes. This enables teachers to come to know their students' cultural practices firsthand and in much more of their true multidimensionality. The teachers then draw upon that knowledge to develop curricula and teaching techniques that have roots in the experience and forms of knowledge of the students and of the community.

While the concept of home visits is not new, entering students' homes with an eye towards learning *from* households is a radical departure from traditional school-home visits. Traditionally, teachers have visited students' homes either to discuss specific, often disciplinary, problems with parents, or to teach the parents how to better support their children's education. In our project, teachers venture into their students' households and communities, not as "teachers" attempting to convey educational information, but as "learners," seeking to understand the ways in which people make sense of their everyday lives. These research visits, in conjunction with collaborative ethnographic reflection, can engender pivotal and transformative shifts in relations between households and schools, between parents and teachers, and between university-based researchers and teacher-researchers.

Genesis of the Project

The Funds of Knowledge for Teaching Project has evolved through several permutations. In 1985-87, Carlos Vélez-Ibáñez, James Greenberg, and others in the University of Arizona's Bureau of Applied Research in Anthropology carried out research and analysis of Mexican-origin households and their exchange systems in Tucson, Arizona. While this research had significant implications for education, teachers and educators were not directly involved. Later, with the collaboration of educational researcher Luis Moll, a grant from the U.S. Department of Education was secured (1987-90) which involved anthropologists and educators in a collaborative effort to investigate the literacy practices of Mexican-origin households. The results of this research were shared with teachers in after-school settings, and researchers and teachers worked together to develop innovations in the teaching of literacy.

During this initial phase, the term "funds of knowledge" was coined by James Greenberg, predicated on the more generally understood "household funds" paradigm advanced by Eric Wolf (*Peasants* [Englewood Cliffs, N.J.: Prentice Hall, 1966]). In his discussion of household economies, Wolf distinguished a number of funds which households must juggle to make ends meet: caloric funds, funds of rent, replacement funds, ceremonial funds, social funds, etc. Entailed in each are a wider set of activities requiring specific bodies, or funds, of knowledge. Funds of knowledge, then, are the historically accumulated bodies of knowledge and skills essential for household functioning and well-being. The recognition that funds of knowledge exist in all households has been critical in reconceptualizing households as repositories of resources that can be strategically tapped to foster education, rather than as the source of barriers to educational attainment.

In 1990-91, with seed money from the Kellogg Foundation, we began to involve the teachers themselves in the fieldwork experience. Ten teachers from three schools participated that year, along with three anthropologists from the Bureau of Applied Research in Anthropology. Funding from the Office of Educational Research and Improvement through the National Center for Research on Cultural Diversity and Second Language Learning allowed one or two teachers from nine different schools to participate the following year. In

1992-93, one school adopted the idea of the project as part of their school improvement plan, and all forty-five teachers from that school became involved, although less intensively than their peers from the other eight schools. That year the project also expanded to include work with African American and Native American households, as well as with the Mexican-origin community of Tucson.

Since 1993 the project has continued to work with the school-wide program as well as with teacher-researchers from other schools and university-researchers. Key to the success of our project has been its three interlocking components: (1) ethnographic research in the community; (2) reflexive teacher study groups; and (3) classroom applications.

Ethnographic Research

Our ethnographic research involves study of the origin, use, and distribution of funds of knowledge among households in the Mexican-origin, African American, and Native American communities of Tucson, Arizona. Teachers from local elementary schools who volunteer to work in the project are given training in participant observation methods, interviewing techniques, and the writing of field notes. Typically, each teacher selects for study three households of children in that year's class and visits each household three times during the course of a year. Some teachers select households randomly; others choose households they believe will have something special to offer. (Our only request is that households not be chosen for disciplinary or punitive reasons.) Teachers who participate more than one year select a new set of households for study each year.

Teachers are provided with interview protocols which include questions on household history, labor history, and daily activities. These questionnaires are open-ended, and teachers are encouraged to adopt a conversational stance with parents. As the interview proceeds, teacher-researchers probe for further insights, especially on topics they see as possible links to the school curriculum. As participant observers, they also attend to material clues within the household which might provide evidence of untapped funds of knowledge. For instance, home remodeling might highlight a household social network with broad knowledge of construction, plumbing, electrical work, etc. Similarly, pictures of *quinceñeras* or weddings often reflect a dense network of exchange in orchestrating the celebration. In addition to interviewing family members (on audio tape when permitted), the teacher-researchers write extensive field notes on each visit.

We have been particularly interested in how families develop social networks that connect them with their environments (especially with other households) and how these social relationships facilitate the development and exchange of resources, including funds of knowledge. Reciprocal practices establish obligations based on the assumption of mutual trust, re-established or confirmed with each exchange. Furthermore, each exchange with kinsmen, friends, and neighbors not only entails practical activities (everything from home and automobile repair to music and exchange of food); it also provides contexts in which learning can occur—contexts in which children participate in activities with people they trust.

The teachers' training in and experience of ethnographic methods has been central to realizing the shift away from the deficit view of households. By interviewing parents and observing in households, teacher-researchers see for themselves that household knowledge is broad and diverse.

Reflexive Teacher Study Groups

After-school study groups provide a setting in which to share and reflect upon research findings and to plan, develop, and support innovations in instruction. Each year's study group includes all the teacher-researchers (from the various elementary schools) and the university-based researchers. Meetings are held every two weeks (insofar as possible), rotating among the participants' schools. Teacher-researchers share the experience of entering the households, as well as the information that has been gleaned, in collective debriefing sessions. Literature pertaining to observed practices is often presented, and collective analyses of the researchers' findings are developed. Applications for classroom practice also emerge during these sessions, as do avenues of access for parent and community involvement.

Within the study group setting, ethnography has surfaced as more than a set of techniques. It has become the filter through which the households are conceptualized as multidimensional and vibrant entities. Although specific techniques in participant observation, field note writing, interviewing, and elicitation of life histories are discussed, the focus is continuously on the constitutive and discursive properties of the joint construction of knowledge. Ethnographic research becomes a collaborative and reflexive process in which teacher-researchers and university-based researchers share insights and information.

Classroom Applications

The goal of the ethnographic research and the teacher study groups is to improve teaching and learning in the schools. In particular, we believe that incorporating household knowledge into tangible curricular activities can enhance student learning. In developing the curricular units teacher-researchers mediate between home and school knowledge and established links between student experiences and the content areas. As they draw on household funds of knowledge in the classroom, teachers academically validate the background knowledge with which students come equipped.

One teacher-researcher learned that many of her students' families had extensive knowledge of the medicinal value of plants and herbs. She was able to draw on this ethnobotanical knowledge in formulating a unit on the curative properties of plants. Building on her students' strengths as the foundation for the unit fostered their increased engagement and their deployment of higher order cognitive skills, especially in language arts.

Another teacher-researcher, after visiting a household which regularly participated in transborder activities in northern Mexico, discovered that her student commonly returned from these trips with candy to sell. Elaborating on this student's marketing skills, the teacher developed an integrated unit on candy. Using an inquiry-based approach, students investigated the nutritional content of candy, compared U.S. and Mexican candy, studied sugar processing, and surveyed and graphed favorite candies. Students used their bilingual language skills in both reading and writing in this unit, building on linguistic funds of knowledge.

In these examples, teachers mediated between home and formal knowledge, and between theory and practice, drawing on their own insights and background knowledge as well as their research to design creative and locally relevant curricula. It is important to note that curricula do not simply reproduce the knowledge of the household, but build on and transform that knowledge for academic purposes. The classroom practice in the content areas of mathematics, science, language arts, and social studies can be greatly enhanced by extending the familiar into the more abstract.

Project Impact

As a result of the research experience, the after-school study groups, and the curricular innovations, teachers came to see culture as negotiated over contested domains, rather than as a static grab bag of tamales, *quinceñeras*, and *cinco de mayo* celebrations. Teacher-researchers were thus able to locate culture in the lived practices of their students. This view made culture "not an object of unquestioning reference, but a mobile field of ideological and material relations that are unfinished, multilayered and always open to interrogation" (Henry Giroux, *Border Crossings: Cultural Workers and the Politics of Education* [New York: Routledge, 1993]). This allowed both teachers and students to construct themselves as agents in the production of meaning.

Although carefully controlled studies of the effects of the project on learning have not been carried out, pre- and post-tests, interviews with students, and review of student products show that students enthusiastically embrace the units based on household funds of knowledge, and teachers judge student learning to be better than that of their previous classes. In addition, what began as an effort to understand households has had unexpected impact at personal, institutional, and structural levels.

The experience of relating family history evinced in the parents a historical consciousness of where they have been, and how they got to be where they are. Mexican-origin households told evocative stories of crossing into the United States on foot, of working in territorial mines and railroads, and of being pulled to Tucson through kinship networks. African American households told stories of relocations and settlements, of grand matriarchs of extended families, and of the splintering of the local community.

The dialogic process of parents "telling their story" to teachers was the basis for transformed relationships of reciprocity and mutual trust between home and school. As teachers validated household praxis as worthy of pedagogical notice, parents came to authenticate their skills as meaningful and productive. Increased parental involvement in the schools is overwhelmingly cited by teachers as one of the beneficial aftermaths of the project.

Within the study groups, teacher-researchers and university-based researchers framed stories which illustrated theoretical and practical insights. A collective story was often formulated which gave coherence and consistency to the research. Just as often, however, the pluralism inherent in storytelling was apparent, as participants constructed competing stories. Discourse on reflective practice illustrated the diversity of sense-making processes among the participants as well as the parents.

This participatory methodology, involving ethnographic research and collaborative reflection, encouraged analysis from multiple perspectives of the ways in which student and household experience is produced and organized, and can be legitimated in schools. This in turn nurtured a critical pedagogy—in which teachers and students think critically about how knowledge is produced, transmitted, and transformed.

Our participatory methodology has shown that social theory is not predicated on distance from the world of practice. At its core is a relationship in which every participant is both learner and teacher. Teacher-researchers learn how qualitative methods can validate the life experiences of their students, as well as their own pedagogical expertise; university-based researchers learn how teachers as qualitative researchers evaluate and weave elements of their own and their students' experience into educational practice. As teachers integrate household knowledge into classroom curricula, students also become teachers as well as learners.

What We Have Learned

The dialogue that ethnography can engender is a powerful and pivotal tool for expanding understanding within a community of learners and improving classroom practice. What are the essential elements for success?

While the recipe will vary from site to site, it is vital, first and foremost, that the integrity of the anthropological approach to households be maintained.

The seductive pull of the familiar home visit mold, in which teachers visit in order to teach or inform, is an ever-present risk. Neither should anthropological approaches be reduced to mere technique. Reflection and analysis are as important as interviewing and note taking.

Second, the theoretical dimension is critical. Without theoretical constructs, the process of visiting households becomes routine and ordinary. Researchers who visit households armed with checklists or questionnaires, but without a theory of households and/or culture, can come away untouched by the experience.

Third, the point of this type of ethnography must be not the collection of data but the development of relationships of empowerment and access between communities and schools. Ethnography is a tool to accomplish this change, and the collection of data is a fortuitous by-product.

Fourth, the curricula developed based on household knowledge must be designed to enhance traditional curricula, not to replace it. The goal is to improve students' engagement in learning by framing the curricula and pedagogy with familiar contextual cues.

Fifth, because of the many demands and constraints on teachers, it is vital that institutional validation and recognition of this work be provided by administrators and school districts. Participating in this type of project is clearly "over and above" the everyday demands of classroom life.

The careful integration of the three main components of our project—ethnographic research, reflexive teacher study groups, and classroom application—has resulted in a successful blend for us. We are cautious, however, of advocating wholesale export of our methodology to other sites. Without experienced and involved anthropologists, the reflexive process of engaging in collaborative sense making would not necessarily occur. Similarly, without committed and involved teachers, the potential for ethnographic awareness to enhance classroom practice can be lost. We are convinced, nonetheless, that in order to effect systemic change, all educational stakeholders—students, parents, teachers, administrators, researchers, legislators, and policy makers— must redefine households as being rich in resources for educational purposes, and schools must validate the knowledge with which students come equipped.

Crossing the Minefield: Politics of Refugee Research and Service

JEFFERY L. MACDONALD

The research and practice of anthropology can have transformative effects not only for the local population but for the anthropologist as well. Working closely with a Southeast Asian refugee community for seven years, Jeffery MacDonald was forced to reexamine his own political and religious views, to adjust his understanding of friendship and professional relationships, to expand his political skills and knowledge, and to become more politically active as an advocate for the refugee community. Although these personal transformations were not always smooth, comfortable, or complete, they contributed significantly, MacDonald argues, to the quality of his research and the effectiveness of his service to the community. MacDonald, like many other anthropologists working in their own home societies with refugee, immigrant, or other disadvantaged populations, ultimately found his research and applied roles to be more complementary than conflicting. P. J. H.

For the past seven years [since 1989] I have worked in dual roles as an ethnographic researcher and an applied anthropologist/social worker in the Southeast Asian refugee community in Portland, Oregon. I began doing research within a single ethnic community of Iu-Mien (Yao) refugees from Laos. Like many refugee researchers, I soon became an applied anthropologist, first providing services for the Iu-Mien. Later, I took a position in a refugee resettlement social service agency where I began to work with other Southeast Asian ethnic communities, providing direct client services and training, doing needs assessment research, and managing and designing culturally specific programs for Southeast Asians.

My research and applied roles necessarily involve me with a variety of political issues both internal and external to the community. I have often likened this to "crossing a minefield," because to be successful one has not only to balance these often opposed, dual roles, but also to understand how one's own political biases, alliances with community leaders, and sensitivity

Jeffery L. MacDonald is Development Director for the International Refugee Center of Oregon (IRCO) (1336 E. Burnside Street, Portland, OR 97214; (503) 234-1541; <iroc@teleport.com>).

Originally published as part of a special section on "Anthropologists Working with Refugees," guest edited by Patricia A. Omidian, in *Practicing Anthropology* 18,1(1996):5-9.

to interethnic political relationships affect each role. One misstep, one personal slight or oversight in dealing with community leaders, or one misunderstanding about political relationships can affect not only your research but your job survival as well.

In the process of learning to negotiate the minefields of internal community, interethnic, and agency politics, my own political roles, views, activities, and awareness were transformed. I became far more politicized in the way I view interpersonal and professional relationships, diplomatic and negotiating skills, and the long-term consequences of my actions and words. In the following pages I explore three levels of personal political transformation I experienced in working with Southeast Asian refugees in the United States and discuss how each affected my work.

Transformations in Political Views

Due to the profoundly political nature of the refugee experience, the researcher must be aware of how the political views and opinions which he or she brings to the field affect and in turn will be challenged by the research and by the refugees themselves. I brought two political biases to the field: a negative view of Christian missionary activity among Southeast Asians and a critical view of American policy and actions in the Vietnam War. Both biases were quickly confronted. I realized that if I wanted to be successful in conducting my research I had to change my attitude, be more open minded, and silence my often outspoken opinions with regard to both issues.

Since my research interests centered on traditional religion, I was especially concerned about how missionary activities were altering Iu-Mien culture. Ironically, my chief sponsor for community entrée and research was a Christian convert who held a vision of a new, Christian Iu-Mien society not only in the U.S. but around the world. I soon became involved with other Christian converts and with Euro-American missionaries as well. They viewed me and my activities suspiciously since I spent most of my research time attending traditional Taoist rituals and relatively little time at Christian activities. I realized that my views needed to be suppressed in order to carry out my research and maintain my personal relationships. I also realized that I needed to broaden and refocus my research interests from simply traditional religion to how religious change interrelated with community politics.

I recorded many reports of Iu-Mien families who had burned their traditional Taoist ritual books and genealogical texts when they converted to Christianity. As a scholar, I found book burning to be abhorrent, and the Iu-Mien variety is all the more shocking when one realizes that these traditional texts were handmade books, many decades old, that families had perilously carried on their backs as they fled through the jungles of Laos and Thailand. (The mother in one family had even sneaked back into Laos to retrieve books left behind.) It was easy to blame the missionaries for encouraging book burning and the destruction of other ritual objects.

Once I realized that casting Iu-Mien converts as victims of the stereotypical culture-destroying missionary was too simplistic, I had to ask *why* people converted to Christianity and subsequently burnt their books. I found an answer in the convergence of the fundamentalist Christian teaching that the Iu-Mien spirit world is essentially evil and the refugees' experience of death, bad luck, disease, and the like which they attributed to vengeful ancestors and angry spirits. Expensive Taoist ceremonies had not solved their spirit problems. Christianity offered them a new, simpler way to control the spirits, and burning their books helped them sever all ties to the spirit world.

The conversion of many Iu-Mien to Christianity had led to a split in the ritual ties that helped bind the community—a split that was mirrored in the political organization, with Christian and Taoist leaders each having their own base of support. Christianity also seemed to confer adaptive advantages in the U.S. context; Christian Iu-Mien received church support in becoming economically self-sufficient and in learning English.

Such insights about the relationship between conversion, politics, and adaptation helped me in my research, analysis, and applied roles with the Iu-Mien. It also gave me more empathy and understanding when working in applied settings with other groups, such as Soviet refugees who had joined Pentecostal denominations.

My views on the Vietnam War were similarly challenged and transformed. Like many who grew up during the 1960s and 1970s, I viewed the war as immoral and illegal and believed the U.S. should have withdrawn far sooner than it did. I saw the suffering the war had brought to Americans. Southeast Asian refugees saw the suffering endured by themselves and their compatriots, and they felt that the U.S. had abandoned them after promising to fight with them to victory.

The conservative, generally Republican, anticommunist politics of Southeast Asian refugees made it difficult for me not to voice my opinions on many occasions. Nevertheless, by keeping my mouth shut, I learned the valuable political skills of diplomacy, tact, and consensus building. Such demeanor was often viewed by my Iu-Mien friends as an expression of humility, a highly valued trait in their society, which in turn advanced my status as a scholar and increased community trust in me.

The tempering of my political views also served me well when I later began to work in the social service agency with former refugees from Southeast Asia. Keeping an open mind when hearing their stories helped build trust between us as well as deepening my understanding. The agency's executive

258

director, a Cambodian, was closely involved with the Cambodian peace process on the side of Prince Sihanouk. Had I not learned to practice some discretion in the expression of my political views, my ability to advance in the agency might well have been blocked.

Transformations in my religious and political views led me to consider how transnational political forces of war and religious conversion had helped create, sustain, and transform refugee identity. My research trajectory and interests were completely altered by my own experience and transformation with regard to these issues. Such transformations also made it possible for me to work closely and supportively with Southeast Asians from all backgrounds in my subsequent role as an applied anthropologist.

Transformations in Political Strategies

The second level of transformation involved political strategies and accommodations adopted in order to negotiate complex political relationships within the Iu-Mien community and to understand how that community fits into the power relationships of the larger Southeast Asian refugee community.

My alliance with a man who was simultaneously a local Portland ethnic leader, a national U.S. ethnic leader, and a Christian leader had both positive and negative consequences. His deep understanding of internal Iu-Mien politics helped me see how the political structure of the Iu-Mien in the United States was a mixture of U.S. political practices and of political institutions and leadership structures from Laos. I also learned how political divisions and factions had grown up in the community between Christians and traditional Taoists. This individual's sponsorship separated me from other rival community leaders, but such a separation was probably inevitable since I could not have functioned in their society without a sponsor.

My relationship with my Iu-Mien sponsor led me to reexamine my own understanding of friendship and professional relationships. His alliance with me as a scholar/researcher fit into his political agenda and enhanced his status. I was often shown off in public meetings as his ally and advisor. In addition, he quickly put me to work writing grants at a time when I really knew little about Iu-Mien culture or how my activities fit into my sponsor's political agenda.

While I recognized the need for reciprocity—in friendship and professional relationships—my rapidly evolving, somewhat competing roles as a researcher and an applied anthropologist caused me some ethical concerns. These concerns expanded when I was appointed to the board of directors of the Iu-Mien Association of Oregon. How can one voice opinions on what a community should be doing while maintaining impartiality as a researcher? While this is a question that has bedeviled many anthropologists, it was not an issue for my Iu-Mien colleagues.

Besides learning to look for hidden political agendas and reciprocal responsibilities in my interpersonal relationships with the Iu-Mien, I gained other valuable political skills and knowledge by working closely with this Iu-Mien leader. He helped me understand the complexities of interethnic politics among Southeast Asian refugees, including how groups viewed themselves relative to others and how these self-perceptions were based upon former relations in Southeast Asia. He also introduced me to many key community leaders among the Lao, the Hmong, the Cambodians, and the Vietnamese, and he helped me understand which leaders were allies and which were enemies and how these relationships could change dramatically in different contexts.

My contacts with these community leaders helped me secure a position at a community-based refugee resettlement agency operated largely by Southeast Asian management. Many of the community leaders were then my coworkers or supervisors, and others were on the agency's board of directors. Knowledge gained from research helped me avoid stepping on interethnic land mines in the agency. At the same time, my work as an applied anthropologist in the agency expanded my understanding of interethnic politics and introduced me to a wider range of community members and leaders.

The agency, which provides employment services, vocational training, and other social services to refugees, was formed in 1984 as a merger of two mutual assistance associations. In this merger, certain ethnic leaders advanced their positions, while others lost their jobs or their agency leadership roles. Anger still lingers, as I discovered recently when a Southeast Asian leader whom I had previously counted as a supporter suddenly became an enemy. His attacks on me were a means to get back at senior management staff from another ethnic community.

As I have become more knowledgeable of interethnic politics and community needs, my roles in the agency have evolved and expanded. From pre-employment instructor I became community researcher and program coordinator of a project for Lao, Iu-Mien, and Hmong teen mothers. I had little knowledge of or personal ability to counsel Southeast Asian teen moms, and I often lay awake at night wondering how a white male could end up in such a position! Based on this experience, however, I began developing new services such as parent education, child care training, intervention with gang-involved youth, and recreational activities for youth and their parents. My current job description includes program development, grant writing, needs assessment research, staff supervision, and provision of cross-cultural training.

Over the years, I have also learned how interethnic politics affect the delivery of social services. For example, ethnic groups not represented in the management structure tend to receive fewer special services—a pattern to which I too have contributed. Although I try to ensure that services are delivered equitably to all groups based on need, I have tended to employ direct service staff from the Lao, Iu-Mien, and Hmong communities because of my previous research. As a result, other communities may be under served. In addition, certain social service needs, such as alleviation of domestic violence, may remain unmet because agency management will either not acknowledge such problems or not address them for fear of upsetting power relationships within the community. As an applied anthropologist/social worker, one needs to know what subjects are taboo and what social service proposals will be dead on arrival.

Knowledge of ethnic power structures is also important in doing interethnic community research. Without such knowledge, it is easy to overlook significant issues or to make the fatal error of not including key community leaders in your research. This detracts from your reputation as knowledgeable and, more importantly, insults community leaders by devaluing their importance and reputation in the community. For many Southeast Asians, a mistake of this kind can create barriers for research as well as for developing and delivering social services.

Another important transformation in my political skills was learning different communication styles. Speaking strategically, being diplomatic and tactful, and building consensus are all part of an indirect or "spiraling" communication style common within many Southeast Asian communities. Being able to practice this style of communication has proven very valuable in my work. Without the necessary cultural background knowledge and skills, many new social workers in our agency do not understand the hidden meanings and agendas being communicated. One learns to look for the implicit, rather than the literal meaning of what is being said.

Transformations in Political Activism

As my reputation has grown in the Southeast Asian community as an expert sympathetic to community needs, and as my job responsibilities have expanded at my agency, I have had to take on the roles of advocate for individuals and of community political activist. As part of my job, I advocate for and assist clients who are not receiving services from other agencies or from the government. I also advocate for individuals as part of my reciprocal responsibilities to community leaders and friends. In addition, I can hardly refuse any requests from my chief sponsor that I take on explicitly political roles as a community advocate.

Serving as an advocate or political activist can generate new research material. For example, a close personal friend and traditional religious leader in the Iu-Mien community called on me to assist his family when wedding plans for his nephew were disrupted by a city official's decision to ban large wedding parties in apartments. I was able to mobilize many Southeast Asian and mainstream leaders to force the city to back down on the basis of racial and religious discrimination. Taking this action allowed me in turn to learn much about wedding ceremonies. The chief priest had to write out a schedule of events, which had never been done before, and explain each step of the ceremony for city officials.

In 1992 I was contracted to conduct a study on the causes of juvenile delinquency in the Southeast Asian community and to make program and service recommendations to solve the problem. This was an explicitly political task from the beginning. Early on it involved me in infighting between Asian American county officials, who had had the money earmarked for Southeast Asian youth, and state officials who felt that the funds should be used for African American youth. The Southeast Asian community was eager to see the study go forward because it would provide them a forum for expressing their needs and concerns to government.

Part of the reason I was given the task was my expertise and good relationships in the community. I could be expected not to weigh the findings in favor of one ethnic group over another. In addition, Southeast Asian community leaders felt I would be discrete in what I revealed about the community as a whole. Knowledge of the complex internal and external political implications of my research findings allowed me to write a report which was accurate but which also discretely skirted sensitive issues.

Since completion of the study in January 1993, its recommendations have been adopted by the county as a blueprint for developing new services for Southeast Asian families and youth. While this is personally gratifying, it has thrust me further into the role of political activist, as I have been asked to testify at meetings and to lend my support in other ways. Despite the faith which many of my Southeast Asian friends and colleagues place in me, I am very uncomfortable in this role. I feel it is neither politically nor culturally correct for me to represent the Southeast Asian community in an activist role at a government hearing or other community forum. Ideally, my role should be advisory, and my knowledge and writings should be used to empower Southeast Asians themselves to advocate for their communities.

The latter has actually occurred in the last two years. A group of Southeast Asian leaders used the study's recommendations to develop a proposal for an Asian Family Center. In May of 1994, they took their proposal to the county board of commissioners and successfully lobbied the board for funding. Following budget approval, they asked me and my agency to develop the center and implement the new programs. Operating since November 1994, the Asian Family Center is maintaining close community ties through an advisory board composed of members of each of Portland's Asian ethnic groups. While the advisory board is still in its infancy, its members have taken on the key advocacy functions which will be critical to community empowerment and to continued funding for the center.

Conclusion

Other anthropologists who work in applied fields while simultaneously carrying out ethnographic research experience similar personal transformations. Many of us slowly move from pure research into applied roles as professional development opportunities arise and as we deepen our awareness of the needs of our research communities. In the process, we learn that research and applied roles may actually be more complementary than conflicting, as advocacy and activism lead to new research insights. Certainly this is true for many of us who work in such multiple roles in refugee communities.

Transformations of this type will become increasingly important issues for all anthropologists as interactions between ethnic, cultural, and linguistic groups expand worldwide. Anthropologists will need to take on enlarged and often multiple roles as political activists, researchers, and designers of social service, health care, and cultural preservation programs. If our vast accumulation of cultural, linguistic, and social knowledge and analysis is to become more than just an internal discourse within our profession, or archival material in a museum or library, we as anthropologists must transform our own political consciousness and activities beyond academia. We must take responsibility for assuring that our knowledge is of use to the communities that we have studied.

Anthropology in the Operating Room

John C. Kolar

Applied anthropometry, sometimes called human engineering, is one of the earliest and most traditional applications of physical anthropology. Indeed, the first twenty years of Practicing Anthropology *include several articles about its various aspects, often having to do with the design of "things" to accommodate variation in human body dimensions. Only recently, however, has the long-standing interest of physical anthropologists in craniofacial biology been directly applied to reconstructive surgery. One hallmark of the growth of biomedical anthropology over the past twenty years has been that physical anthropologists have come to work with physicians in clinical settings. John Kolar's work, an excellent example of the positive benefits of such collaboration, is based on a fundamental focus of physical anthropology—normal biological variation in living people, something less frequently considered within the framework of the "medical" model. His comment on the legal implications of his professional practice merits special thought, for practicing anthropology may entail "jeopardy" not characteristic of anthropologists employed in academic settings.* C. W. W.

The idea of applying anthropometry to medical clinical practice was first proposed by Ales Hrdlička in his monograph, *Anthropometry* (1920). His suggestion was largely ignored, except for studies of overall growth and development, primarily height and weight, which had begun generations earlier and which continue to this day. The idea was resurrected by physical anthropologists like Wilton M. Krogman and J. Lawrence Angel in the 1950s and 1960s, but such use of anthropometry is still rare. Among craniofacial treatment centers, for example, only Medical City Dallas has a professionally trained, full-time physical anthropologist doing clinical work with patients undergoing reconstructive surgery.

Anthropometry and Reconstructive Surgery

Little more than a generation ago, a child with congenital deformities of the head and face had very little hope of leading a normal life. There were

John C. Kolar is Clinical Anthropologist with the Dallas Craniofacial Center at Medical City Dallas Hospital (777 Forest Lane, Dallas, TX 75230; (972) 566-6721; <emsalter@flash.net>).

Originally published in *Practicing Anthropology* 18,2(1996):18-21, this article has been edited for republication here.

264

only a few surgical techniques available to repair the physical defects, and public reactions to these deformities led to social withdrawal by the child and its family. Institutionalization was not unusual, based on an assumption that physical malformation must be accompanied by mental defect.

The situation started to improve in the late 1960s, due to the pioneering efforts of a French reconstructive surgeon, Dr. Paul Tessier. Tessier began to experiment with surgical techniques for radical disassembly and reconstruction of the head and face in patients with a wide range of congenital anomalies. He advocated a strong multidisciplinary approach, recognizing that there were often other medical problems that could not or did not need to be corrected surgically. He also recognized that the psychological and social needs of the patient had to be addressed. Tessier's approach revolutionized the treatment of craniofacial patients and greatly influenced subsequent generations of reconstructive plastic surgeons.

At about the same time that Tessier was developing his surgical techniques, the Department of Plastic Surgery at Charles University in Prague, Czechoslovakia, began an extensive treatment program and multigenerational study of children born with cleft lip and palate. They recruited Dr. Karel Hajniš, a member of the Anthropology Department, to develop a quantitative assessment system to measure the severity of these clefts and the results of their repair. Hajniš developed his battery of measurements, based on traditional anthropometric techniques, with the assistance of plastic surgeon Dr. Ladislav Farkas. They worked together until Farkas left Czechoslovakia in 1968 to take a research fellowship at the Hospital for Sick Children, Toronto, Canada.

In 1970 Dr. Ian Munro joined the medical staff of the Hospital for Sick Children in Toronto and began applying the reconstructive techniques of Tessier to patients with congenital defects of the head and face. Such surgery was new, controversial, and risky, and it was opposed by many senior surgeons who did not observe any significant benefit to it. Farkas offered to measure Munro's patients before and after surgery, using the techniques he had learned from Hajniš, in order to provide objective evidence that the new surgical techniques actually changed the heads and faces of these children. When the data showed this, the next objection was that such changes did not necessarily mean improvement. To determine that, comparison to objective normal standards was needed.

The most extensive study of normal children was one carried out by Hajniš in West Germany in 1967 and 1968. Although the study encompassed the entire growth period, from birth to twenty years of age, it involved only a small battery of measurements made on a much more homogeneous population than is found in North America. The results were useful but not sufficient to answer the kinds of clinical questions presented by reconstructive surgeons.

Farkas developed a more extensive system of measurements which he used to study Toronto schoolchildren in the 1970s. This included a large series of paired measurements of the face, which allowed for a study of normal asymmetry. Clinically, this was important because many of the craniofacial patients had unilateral growth defects. (The standards for younger patients were adapted from the West German study.)

Measuring Craniofacial Anomalies

Most of the anthropometric data on craniofacial anomalies are descriptive rather than predictive. At the simplest level, a single examination of a single patient is compared to the appropriate sex- and age-matched normal standards. This provides an objective picture of the deformities which is much more precise than visual examination.

The use of proportions calculated from clinical measurements is important because the proportions help explain our subjective visual impressions. We do not perceive objects, including the head and face, as a series of independent linear measurements. Instead, we perceive shape, the *Gestalt* of the object. The proportions represent the shape, while the measurements are the components which produce that shape.

When sufficient numbers of patients with a specific diagnosis are available, we can look at the pooled anthropometric results to get a broader picture of each syndrome. Because craniofacial syndromes are so rare, it is very difficult to get enough patients to do this kind of analysis except at specialized facilities designed to treat these patients. Even then, it may take several years before there are enough patients with a particular syndrome to be able to identify consistent patterns of malformation.

When we do have a sample of patients with a single diagnosis, we often find that the quantitative data do not necessarily match the clinical literature. Eyes can play tricks on specialists as well as lay persons, making us see things that are not there and missing others that are present.

For example, one of the rarer conditions that we see for treatment is Treacher Collins syndrome. Children with this syndrome have underdeveloped cheekbones, jaws, and ears, among other problems. In fact, the cheekbones are usually completely missing and the external ears frequently are represented only by small rudiments of soft tissue. The clinical literature often mentions the large size of the nose in these patients. However, the anthropometric data indicate that the nose generally is of normal size and shape. The root of the nose, between the eye sockets, *is* large. This obliterates the normal angle between the nose and the forehead, making it difficult to separate these two areas visually, so the nose appears longer. Also, the entire face is abnormally small, making the nose look relatively large.

The amount of information we have about growth patterns in children with craniofacial anomalies is very limited, for practical and ethical reasons. Treatment, including full team assessment, is expensive. As a consequence, children frequently appear for examination just before reconstructive surgery. After surgery, financial restraints may limit the number of follow-up visits. Even when we have records of postoperative growth, that growth reflects both syndromic and surgical effects, and it is extremely difficult to identify what each contributes to a child's development. Occasionally, a child is not a candidate for immediate surgery and it is possible to obtain a small amount of information about growth, but this is rare. Treatment cannot be delayed when it is needed, so our understanding of the growth processes in these patients ends up being based on a patchwork of bits of clinical data, scattered by sex, age, and clinical opportunity.

(While predictive models of abnormal growth are still being developed, the normal data already have been used for predictive purposes in at least one quasi-forensic application. Several years ago, Lou Sadler, then of the Medical Illustration Department of the University of Texas Southwestern Medical Center at Dallas, later at the University of Illinois-Chicago Circle campus, developed a program for simulating the growth of children's faces. Photographs of children who had disappeared were altered to reflect normal changes in facial shape over a specified period, based on anthropometric data. The validity of the technique was tested by preparing a series of age reconstructions from photographs of children who were not missing, and comparing the reconstructions with the actual children. These tests confirmed the usefulness of the technique, and the program was responsible for identifying over thirty children.)

Assessing Effects of Reconstructive Surgery

Pre- and postoperative anthropometric measurements can be used to judge the effectiveness of the surgical procedures. Except for very young infants, growth will not have had time to obscure the effects of surgery if the examination is repeated within six months of the operation. Comparison to the appropriate normal standards will show whether the changes represent improvement. Because many craniofacial syndromes require repeated surgery, it is sometimes necessary to overcorrect a defect, producing a new, temporary deformity which provides a platform for the next stage of reconstruction. Interpretation of the anthropometric data requires knowledge of these surgical needs.

Each syndrome has a characteristic set of deformities which are treated with a distinctive set of surgical procedures, adjusted for the specific needs of each patient. Analysis of the postoperative measurements in a group of patients with the same diagnosis can show how effective the procedures are in correcting the deformity.

In the early 1980s, several West German surgeons suggested that a fairly simple set of cosmetic surgical procedures could mask the craniofacial deformities of children with Down syndrome (trisomy 21). They believed that removing the obvious signs of the syndrome would alter people's perceptions of these children and allow them to become better integrated into society. As they promoted this technique in public lectures across North America, parents of children with Down syndrome flocked to craniofacial centers all over the continent, including the Hospital for Sick Children in Toronto.

The patients in Toronto were seen by the entire craniofacial team, and they received preoperative and postoperative anthropometric examinations. Postoperatively, the children were still recognizable as having Down syndrome. This was puzzling until the preoperative data for the group were analyzed statistically. The results showed that the most severe and most characteristic craniofacial defects associated with Down syndrome--underdevelopment of the upper face and the eye sockets—were not corrected by the cosmetic surgical procedures. These anomalies produce deformities which require major reconstructive surgery to correct. Presentation of these findings at surgical meetings, together with the experience of other craniofacial centers, led to the abandonment of the procedures by most surgeons.

Clinical Advantages of Anthropometry

Anthropometry has several advantages in clinical use. It is relatively fast, simple, inexpensive, and noninvasive.

A full examination by an experienced anthropologist, involving up to 120 measurements, can be completed in half an hour. Computer analysis of the data, including calculation of a full set of 131 proportion indices, comparison to the appropriate normal standards, and a printed copy of the results, arranged in a logical sequence easily readable by a nonanthropologist, takes less than two minutes. This leaves ample time for the anthropologist to interpret the clinical significance of the results for the surgeon. By comparison, a 3D CT analysis, including scan, three-dimensional computer reconstruction, and measurement, requires several hours and produces a very small amount of quantitative data, fewer than a dozen measurements. (These computer-simulated images do show important details of internal anatomy that cannot be seen in any other manner, however.)

An anthropometric examination can be done in such a short time in part because the measurement techniques, and the instruments themselves, are relatively simple. The basic calipers have been used for over 150 years, and many of the measurements are of the same age. The simplicity of the instruments contributes to the relatively low cost of anthropometry. Even the cost of the computers used in clinical anthropometry is small when compared to a CT scanner. The main cost of clinical anthropometry is the salary of the anthropologist. Although the techniques and instruments are relatively simple, formal training is essential to assure accuracy and efficiency in their use.

Because anthropometry is noninvasive, the examination can be repeated as often as needed without putting a patient at risk. This has been especially important in developing the normal standards needed for clinical comparisons. Radiographic techniques ethically cannot be used on children with no clinical problem.

The limited normal standards available based on radiographic techniques come from data on children who have had CT scans for conditions which are not congenital and which are not believed to have affected the normal growth of their head and face. Even with time-consuming surveys of radiological records, a suitable patient sample is likely to be small and may be unevenly distributed by sex and/or age. The sole CT-based normal study involved only 15 measurements of 545 children, took more than a year to compute, and produced only about 8200 individual measurements.

In measuring normal children using anthropometric techniques, the sample size is limited only by the time available and the statistical requirements, so the number of measurements can be much larger. Collecting these data remains very time consuming, however. Hajniš, for example, took a year and a half to gather his West German data, resulting in about 76,000 individual measurements. Farkas spent four years assembling a database of about 190,000 individual measurements.

Surgical Planning

Clinical anthropometry has proven helpful to reconstructive surgeons by providing more objective and precise descriptions of the patients and their syndromes and the results of the surgery. Active involvement of a clinical anthropologist in planning reconstructive surgery of the head and face is a very new idea, being developed at the Dallas Craniofacial Center. It is a logical extension, however, of the analysis of preoperative dysmorphology. Comparison of the patient's preoperative measurements and proportions to the normal standards produces a quantitative description of the deformities and furnish a framework for calculating the changes needed to correct the deformities.

The planning process begins with analysis of the proportions which will be directly affected by the surgery. Most of the proportions for which normal standards have been developed involve only two measurements, so the initial calculations are relatively simple. With the normal proportion index, selected as the average for the appropriate sex and age, and the patient's preoperative measurement, it is easy to calculate how much the abnormal measurement needs to be changed to reach the normal proportion.

The process is much more complicated than that, of course. Each measurement being changed needs to be compared to a series of other measurements. Changing one thing may produce effects in other areas which then need to be adjusted. In the end, the final recommendation should fit as many of these variables together as close to the averages as possible.

This kind of surgical planning requires a knowledge of reconstructive surgery, which is not taught in anthropology departments. Such knowledge can be gained partially by reading surgical atlases, but it also requires discussion with reconstructive surgeons and direct observation in the operating room. Any kind of quantitative result can be calculated, but the surgical techniques available may not be able to produce the results. In addition, many patients need multiple staged surgeries to correct their deformities. Some procedures need to coincide with specific stages of development; others need to be done to prepare the framework for later operations. Understanding these limits is necessary to provide the proper information in an efficient manner.

Cautions and Limitations

Being able to evaluate a patient's anthropometric results before and after surgery suggests some medico-legal ramifications that are barely recognized so far. Comparison of these findings can show objectively whether the patient's dysmorphology improved after surgery, stayed essentially the same, or even worsened.

The legal aspects of the last situation should not be exaggerated. Anthropological judgement has to be weighed against the limitations set by surgical techniques before criticizing the results, especially when a patient or family has unreasonable expectations for the surgery. Furthermore, the interpretation of postoperative results is virtually impossible when a patient has had surgery at another center, where anthropometry is not part of the assessment process, then changes surgeons and centers after dissatisfaction with the results. However, this is exactly the kind of situation where anthropometry is most likely to meet the legal system.

Another limit to the interpretation of postoperative results is the lack of good predictive models of craniofacial growth in children with congenital malformations of the head and face. Models of normal growth cannot be used when evaluating postoperative results, particularly in the long term when surgical results are blended with the effects of growth. Clinical necessity dictates that predictive models of abnormal growth will have to be built slowly and carefully from small bits of data from large groups of patients. Each syndrome or malformation will have different patterns of growth, which makes the collection of such data even harder.

Unfortunately, very few craniofacial centers have trained physical anthropologists who can carry out these examinations accurately and efficiently. The few centers that attempt such a clinical anthropometry program almost all rely on clinicians who practice anthropology as an avocation, with little training in anthropometric techniques. Professionally trained physical anthropologists need to make their availability known to such centers to increase and improve this clinical approach on a national basis.

A Space of Our Own: The Case for Masters-Level Professional Anthropology

MARSHA JENAKOVICH AND R. OWEN MURDOCH

In the twenty years since the founding of the publication Practicing Anthropology, *a new type of practicing anthropologist has emerged— largely created by the same forces (and often the same people) responsible for the publication. Graduates of the growing number of programs offering master's degrees in applied anthropology have been joined by some graduates of more traditional programs to swell the ranks of persons practicing with a master's degree. In this article, Marsha Jenakovich and R. Owen Murdoch focus not so much on the successes or difficulties this group has faced, as on their potential to transform the discipline of anthropology. In making a space for themselves in the profession, as well as in the job market, they are pressuring anthropology to expand its borders to include not just knowledge production (research—pure or applied), but also knowledge application. Thus, "master's practitioners" can contribute substantially to the professionalization of the discipline.*

P. J. H.

In seven years of attending professional anthropological meetings, we have listened to and participated in similar conversations time and again. Those with jobs wonder how to increase the discipline's visibility and make it a more valued, recognized commodity. Those without jobs wonder how to accomplish this on an individual level, many feeling as if they are "recreating the wheel" with each job search. Apparently, anthropology is the best kept secret in social science.

An increasing number of individuals with master's degrees in anthropology are doing (on a daily basis) what everyone at these professional confer-

Marsha Jenakovich is a Research Associate with LTG Associates, Inc. (6930 Carroll Avenue, Suite 410, Takoma Park, MD 20912; (301) 270-0882; fax: (301) 270-1966; <ltg@earthlink.net>).
R. Owen Murdoch is a development and evaluation specialist with Wright Focus Groups. He can be contacted at 1533 Polo Road, Winston-Salem, NC 27106; <romurdoc@uncg.edu>.

Originally published as part of a special section on "Mastering Anthropology: Anthropologists Practicing with Masters' Degrees," guest edited by Kathleen M. Quirk and Marsha Jenakovich, in *Practicing Anthropology* 19,2(1997):17-21, this article has been edited and abridged for republication here.

ences is obsessing about. Largely in isolation, in jobs that are not high profile, we are quietly accomplishing what conference-goers bemoan—finding new way to apply anthropology. And people are buying what we sell—our concepts of culture, our qualitative methods, and our approach to problem solving. Most master's practitioners are graduates of academic programs offering little or no applied training at the master's level; others are graduates of specifically applied programs. Despite their anthropology degrees, they carry out their daily work largely without the legitimization of the discipline in which they were trained. They are therefore unlikely to publish in professional anthropology journals or present at anthropology meetings (though they often do so in "other fields," e.g., prevention, public health, AIDS). Some have difficulty articulating what is recognizably anthropological about their jobs, because, they reason, they do not do research (which is what they were taught is the measure of anthropology). Many have allowed their memberships in professional anthropological organizations to lapse, and few have had much contact with other professional anthropologists with master's degrees. Yet many would like to see themselves included in an expanded profession and discipline of anthropology.

Alternative Views of Applied Anthropology

Some master's practitioners have sought legitimacy within anthropology by trying to demonstrate what master's anthropologists have in common with Ph.D. anthropologists. This exercise is of limited utility because without the requisite rite of passage, one is, after all, not the other. Rather than compare ourselves to Ph.D.s, master's practitioners should be talking about what applied master's practitioners can do better than Ph.D.s.

Traditionally, attaining the Ph.D. has been seen as the defining moment in the discipline; once you have that, you are an anthropologist. It is not so much the degree itself as the experience of fieldwork and research that make one an anthropologist and constitute a rite of passage. This has also meant that the production of knowledge has become the hallmark of anthropology. Those who hold this view define an "applied" anthropologist as one who is engaged in research that is conducted in order to obtain information useful to a client, rather than "pure" research (whatever that means).

Within this framework, both master's and Ph.D. students are primarily trained in anthropological methods of qualitative research, and it is assumed that those who seek employment outside of academia will participate in some form of applied research. Since this kind of work has been most highly valued by the discipline, those working in more practice-based settings must be doing so due to an inability to secure "real" (i.e., research-based) anthropological positions. This bias has historical and understandable roots in a discipline that was originally academic.

There is, however, another school of thought that is redefining the practice of anthropology. By this progressive view, applied anthropology has more to do with mediation, translation, and interpretation; it is the application of knowledge rather than the production of it. Research may be a part of practice, but when it is, it is limited in scope and produced for immediate institutional consumption. Anthropologists who practice within this framework play an active role in planning and implementing policies and programs, which leads to more integral, continuing roles in the institutions for which they work.

Many master's practitioners inhabit this realm successfully, especially those trained in applied programs. But the work they do is often not recognizably "anthropological" to those who hold the traditionalist view. Some traditionalists even find it difficult to consider these practitioners "anthropologists" without clear involvement in anthropological research.

In fact, these master's practitioners are exploring the frontiers of applied practice. They are creating a space for themselves (and often by themselves) which, because of their success and diligence, will expand to include others. In the process, they are changing the face of anthropology. Virtually any discipline that has professionalized itself away from its academic roots has something to offer which has nothing to do with research. A mature discipline has the potential to grow beyond its boundaries, and the progressive view of applied practice offers a source for this growth.

A Space of Our Own

Master's practitioners occupy a unique space within the discipline and the profession, as well as within the employment sector. They are at an increasingly important professional nexus where utility, relevance, and anthropology meet. Institutions are being challenged to prove the money they use has been well spent. Additionally, the radical idea that initiatives need to be based at the community level and tailored to fit community needs is catching on in many institutions (which is great news for anthropologists). Interest in anthropology's concept of culture is also in greater demand as more and more of our daily existence becomes a cross-cultural experience.

Master's practitioners have an opportunity to work with many different groups in technical assistance positions, in advocacy, and in policy positions. More opportunities could well open in the near future for people working at the state and local level. Within these organizations, private and public, master's practitioners are likely to define needs, plan and implement programs, disseminate information, advocate for change, fight for funding, etc.

Working in and around the Washington, D.C. area, we have noticed employment trends among master's practitioners that exemplify this new space. While the realm of consulting seems to be overwhelmingly staffed by Ph.D.s, nongovernmental organizations are staffed largely by people at the master's

274

level, drawn from many disciplines. Applied anthropological skills—mediation, translation and interpretation—are welcome additions in program planning, implementation, evaluation, training, advocacy and policy development. Yet "creating a space" for applied master's practitioners is still largely being done one practitioner at a time.

Self-definition and Identity Formation

Master's practitioners need to come together to discuss what they do. From this discourse will arise concepts and words that are specific to their experience and that more closely capture the essence of their work. Our resulting self-discoveries may well give the profession and the discipline new directions for the future.

It has been difficult, however, for master's practitioners to identify and locate one another. We have a tendency to become less visible as anthropologists as we become more successful professionally. We rarely have or use "anthropologist" in our professional titles, even in informal settings. We work in what some like to call "other fields," so our success rests upon our becoming effective "crossover artists." We are the chameleons of the social sciences.

Because we have few opportunities to compare our experience with one another, we share no common language to express ourselves, even with those who share our background and interests. Master's practitioners are in the same position that ethnographers were twenty years ago. To forge a stronger identity we need to develop a common language and to elucidate concrete models of the "methods of application" that we use (those that deal with mediation, translation, and interpretation). In the same way that researchers have made ethnography explicit, so must master's-level practitioners take the initiative and set down what it is that we know and do on a daily basis.

The Business of Anthropology

What is it we really do for a living? Even those master's practitioners who are fortunate enough to do some form of applied research only do so (by several practitioners' estimates) for about 25 percent of their time.

What is done for the other three-quarters? Administrative work: attending/facilitating meetings, giving presentations, writing reports and grants, managing/supervising other personnel, planning organizational activities, managing fiscal responsibilities, and other standard institutional endeavors. While most applied anthropology training programs address methods for producing knowledge, "methods of application" (methods of applying knowledge) seem harder to define and less likely to be clearly articulated in training programs. Administration is not necessarily anthropology, but it is precisely these "methods of application" that occupy the largest part of a master's practitioner's professional life.

Similarly, while training programs are increasingly responsive to the needs of professional anthropologists, the most vital skills required to secure employment are not considered anthropology at all, so students are rarely taught how to do these things specifically (e.g., networking, "marketing oneself," and interpreting one's anthropological skills in the context of the employer's expectations). While essential for obtaining employment, the development of these skills is often left to the individual practitioner—and trial and error discovery. Clearly, these are skills that can be taught and learned; why should they not be an integral part of the training curriculum?

Since the ability to "apply" anthropology is continually being invented and reinvented by the individual practitioner, it is practitioners who must develop models of application. With the formation of an interest group within the Society for Applied Anthropology, we have begun to talk about the specifics of what we do, what we have in common, and what it is about what we do and how we do it that makes it "anthropological."

Conclusion

Master's practitioners are creating a new space for themselves professionally, a space that is within the anthropological tradition and reflects many of the current concerns of the discipline. Master's practitioners who utilize the progressive view of applying anthropology may be better prepared to occupy this space than Ph.D.s. This type of practice is not just about knowledge production but about the genuine application and uses of knowledge. As practitioners engaged in a daily effort to apply anthropology, master's professionals are uniquely suited to define and refine methods of application.

Unfortunately, the contributions of master's practitioners have as yet not gained much recognition within the discipline. This is in part because there is no language to use and no place to talk about it within a professional anthropological context. The challenge for master's practitioners is to create this language and this place. This endeavor is important because the future of the discipline and the profession may very well lie in the uses and application of anthropological knowledge; if so, master's practitioners are already on the cutting edge.

Practicing Anthropology on the Frontiers of Humanity: Interspecies Applied Anthropology

ANDREW J. PETTO AND KARLA D. RUSSELL

Studies of nonhuman primates have long captured the imagination of the public as well as the attention of anthropologists and others seeking to understand the intersections of nature and culture. Rarely have experts in primate behavior found an immediate, practical need for their knowledge, however. More stringent regulations concerning the care of nonhuman primates in captivity have changed that, just as laws and regulations concerning cultural resources have created a demand for archaeological skills and expertise. Andrew Petto and Karla Russell's work at the New England Regional Primate Research Center addressed the requirement that research facilities provide an environment conducive to the psychological well-being of the nonhuman primates in their care. Having identified interactions between human and nonhuman primates as a key variable in the animals' lives, Petto and Russell used observational techniques common to sociocultural anthropology and primatology as well as knowledge of primate behavior (human and nonhuman) to design ways to lessen interspecies conflict at the facility. Their effectiveness in applying similar research techniques, modes of analysis, and principles of behavior modification to human and nonhuman primates illustrates once more both the usefulness of anthropology and the close relationship that exists between primate species. P. J. H.

Whenever there is friction between two social groups, anthropologists can usually identify a few characteristic actions that might improve relations between them. Anthropologists are valuable in such situations because our expertise and training allow us the possibility of understanding the specific interactions between groups in a larger context. This may result in the discovery

Andrew J. Petto teaches natural science at the University of the Arts in Philadelphia and is also editor for the National Center for Science Education. He can be reached at the Division of Liberal Arts, University of the Arts, 320 S. Broad Street, Philadelphia, PA 19102-4994; (215) 717-6276; <editor@natscnscied.org>.
Karla D. Russell is a wildlife biologist in Idaho.

Originally published in *Practicing Anthropology* 20,2(1998):26-29, this article has been edited and abridged for republication here.

278

of a set of principles and prohibitions that gives meaning to the interactions among individuals and between groups.

In intergroup conflicts, the members of one group may misinterpret the specific behaviors of those in the other group as hostile or threatening. The range of allowable and acceptable actions and their motivations may differ between the groups. At a deeper level, the social organization and prescribed relationships within one group may be misunderstood by the other as insulting or demeaning. Individuals may wrongly ascribe status and roles to others as well as misinterpret meanings. Finally, the physical environment and how each group interprets and relates to it may also put them at odds. What one group regards as a practical and safe living area may be perceived by the other as dangerous and threatening. Resolving such situations means addressing the conflict between groups at each of these levels.

Our project, like many others in applied anthropology, dealt with all these characteristics—intergroup communications, unintended or misconstrued hostility, and conflicting interpretation of the physical environment, its use and ownership. What is different about this project is that only one of the social groups was human. The other consisted of nonhuman primates at the New England Regional Primate Research Center (NERPRC), a department of Harvard Medical School, located in Southborough, Massachusetts. The nonhuman primates lived in social groups of various sizes in both indoor and outdoor enclosures that served as breeding colonies for animals to be used as research subjects by the medical school. The humans were responsible for feeding, basic care, medical treatments, and maintenance of the physical environment.

Project Description

The main impetus for our project came from amendments to the Animal Welfare Act (AWA) passed by Congress in December 1985. One of the most significant of these amendments requires animal research facilities to provide environments that promote the "psychological well-being" of captive nonhuman primates. This amendment and the regulations later issued by the U.S. Department of Agriculture focused attention on how nonhuman primates in research colonies function in captive environments. An important part of these environments and the animals' lives in them was the quality of the interactions between the nonhuman primates and their human caretakers.

At the time that we began our project—a training grant directed at improving the quality of care for research animals (supported by the Edna H. Tompkins Trust and NIH grant RR00168)—the two groups could best be described as struggling for social and behavioral dominance of the situation. The humans were of the mind that these animals were a force to be controlled and should be "trained" to obey and not to resist human commands. This was accomplished by superior force, technology (traps, cages, nets, tranquilizer guns), and control over the physical environment. Although this strategy succeeded after a fashion, it did so at some risk to the animals and to the humans. The injuries and illnesses associated with this struggle were generally minor, but concern about the rates of injury associated with "routine" animal handling rose throughout the 1980s. Early in the decade, interspecies transmission of simian immunodeficiency viruses alerted colony managers to potential cross-contamination. Near the end of the decade several humans were fatally struck by monkey-to-human transmission of viruses that had little impact on the health of their simian hosts.

The animals for their part seemed to rely on their superior agility, larger numbers, and recruitment of allies (especially larger adult males) to frustrate the humans' intentions. The monkeys typically used parts of the environment that were inaccessible to humans, such as climbing upside down across the ceiling of an enclosure while humans had to clamber over or walk around structures designed for climbing, hiding, and manipulation that were on the floors. They also allowed their "targeted" groupmates to hide behind others or to be secreted in inaccessible areas of the enclosure. In the extreme case, members of a social group would join to threaten the humans who entered the enclosure and, only in the rarest circumstances, to attack humans physically. Although this provided the monkeys with some short-term gains, in the end, the humans always succeeded by escalating their application of technological solutions or by increasing their control over the physical environment, reducing the space for maneuvering, and decreasing possible avoidance/escape routes.

Our first assessment of these interactions was that a realignment of management practices by humans could reduce the risks of injuries, lower the general stress levels for both animals and humans, and produce the desired outcomes with less-intense activity by human caretakers. This realignment had three main components. First, we had to assess and understand the behaviors and motivations of each party in these interactions. Second, we had to assess options for changing those behaviors when they instigated or intensified the conflict between parties. Third, we had to assess the ways in which the physical environment structured or promoted behaviors that contributed to the conflict.

As a practical matter, we decided that behaviors and motivations would be the most difficult to change. It was useful to study these variables because they helped us to understand the interactions between the parties, but it was clear that training of the animals and educational programs for human caretakers would have limited effect if they were not compatible with the existing contexts. On the other hand, the new federal regulations for care, housing, and research use of nonhuman primates provided several opportunities to redesign animal housing environments in such a way as to promote more desirable interactions between humans and the other primates.

280

Restructuring the Environment

The first changes in the physical environment reduced direct contact between humans and nonhuman primates. These included a number of tunnels, passageways, and doorways that directed the animals into temporary quarters or specialized transfer cages in which they could be removed from one enclosure to another. These physical changes were based on the observed responses of monkeys when caretakers entered their enclosures. All except the most terrestrial species tended to climb to the top of the enclosure for safety.

For some species, that meant that nesting boxes with removable covers would be placed flush with the ceiling of the enclosure so that, in seeking the highest point in the environment, the monkeys would enter the nesting box (rather than hiding on top of it). Once in the nesting box, the monkeys could be contained by sliding the cover closed and removing the whole nesting box. The animal(s) could then be transferred to a new enclosure or to a laboratory and released again by sliding the cover open without physical contact with humans.

With the more terrestrial species, the changes included transfer doors and short connecting passageways between housing units or areas. In these cases the caretakers needed to ready these structures and then enter the enclosures in a way that would normally induce the monkeys toward the desired structures. In some passageways there were removable barriers or space restrictions that would allow caretakers to single out one or a few of the animals for removal or transfer to another group.

The objective of such structural changes was to minimize threatening situations. Monkeys seeking to avoid direct contact with a human would move from the enclosure without being threatened, restrained, or captured. Then caretakers could clean and sanitize the enclosures or perform medical exams or treatments. Furthermore, both humans and nonhumans were less likely to be involved in prolonged, antagonistic interactions during these routine animal care activities. With the general level of tension lower, the chances of injuries to either party are also reduced.

Refocusing Interactions

One important aspect of improving intergroup interactions is to help group members to identify and recognize members of the other group as individuals. Monkeys seemed to relate to human caretakers as classes of individuals identifiable by work clothing of various types and colors. Clinical staff tended to wear white lab coats or green or pink scrubsuits. Animal care staff tended to wear blue work pants with a lighter blue shirt, and maintenance staff wore a similar uniform in green. Student interns and our staff wore brown coveralls when interacting with the animals and street clothes when observing from a distance.

The humans tended to identify only a few monkeys as individuals—mostly based on the monkeys' reactions to humans or unusual behavior from the past. Many of these interactions could be regarded as antagonistic, especially in those cases where group members were removed from an enclosure for medical treatment, research, or other reasons. Adult males commonly reacted with threats or overt aggression in these cases, and this behavior was made even more noticeable in groups composed of a single adult male with several adult females and immature monkeys. However, a few monkeys gained the reputation of being particularly friendly or at least indifferent toward humans.

Both positive and negative lore about individual monkeys was passed down from one caretaker to the next as new staff came on the job. In a few cases, the exact identity of the animal in the "legend" was obscure, and the name of the legendary monkey was reattributed to other individuals who had the same or similar behaviors. This was the case for a Taiwan macaque named "Goober, Jr." who had the "look" and behavior of a legendary adult male that had been named "Goober." However, when we examined the pedigrees of all the animals of this species in the breeding pool, we discovered that Goober, Jr. was not at all related to the legendary Goober.

When all monkeys look "alike" or when temperamental and behavioral characteristics are inaccurately attributed to individuals, then stress and tension between parties is heightened. The time and effort necessary to locate and capture a specific individual are increased, and if follow-up observations or examinations are necessary for these individuals, it is difficult to carry out these activities without disturbing the group again.

By federal regulation, research facilities must have a permanent system of identification for all animals. For nonhuman primates this system frequently relies on tattoos on the abdomen, arms, or inner thigh. However, the combination of the dark pigmentation in the skin and the density of hair covering the body often makes these tattoos difficult to read accurately in normally acting monkeys. The problem is complicated when they are being pursued around a large enclosure by humans. To be completely certain of having selected the desired individual, several monkeys often had to be pursued, captured, and restrained in order to read their tattoos—and then released if not the individual intended for capture. To improve human ability to distinguish among individual animals, we began using systems of "remote" identification.

The "remote" identification consisted of small quantities of hair dye applied to the monkeys' fur in a limited number of patterns during the times when the monkeys were being restrained for routine clinical procedures or physical examinations. After all the members of a social group were marked, caretakers posted a key that related the pattern of dyed hair to the permanent identification number for each monkey. This meant that the efforts of caretakers were focused only on the monkey(s) that were being selected for study or medical care and that the others in the social group were less likely to be unnecessarily captured, restrained, then released. It also meant that once the intended animal was captured then the pursuit of animals would cease.

Observations Replace Lore

The final phase of the program was to change the interactions between the groups based on short-term research supplemented by insights from the broader literature in animal behavior. We began informal instruction of the caretakers by pointing out how the animals were reacting to events and activities around them—especially to the behaviors of the humans going about their daily routines. Later, we included information about animal communications—vocalizations, postures, facial expressions that could be used to monitor the animals' reactions to the humans.

In part this instruction was accomplished simply by having a number of students available on site who were regularly observing and recording animal behavior. From that point it was fairly easy to demonstrate that certain ways of going about one's routine would increase tension, stress, and antagonistic behavior between humans and nonhumans, while others would tend to defuse the situation or even decrease the tensions.

In addition, observers were also recording the events and activities in the environment around the animals—including the behaviors of the human caretakers. These observers, of course, had an effect on the behavior of the observed—normally a condition that we try to avoid. Yet, here we actually hoped for this to happen. We wanted both the caretakers and the monkeys to observe each other and start to experience different ways of interacting with each other. Eventually, a number of caretakers began to take an interest in the behavioral observations, and several used them to learn more about the monkeys.

Finally, we instituted short-term formal studies on the ways that animals responded to their new structures and the addition of new group members. These were complemented by studies of singly-housed animals presented with novel objects and other diversions in their cages. One of the encouraging results of the studies was that some caretakers themselves began to notice the ways in which individual animals responded to new situations. They also began to think about their tasks in terms of accommodating different animal temperaments and group dynamics. These observations allowed them to vary their approaches to colony management.

Project Outcomes

The transition to new interspecies relations was not complete in the short span of our training grant, but several positive outcomes remained. First, the structural changes incorporated into enclosure and building designs to take advantage of normal animal behaviors and help humans to use these behaviors in animal care activities will remain in place for several years before renovation or updates are needed. Furthermore, a number of the design modifications were reworked or improved in later building projects.

Second, key technicians came to appreciate better the ways in which understanding and incorporating the animals' behaviors into their work planning can make their jobs easier. One example involved "timed mating." In this colony, individual females are monitored for their reproductive status and then paired with males during the most likely time for conception. New routines we suggested and helped to implement resulted in less handling of the animals, lowered costs, and a dramatic increase in fertility among females in the colony each year.

Third, caretakers became more aware and alert to individual differences in temperament and behavior among monkeys and to how their own behaviors in their daily duties affected the monkeys' reactions to them. Humans learned to read some important signals more accurately (for example, some postural and behavioral reactions to humans in the enclosure that are defensive rather than hostile or aggressive). Caretakers also learned to assess empirically the temperamental characteristics of different groups and so could vary the husbandry practices based on how different groups reacted to interaction with humans.

Fourth, formal studies carried out by student interns led to a program of environmental enrichment. Our staff and the student interns would make certain behavioral observations of monkeys in specific environments and recommend structural changes that might improve relations between humans and nonhumans. As a part of the assessment of this approach, caretakers began completing a short behavioral inventory that accompanied the "routine" physical condition/health inventory at the beginning of each day. One staff member was eventually assigned the permanent tasks of assessing the situations, devising interventions, and following progress in each case.

The positive outcomes of this project show that identifying behavioral interactions between groups, social relations within groups, and the ways in which individuals in each group perceive and respond to the environment can be used effectively to address and relieve intergroup tensions. The application of such principles of applied anthropology can be adapted to work well even when the conflicting groups include both humans and our nonhuman primate cousins. This approach and its success in interspecies social relations has extended the reach of applied anthropology to frontiers of our humanity.

Afterword

LINDA A. BENNETT
SfAA PRESIDENT, 1999-2001

Looking forward to the twenty-first century, I envision a central role for applied anthropology in both academic and nonacademic domains. In reflecting on the papers in *Classics of Practicing Anthropology*, I see maintaining a professional identity as an anthropologist as particularly important. Where we work and our specific job title matter less and less, but the expression of an anthropological identity will continue to be transformed.

Four significant trends in anthropology that have begun already at the end of the twentieth century will have a major impact on the field in the new millennium. These changes involve the way in which we behave as anthropologists and the way in which the discipline will operate in the future.

Movement of Anthropologists into Nonacademic Domains

In the 1970s, many anthropologists took a negative view of the necessity or the preference for positions outside of academia. In time, though, a plethora of case reports and surveys demonstrated that job satisfaction, on average, is at least as good if not better among anthropologists working in nonacademic positions as among those in higher education. A large percentage of anthropologists employed outside of academia are functioning as applied anthropologists, even when the specific job title does not reflect this reality.

The increased responsiveness of anthropological organizations to the needs and interests of nonacademically based anthropologists may contribute to this job satisfaction. Such responsiveness has required a major shift from the days when we thought we could look in the American Anthropological Association (AAA) *Guide* and find most of our anthropology colleagues listed in academic departments. A large percentage of the anthropologists with advanced degrees may still be listed in the AAA guide, especially if they are members of the association, but the AAA has had to substantially modify and expand the types of organizations that the guide encompasses in order to accommodate the diversity of settings in which anthropologists work today. Other directories have been developed to help identify applied anthropologists, such as the 1996 *Directory of Members* of the Society for Applied Anthropology and the National Association for the Practice of Anthropology. In the future the Internet will no doubt be especially useful in identifying and communicating with anthropologists working in a variety of contexts.

The Visible and Critical Role of Master's-level Anthropologists

The number of anthropologists with master's degrees who are practicing anthropology in a vast array of positions will grow even more in the future, as will their impact upon the discipline and upon the visibility of anthropology. While many—perhaps most—are in archaeology, master's practitioners from other subfields of anthropology are increasingly common. Any of the applied anthropology M.A. programs around the country could testify to the significance of their "alums" for helping in critical ways to "deliver" their graduate and undergraduate programs. These anthropologists are particularly important in the placement of current students and future alums in meaningful practica or internships and paying positions in the community.

Anthropologists often complain that our visibility is not good; this is certainly true in most parts of the United States. Most people have a very incomplete view of all the spheres that anthropology encompasses. One of the most effective ways to reverse this trend is through the placement of anthropologists with master's degrees in positions where they apply their anthropological knowledge and skills *and* where they articulate to their nonanthropologist colleagues the connection between their education and training as anthropologists and their current work. This articulation is much more likely to occur when they have maintained an active anthropological identity.

Local Practitioner Organizations

The establishment of local practitioner organizations (LPOs) over the last three decades of the twentieth century has been critical in increasing the likelihood that anthropologists working outside of academia will maintain an identity as anthropologists. While our national and international anthropology organizations pay much greater attention today to communicating with nonacademically based anthropologists, to encouraging their meaningful participation in our various activities, and to providing desired services, there are definite limitations on how much these organizations can accomplish. Fortunately, some of the "void" in direct communication between national-level organizations and nonacademically based anthropologists has been filled by local practitioner organizations.

The Society of Professional Anthropologists (SOPA), the first LPO, was established in Tucson, Arizona, in 1974. The Washington Association of Professional Anthropologists (WAPA) was established in 1976, drawing upon the very substantial number of anthropologists working in the Washington, D.C. area in the nonacademic sectors such as the federal government as well as in academic departments. These two were followed in 1979 by the Sun Coast Organization of Practicing Anthropologists (SCOPA) in Tampa, Florida, and the Chicago Organization of Professional Anthropologists (COPA). While SOPA disbanded in 1983, WAPA recently celebrated its twentieth anniversary and continues to draw local, national, and international members.

The earliest LPOs were formed in areas with a substantial "critical mass" of anthropologists within commuting distance. Later, some LPOs began as regional organizations, such as the High Plains Society for Applied Anthropology (HPSfAA), formed in 1980, and the Southern California Applied Anthropology Network (SCAAN), formed in 1984. By the later 1970s, this pattern began to change. Throughout the later 1970s, the 1980s, and the 1990s, an impressive array of LPOs has been scattered through all parts of the country. In addition to those mentioned already, the list includes the Mid-South Association of Professional Anthropologists (MSAPA), Memphis, Tennessee, formed in 1983; the Detroit Association of Practicing Anthropologists (DAPA), formed in 1986; the New Jersey Association for the Practice of Anthropology (NJAPA) begun in 1987; the North Florida Network of Practicing Anthropologists (originally the North Florida Group), established in 1988; and the Ann Arbor Area Association of Applied Anthropologists ("A-6"), also established in 1988 (Linda A. Bennett with commentaries by Karen J. Hanson and Omer C. Stewart, *Bridges for Changing Times: Local Practitioner Organizations in American Anthropology* [Washington, D.C.: American Anthropological Association, National Association for the Practice of Anthropology Bulletin 6, 1988]). Some of these LPOs have not survived to the present, but this partial listing indicates the broad geographical spread across the country. Currently there are nine active LPOs, including one in Nebraska and one in the northeast United States, and another three LPOs with a less active status.

Participating in a local practitioner organization gives nonacademically and academically based anthropologists an opportunity to interact regularly with fellow anthropologists. Even with the seemingly boundless possibilities in communication through the Internet, this is an inadequate substitute for face-to-face contact for meaningful communication. Given that many anthropologists—whether located in academic or nonacademic positions—cannot attend national meetings, the availability of these local practitioner organizations will continue to make such communication possible and necessary.

Policy Arena Work

In the long-range planning goals of the Society for Applied Anthropology, "the capacity to respond to policy issues" has been identified as the number one issue for the future. Making advances with respect to this fourth trend for the twenty-first century is feasible only because of successes in the three trends described above. Without the movement of such a major segment of anthropologists into nonacademic positions, the notable increase of M.A. practicing anthropologists, and the presence of local practitioner organizations, our ability to respond to policy issues would be severely limited. Furthermore, while many of us tend to think in international and national terms when we talk about policy issues, anthropological impact on policy is likely to be greatest at the local and regional levels, through the work of M.A. and Ph.D. anthropologists. In addition, our effectiveness in the policy arena will be much greater if our national, international, and local anthropological organizations carefully target policy areas.

The future for applied anthropology holds tremendous possibilities for visibility, relevance, and effectiveness. To ensure such success, it is crucial that we work cooperatively with each other and with our academic colleagues in other disciplines and that we effectively communicate our perspectives and our accomplishments to the wider society.

Index

290

294

and business, 80–81
and development, 181–82
Grand Teton National Park, 235
grants, 26
Great Depression, 3
Green, James W., 54
Greenberg, James, 249
Grobsmith, Elizabeth S., 183–90
grounded theory approach, 241
groundwater contamination, 135–42
group interaction, 277–83
"Guardians of the Land: Indigenous Peoples and the Health of the Earth" (Durning), 229

Hajniš, Dr. Karel, 264, 268
Halper, Jeff, 191–97
Hamada, Tomoko, 119–26
Hanna, Joel M., 87–93
Hanna Mining Company, 39
Harris, Marvin, 82
Harshbarger, Camilla L., 127–33
Hatch Act, 164
Hawaii, 89, 90, 91, 92
health sciences, 87–93
Hernandez, Hilda, 100
Herskovits, Melville, 82
Hester, James, 203
Hickey, Gerald, 54
Higgins, Patricia J., 1–9
High Plains Society for Applied Anthropology (HPSfAA), 287
historic preservation, 3
    Zuni and, 151, 153, 154, 155
historic resources, 236
HIV, 207–13
    See also AIDS
Hodge, Frederick, 152
home visits, 248–49, 254
homelessness, 143–50
    and mental illness, 146, 149
Hornick, Conrad, 92
Hospital for Sick Children (Toronto),

264, 267
household funds, 249, 252
"How Agencies Can Use Anthropology in Advertising" (Marcus), 83
Hrdlička, Ales, 263
Hudson, Chris, 215–21
human engineering, 263
Human Organization, 4, 5, 15, 16, 17, 19
Human Relations Area File, 162
human remains, 232–33
human rights, 32, 34
    and the environment, 223–30
"Human Rights and the Environment: Examining the Sociocultural Context of Environmental Crisis," 229
Humphrey, Hubert H., 35
hunting, 235–36
Hurston, Zora Neale, 191, 192
Hymes, Dell, 192

ICA (International Cooperation Administration), 51, 53
identity
    American Indian, 233
    anthropological, 285, 286
    community, 217
    cultural, 215–21, 236
    and environmental protection, 223
    of master's practitioners, 274
    professional, 285
    spiritual, 234
impact assessment, 234
imperialism, 227
    Japanese, 3
inmates. *See* prisoners
Integrating Multicultural Perspectives into Teacher Education: A Curriculum Resource Guide, 100
integration, 35
intentions, 83
interethnic politics, 259–60

298

300